Wasted

How Misunderstanding Young Britain Threatens Our Future

GEORGIA GOULD

Little, Brown

LITTLE, BROWN

First published in Great Britain in 2015 by Little, Brown

1 3 5 7 9 10 8 6 4 2

The graph on p. 182 is from Steve Strand, 'Ethnicity, Gender, Social Class
and Achievement Gaps at Age 16: Intersectionality and "Getting It" for
the White Working Class', *Research Papers in Education*, 29:2 (2014),
published by Taylor & Francis Online.

A CIP catalogue record for this book
is available from the British Library.

ISBN 978-1-4087-0452-3

Typeset in Bembo by M Rules
Printed and bound in Great Britain by
Clays Ltd, St Ives plc

Papers used by Little, Brown are from well-managed forests
and other responsible sources.

MIX
Paper from
responsible sources
FSC
www.fsc.org   FSC® C104740

Little, Brown
An imprint of
Little, Brown Book Group
100 Victoria Embankment
London EC4Y 0DY

An Hachette UK Company
www.hachette.co.uk

www.littlebrown.co.uk

For the young people who shared their stories with me –
I hope this book does them justice

Contents

Introduction

It is six o'clock on a cold November evening in Camden, and I am sitting waiting for a group of young volunteers. They turn up en masse and suddenly the committee room is full of food, laughter and fifteen teenagers all talking over each other to tell me about their work. We are in the middle of a debate about the media when a girl rushes in late, school bags flying. 'Sorry,' she tells us, 'I was stopped and searched three times on the way here.' I ask her if the police gave a reason. 'They said I looked thuggish,' she replies with a bemused laugh. No one apart from me looks surprised. This is their daily experience: security guards that tail them in shops, curtains that twitch as they walk home, people who avoid their gaze as they walk down the street. As a society we have begun to demonise our young. We label them 'thugs', 'hoodies', 'feral', and define them by what they are not – Not in Education, Employment or Training – until the word 'youth' becomes synonymous with antisocial behaviour. At the extreme, we begin to question their very humanity.[1]

Older generations have always watched with some trepidation as young people challenge the status quo. However, as the story of our teens and twenty-somethings became intertwined with the story of the internet, the gap between their generation and all who came before widened into a chasm in workplaces, in communities and in politics. Businesses rail at the entitled and unemployable young people they are asked to give jobs to. Politicians complain about the apathy of the young people they have to try to win over. Commentators worry that we are bringing up a generation of shallow, lazy, self-obsessed narcissists who are abandoning their empathy, their morality and their values in the relentless pursuit of attention and consumption.

As a society we try to mould the next generation into our failing institutions, rather than asking them how to transform them. If we call young people who are registering a protest at our political institutions apathetic instead of listening to their critique, we lose the opportunity of reform. If we describe young people left angry and disillusioned by the lack of opportunities they face as feral, it stops us addressing rising inequality. If we label young people who have been failed by our education system 'entitled' and 'lazy', it leads to policies that sanction, penalise and criminalise the young rather than support them.

This is a generation that has grown up with a social contract straining to keep up with a changing world. In many ways they have inherited their parents' aspirations. They want to find a good job, eventually buy their own home, get married and have children. Yet the reality they are facing is a lower standard of living than their parents,[2] stagnating wages and massive youth unemployment. Young people struggling to get on the housing ladder are forced to navigate an expensive private rented sector, which offers little stability.

This is a long way from what they want. As we will see throughout this book, many young people growing up in Britain today are highly entrepreneurial and aspirational both for themselves and for society. Yet there is a huge gap between young people's aspirations for their own lives, for society at large and the reality they face. Rather than setting up new businesses, most are focused on getting by. They are forced into trade-offs between education and housing, career and family, making a difference and paying the bills. They need more education than ever before to do the same jobs and some are finding it difficult to enter the labour market at all.

We could ignore this. Young people are less likely to vote, to identify with political parties, to join trade unions, to turn up to community meetings or planning committees. It isn't difficult for the whole system to churn on without taking the protest of the young seriously or listening to their concerns. Yet as it does, young people become more disengaged – and none more so than young people from disadvantaged backgrounds who watch as opportunities slip further from their reach. As their voices become more and more marginalised they bunker in, retrenching further and further away from communities and institutions. We end up with an atomised society where young people retreat to a harsh individualism or fall prey to an anti-democratic political force that gives voice to their frustration at the whole system.

The challenges facing this generation present a bleak picture but this is not a pessimistic book. If you spend even a small amount of time with young people it is impossible to be pessimistic. As a Labour Councillor and Cabinet Member for Young People in Camden I am lucky enough to spend a lot of time with different groups of young people and I am constantly lifted and inspired by their optimism, creativity and energy. They are far more likely to express grand ambitions than hopelessness, whether they are describing their own lives or their mission for society. Young people in Britain today may face huge challenges but they are also offering up new solutions.

If we waste this optimism, we waste one of the greatest resources we have as a country. Research by the Office for National Statistics shows that while only 41.5 per cent of the working-age population are under thirty-five, they represent 66.2 per cent of the country's human capital stock[3] – the value to the economy of their future earning potential. We will need every bit of young people's creativity, energy and optimism to realign our economy, reignite growth, care for an elderly population and reduce energy consumption. Young people must be active partners, but at the moment they are largely absent from the debate about our future

The lost voices of young Britain are the real tragedy and why I called the book *Wasted*. In our obsession with identifying everything that is wrong with the next generation, we miss how much they have to teach us.

We need to break down some of the negative myths that pervade public debate about the young. In Chapter 1, I explore how young people end up as the scapegoat for society's problems and take on some of the myths about the next generation.

One of the most dangerous myths mistakes young people's anger about politics for apathy. This is dangerous because it allows young people's legitimate critique of our political institutions to be ignored. In Chapter 2 I make the case that the real apathy comes from politicians who have failed to acknowledge that young people's alienation from political institutions should be a wake-up call. Many young people no longer express their political beliefs in collective movements but in highly personal choices about how they live, where they work and what they consume. This should be celebrated and encouraged as the starting point of a new empowered citizenship.

In Chapter 3 I come to the crux of older people's fears about the young. Talking about my book with baby boomers I hear again and again about their fear that, through liberating themselves from their parents' communities and their own search for personal liberation, they inadvertently created the circumstances where their own children developed into a generational monster, too selfish and individualistic to partake in community or political life. I show that while individualism is here to stay, the nature of this is open for debate. For some young people this can be a positive and liberating force. Research shows that many young people are highly entrepreneurial, driven by a desire to make a personal impact and more accepting of others' individuality than older generations. However, for some young people individualism expresses itself as a need to put themselves first in a zero-sum game. The more young people feel like they have been left behind, the less they will feel they have an obligation to others. Wider society has a big part to play in whether the individualism the next generation grows up with is a 'put-myself-first fight for survival' or one that equates personal fulfilment with the pursuit of something bigger than oneself.

In Chapter 4, I explore what this individualism means for community life. Traditional collective identities, whether class or religious, are declining. However, I show that far from rejecting solidarity and cooperation, young people are forming new communities built through relationships and empathy. They are proving that individuality and solidarity do not have to conflict but that true personal empowerment takes place within a collective.

While some young people are creating new communities and shared experiences, others are struggling to form connections. A central theme that comes up in every chapter is the growing disparity between young people based on their background. Young people growing up in poverty have tended to bear the brunt of the negative stereotypes; they also experience the greatest sense of alienation and lack of power. In Chapter 5 I show how our education system is not fit for purpose and is failing to produce social mobility or give young people the skills they need to succeed in the labour market.

We are also failing to give young people the tools they need to deal with a society and economy that is ever more reliant on the internet. At the same time as it liberates and empowers, technology disrupts and polarises. In Chapter 6 I show that young people are on the front line of the battle to understand and shape the internet. It is only by listening to them and giving them the support they need that we can ensure it is a progressive force in their lives.

In the second section of the book I set out a path for the future based on the ideas and example of the young people I have met. It is a vision of a modern, empowered citizenship actively expressed by young people in their work, their communities and the way they engage with services. In return, we need to give every young person the support, opportunity and investment they need to flourish.

The institutions of civil society will be key to this. It is no longer acceptable in the post-recession world to talk about businesses and banks as merely the engines of growth, with government worrying about everything else: the future is businesses creating shared value for themselves and society. To meet this vision will require leaders committed to unlocking the leadership capacity of their citizens and a new uniting purpose for society.

What do I mean by young people?

Before I go much further I want to clarify some of the key terms I use in this book.

First and most importantly, who am I talking about when I refer to 'young people'? Alongside the idea of 'youth' as a problem, 'youth' has become a drawn-out process. Because of the challenges young people face, they take longer to settle down than their parents' generation and the twilight zone between adolescence and full adulthood can go on well into the twenties and early thirties.

As I explore in Chapter 1, there are some universal features of youth and indeed other life stages that hold true across generations. We can still identify with Shakespeare's seven ages of man: from the mewling and puking infant, through the whining schoolboy, the lover, the soldier, the justice in fair round belly, the lean and slippered pantaloon to the second childishness. We play many roles as we move through life, roles that have some kind of universal quality across time.

However, the social conditions that exist through our formative years are powerful in shaping an individual's values. Napoleon said if you want to understand a man then look at the world when he was twenty. Karl Mannheim, in his 1928 essay 'The Problem of Generations', was influential in developing the idea of generations as distinct social categories where those growing up under similar sociological and historical circumstances share a certain view of the world that they will carry throughout their lives.

William Strauss and Neil Howe took up the modern discussion of generations in the US: 'As each generation ages into the next phase – from youth to young adulthood to midlife to elderhood – its attitudes and behaviours mature, producing new currents in the public mood. In other words, people do not "belong" to their age brackets. A woman of forty today has less in common with forty-year-old women across the ages than with the rest of her generation, which is united by memories, language, habits, beliefs, and life lessons.'[4]

Today we commonly divide society into five generations defined by the conditions of birth – the pre-war generation born before 1945, the baby boomers born between 1945 and 1965, Generation X born between 1966 and 1979, Gen Y born between 1980 and 2000 and Gen Z born after 2000.

This book focuses on Generation Y, otherwise known as the 'millennial generation', those born between 1980 and 2000. Within this group I look particularly at the younger half of this generation, those in their teens and twenties, and most of my interviews were with fifteen- to twenty-four-year-olds.

What, then, are the shared reference points and the unique context of this generation? It is a generation brought up in a diverse country and a globalised world. They are growing up one step further along the curve of modernity and therefore one step further away from hierarchy, deference and traditional identities. They are more familiar with rapid change and flux than they are with stability. They have also grown up alongside the internet. It has allowed them to choose their identity and shape their communities in a way that was unimaginable for their grandparents. They are growing up in a world where knowledge and power are not locked away in corporate headquarters and parliamentary institutions, but dispersed across society for good or for bad. They live in a world where every Goliath can find himself trumped by a smaller and more nimble David.

Yet paradoxically they are growing up in a world where it matters more than ever what kind of family you are born into – not just how much money your family has but where they live, the premium they put on education and the stability they can give you when dealing with an unstable world. As inequality grows, for some the world genuinely is their oyster, for others the world contracts to the couple of streets they grew up on.

The themes I explore in this book impact on young people differently depending on their class, gender, race, religion, region and many other factors. I chose to focus in particular on how social class impacts on young people's experiences and opportunities because I see this as a fundamental issue in politics, education and community life.

Many of the themes I look at, from youth unemployment to rising inequality, are very much global trends, but in these pages I look at what they mean for young people in the UK.[5]

This book is not here to answer every question or speak for every young person.

There will be many perspectives that I haven't explored and so many brilliant projects that I haven't mentioned. The fact that this can only offer a snapshot is testament to the huge range and diverse experiences of young people in Britain.

I do hope that this book can provide a guide to start exploring the challenges young people face and how to meet them. I strongly believe this debate has to happen but it needs to be a debate *with* young people not *about* them. If this book does one thing I hope it gives a platform to some of the exceptional young people I have met. They have so much to contribute and deserve to be heard.

My journey around Britain

In order to write this book I spent two years travelling round the country talking to young people and researching their attitudes. I started off by reviewing as much of the polling and attitudinal surveys of young people as I could find from a whole range of sources – the British Social Attitudes survey, Ipsos MORI, the Prince's Trust, the RSA, YouGov, Hansard, the Joseph Rowntree Foundation, academic journals and studies and too many more to mention. I was helped in this by two brilliant young researchers, Jake Leeper and Helen Williams, who in different ways embody everything I am saying in this book about the energy, purpose and commitment of young people. I then set out to discuss some of the findings with young people themselves. I visited schools, youth centres and university campuses. I visited some of the most prestigious schools like Eton and Wellington College and some of the most deprived estates.

I particularly focused on six parts of the country, which I felt said something important for what is happening in Britain today:

Camden, a multicultural central London borough with a diverse social mix – the internationally wealthy, an asset-rich middle class, floating young professionals, large and aspirational immigrant communities and a shrinking white working class. I chose Guildford and Woking to represent a predominately white, middle-class suburban life. Areas like this part of Surrey had been a core audience for New Labour: the aspirational voters who have become the focus of much modern political campaigning. Bradford, a faded industrial giant, once leading the world in cotton-spinning, now more notable for racial conflict and economic stagnation. Glasgow, one of Britain's great cities, combining new growth and huge poverty, and central to the debate about the future of Scotland. Finally, the Valleys in South Wales, bringing together a mix of rural and town life and a rich political, industrial and cultural history. These places all say something about Britain's political and social past, but the question I had is, what do their children say about Britain's future?

I approached youth clubs, schools, young people in care, pupil referral units, youth MPs, young religious groups, young volunteers and youth employability schemes. There was a danger that young people taking part in an organised activity of any kind would be more engaged than the average so I also wanted to reach young people who weren't necessarily engaging in any kind of institution, who were just going about their daily lives. Here I sought the help of Leftfield, a brilliant independent field agency specialising in recruiting focus groups and in-depth research. They worked with me to develop a research plan and arrange focus groups in each location with eighteen- to twenty-four-year-olds, deliberately excluding those who were members of a political party or active in politics or community life. I asked everyone I met the same questions about politics, their community, their aspirations, their hopes and fears, their schools, their view of welfare, class, the difference between the generations, inequality, business, the responsibilities of state and citizen. The themes I pick up in this book are where the quantitative and qualitative research tally to show a general trend.

At the same time I went out looking for examples of where young people were doing things differently, whether it was creating new business models, social movements or leadership styles. I did this in any way I could. I went to hundreds of events, debates and youth celebration awards and I spent a lot of time on social media. I found Charandeep, who I write about in Chapter 8, on a Sikh message board and contacted him through Facebook. I saw Franklyn (Chapter 1) perform at an awards ceremony. I found Natalie (Chapter 2) through her blog. The young people I met told me who they admired and I followed the chain of recommendations, discovering some amazing stories along the way. I also bring in my own experience of working with young people in Camden.

I have used the stories of some of the young people I met as case studies throughout the book, illustrating and bringing to life the themes I want to discuss. Many of these case studies are not typical but I choose them because they point to how things could be, to the green shoots of a different kind of future.

Sitting in an empty stadium

Three years ago I organised an event about Stop and Search and one of the young people I had invited stole the show. He spoke passionately about the experience of being regularly stopped on his way back from university, the frustration and powerlessness he felt. Afterwards I asked him if he had considered getting involved in politics. He told me that it wasn't for him; he would have no idea where to start.

I seemed to be hearing the same story all the time. Young people with powerful messages didn't see politics as the forum to express them. The debate I was hearing in the media and many policy forums about what to do about the problem of the young seemed to miss the point. The energy, optimism and ideas seemed to be with the young people I was meeting, the apathy and boredom in the political forums.

I was twenty-six when I first started working on this book and when it is published I will be twenty-eight, but I didn't write this book from the perspective of 'we' because although I am a member of Gen Y I had a more political upbringing than most. I was featuring on Labour Party leaflets before I could speak; I was waving a flag on the steps outside Downing Street in 1997 and by the time I was fifteen I was travelling round the country to campaign for Labour. When I was eighteen and all set to go up to university, my new pots and pans packed, I was offered the opportunity to spend the year as a Labour Party organiser during the 2005 election campaign. I took a train up to Oxford and begged my tutors to let me take a year off and amazingly they agreed, much to my mum's horror. If there is a traditional political or community institution then I am probably a member of it. I am a trustee of my local community centre, governor of a school (even though I have no children), member of a trade union, cooperative party, women's network, Fabians, Progress. I think you probably get the gist.

My friends and in fact the vast majority of my generation have done none of these things. They are highly political, creative and community-spirited, as I hope this book will demonstrate, but they are not party political and they are not working through formal political institutions.

I was brought up to believe politics is a noble endeavour led by people who want to make a difference. I still believe that. It is why I cared enough to write a book about why it needs to change. As a councillor I know politics is full of people who care deeply about their communities but who are trapped in a set of institutions that are failing to let them fulfil this promise. This is no individual's fault but a systemic failure. I know that the young people I work with want to change the world. If politics isn't giving them that chance then there is something wrong with politics. We need radical change and in my view listening to young people is a good place to start.

This book is not a party political pamphlet – that would not be fair for the young people I met, many of whom have rejected the whole idea of party politics. I have tried to put forward what I've found as dispassionately as possible and I hope that people from all political persuasions will get something out of it.

My attitude to politics has everything to do with my family. My dad was a political strategist for the Labour Party from 1986 until his death in 2011. I watched him dedicate his life to political campaigns because he wanted to make the world a better place. I saw first-hand the difficulties and trade-offs he and his colleagues faced but I never doubted that they were there because they wanted to make a difference. My dad taught me three big lessons that shaped my approach to this book. The first was his driving motto and core belief: 'trust the people'. I know the reason he went round the country conducting focus groups was because he believed that politics should be rooted in the voices of ordinary people. In his latter years he became increasingly concerned that politics was operating in an empty stadium. I try to root the ideas in this book in the reality of young people's views and not in what I would like them to be.

The second thing he taught me was to keep a progressive mindset – not to be scared of change but to keep up with it. He saw constant renewal as the only way to ensure that our values stayed relevant in a changing world. This means that I don't always agree with him but he would have been disappointed if I did. He would expect the solutions to be different and shaped by the world as it is.

The third was really a lesson from both my parents, which is the importance of a life lived in the service of others. They brought a deep sense of purpose to everything they did and they asked the same of my sister and me. It was that sense of purpose that I brought to this book and to telling the stories of the young people I met.

However, my most formative political experience had nothing to do with my parents. It was being a middle-class kid at a comprehensive school. From very early on I was acutely aware of the advantages I had by virtue of the lucky chance of being born into an affluent family. Growing up I saw friends who were far smarter than me fall behind and be let down by our education system. That was what pushed me to get involved in the first place, to stand for office, to become a school governor. Politics seemed to be the natural place to fight those battles. The work I do as a councillor focuses on this wasted potential and it is really why I wrote this book. It is a book for the girls I grew up with who deserved more than they got.

It is a book that calls for politics to change but it isn't just a book for politicians. One thing I have learnt from the experience of New Labour and working for five years as a local councillor is that political decision-making alone cannot solve the problems we face. Direction from the centre can only do so much; real solutions have to go beyond politics and empower people. If we want to stop papering over the cracks of unequal opportunity and unleash the true potential of young people then it will take the energy of every member of society.

It will need older generations to get behind young people. I did not write this book to start a war between generations— the last thing young people want is to wage war on their parents and grandparents. The challenges we face require generations to work together, to learn from each other and to find common narratives. I wrote it for my constituents who desperately want to do right by young people but don't know where to start. But most of all I wrote it for the young people who want a say in how their communities are run and don't know how to have their voices heard.

Chapter 1

The Myth of a Problem Generation

The reluctant role model – Franklyn Addo, 21, London

I met Franklyn Addo at a café down the road from the LSE. Fresh from the library, towing a backpack, laptop and several books about injustice, there was little to distinguish him from the hundreds of other students thronging the streets of Holborn on a Friday afternoon. But he is not just another student. Brought up on one of the toughest estates in the country, an estate in Hackney known more for its prison population than its university students, he has become a poster boy for social mobility, the power of hard work and personal responsibility. He is the archetypal 'striver'. But he's uncomfortable with the label. He says that while his family didn't have much money he considers himself deeply privileged because he grew up with security, with parents who encouraged his education and an older sister who gave him a roadmap by being the first member of their family to go to university. He doesn't want his story rammed down the throats of school children growing up on his estate, for them to be told 'work hard, dream big and you can get to LSE or Cambridge'. He says that for too many of them this would be a

lie: the barriers they face are too big to be overcome by hard
work alone, and putting the responsibility in the hands of the
child sets them up to fail.

He thinks society needs to look more closely at how young
people end up in criminal activity rather than just branding them
as thugs: 'Take a young person born on an estate where criminality is rife, the only jobs available are telecommunications or
retail that are hard to get anyway. He does all right at school initially but his mum doesn't really know how to support him. He
still tries his best but he goes to secondary school and gets discouraged, he's got some behavioural issues and ends up getting
permanently excluded. He's left with a lot of free time, ends up
hanging out on the streets. He chooses to sell drugs, eventually
ends up in prison or on probation. His name is already tainted,
making it even harder to get into employment. Of course, the
decision to sell drugs is a choice that is wrong but it takes place
in a context well beyond his control.' Franklyn is keen to point
out that despite these challenges the majority don't follow this
route; his point is that society should have more to offer young
people than criminality or unemployment.

Franklyn is calling for a change of public discourse from one
that is quick to condemn to one that has some empathy for the
challenges of disadvantage.

'No one rationally chooses a life of misery when there is an
alternative. It's a mixture of structural factors and individual
responsibility but I come down on the side of structure. Some
people don't stand a chance from the outset; if they were born in
Kensington they wouldn't have these issues. Some get through
but these are the anomalies, the majority won't have the opportunity. Even those who escape the system are disadvantaged.'

Franklyn wasn't always hailed as a positive role model. His
story first attracted attention when he turned down a place at
Cambridge, deciding that he would study straight sociology and
save money in London rather than take up the joint course on

offer at Cambridge. 'I don't even understand why it was news-worthy,' he says. So deeply ingrained are cultural stereotypes about young black disadvantaged men wearing hoodies and pro-ducing music that any challenge to this stereotype is news. And the reporting of this told its own story. 'Gangster rapper turns down Cambridge' read the *Sun*.[1] The *Daily Mail* likewise led with the negative and the comments made disturbing reading: 'No wonder they never achieve anything in life. I am sure we will be reading about his demise soon. And then moaning about how he wasn't given opportunities in life.'[2]

No one had listened to his songs – a mixture of poetry, story-telling and politics, with not so much as a swear word. His reality was ignored. He fitted neatly into a stereotype and that was enough. It was at this point he began to take matters into his own hands, starting a blog called 'thisis2020' to give voice to his frus-tration.

Whatever his background, Franklyn would be worth writing about. He is a modern-day Renaissance man – poet, musician, academic, writer and philosopher, all while holding down a part-time job in John Lewis. He has set up a collective called 'anomaly', of artists, producers and photographers he met over social media. They come together to produce music, videos and artwork. He has just completed a new set of songs based on real-life news stories and is researching a book about young people and crime.

At the heart of everything he does is a powerful sense of pur-pose. He is an evangelist for his community and the young people he grew up with. He says that while there isn't a strong sense of community in his estate – in fact, there isn't a whole lot of communication at all – there is a common experience of poverty and disadvantage.

And giving voice to those young people drives everything he does. 'I feel like my life is genuinely not my own. I live for these young people. If I don't have a platform to give them a voice I've failed them. I could go for a Goldman Sachs internship, get a decent graduate role, live normally, but so many people are not going to get that opportunity I feel like I need to try to do something.' He says this isn't about charity, he is fed up of young people being seen as helpless or in need of saving. It is about working alongside them to campaign for social justice.

He is determined to challenge the structural reasons for poverty and to change the discourse from blame to empathy and a shared sense of responsibility.

He says there are days where the challenges seem too big, but if he can change the course of one person's life then he will be a success.

Franklyn's story shows how distorted our view of young people becomes when we accept the myth of a problem generation. If we continue to blame them for the problems they are facing rather than asking how to support them we are in danger of turning these myths into a reality.

'Young people these days'

There is nothing new about a moral panic about the nation's youth. Young people have always been used as a proxy for society's fears about social change.

Part of this cyclical story is the reality of adolescent behaviour and development. We now know that the brain continues to be incredibly malleable during teenage years. While our cognitive processes expand in early adolescence, it takes much longer for the prefrontal cortex – the part of the brain that regulates risk and helps with planning, reasoning and judgement – to fully develop. And for those wondering why twenty-somethings sometimes behave like teenagers, this is a process that scientists now think only ends in the mid-twenties and thirties.[3]

Teenagers, therefore, have a developing brain that encourages risk taking and impulsiveness and can make it harder for them to read social cues.[4] At the same time, they are trying to work out their identity and test their boundaries. This is before we have even accounted for the impact of hormones. Teenagers may start to look and sound like adults but in fact the care they receive is as important now as early in childhood.

Marcel Proust's reflections on adolescence in the nineteenth century still ring true today: 'One lives among monsters and gods, a stranger to peace of mind. There is scarcely a single one of our acts from that time which we would not prefer to abolish later on. But all we should lament is the loss of the spontaneity that urged them upon us. In later life, we see things with a more practical eye, one we share with the rest of society; but adolescence was the only time when we ever learnt anything.'[5]

This process of brain development doesn't happen in isolation from the environment but is deeply linked to it. Emerging research shows that the stresses associated with poverty can hinder the development of a healthy brain.[6] In the right circumstances adolescence can be a time of great flourishing, growth, learning and healthy experimentation. In the wrong circumstances it can be a time of chaos, violence and lack of control.

At the same time as sharing some universal features of youth, each generation is a product of a social moment. These are the economic and social forces that shape a particular generation's worldview.

The history of the teenager

The 'teenager' as a consumer with unique drivers and spending habits is very much a modern social construct. In *Never Had It So Good* the social historian Dominic Sandbrook shows that unlike their parents and grandparents, young people reaching adolescence in the 1950s were living in a time of relative prosperity. The post-war austerity was loosening, Britain was at peace, unemployment was low and the welfare state provided security. This was a generation with money in their pockets, time on their hands and opportunity at their doorstep.

At the same time the development of mass media and growing urbanisation gave new opportunities for trends to capture young imaginations. The term 'teenager' came from the US, as did many of the new products appealing to the 1950s adolescent. Young people were creating their own markets in records, bikes and fashion.[7]

For older generations that had endured the hardships of rationing and the self-sacrifice of wartime Britain, this new aspirational consumerism seemed distasteful and sometimes threatening. Accompanying this was the first 'folk devil'[8] of the post-war period. The Teddy boys were working-class boys associated in the public consciousness with a distinctive Edwardian dress, flick knives and a proclivity for violence. They made headline news in 1954 when forty young men were held overnight after a fight at St Mary Cray train station in south-east London. In their carefully put-together Edwardian outfits they represented both the evils of consumerism and the fears of social breakdown. One letter to the local paper after the St Mary Cray fight read, 'It is about time drastic action was taken to put a stop to these scenes of violence caused by irresponsible youths called "Edwardians". The only remedy now is imprisonment and the birch.'[9]

As Sandbrook put it, 'For many people, the teenager was simply the personification of all these concerns: a figure who represented modernity, energy, sexuality and ambition. Rather than teenage subcultures representing a genuine attempt to challenge the values of mainstream culture, what had happened was that people had projected on to the teenager their own fears about the modern world.'[10]

The Teddy boys were swiftly followed by the new youth problem of the early 1960s, the Mods and Rockers. These two groups represented the class divides that still cut deeply among Britain's young: the Mods tended to be middle class, modelling themselves on the Continent, and the Rockers tended to be long-haired, leather-jacket-clad bikers taking their inspiration from the American Hell's Angels.[11] In *White Heat* Dominic Sandbrook shows how small-scale clashes, this time in Margate, were once again blown out of proportion by the press. The *Telegraph* declared them, 'grubby hordes of louts and sluts', the *Express*, 'ill-conditioned, odious louts', and from the magistrate who presided over the resulting court case, the most damning criticism of all: 'These long-haired mentally unstable, petty little hoodlums, these sawdust Caesars who can only find courage like rats, in hunting in packs, came to Margate with the avowed intent of interfering with the life and property of inhabitants.'[12]

It was during the 1960s that the tension between young people and older generations really exploded. A post-war baby bulge suddenly hit adolescence, so they represented a bigger section of the population. Growing numbers were going on to university, so 'students' became a tribe of young people with their own values and worldview. The trends of the late 1950s of growing affluence and consumerism among the young accelerated and saw the birth of 'Swinging London' and the 'Alternative Society'.

My dad was born in the 1950s to two teachers in a typical sub-urban family. He failed his eleven-plus and spent his teenage years bristling against an education system seeking to cane him into a life of metalwork. He left home at sixteen looking for an escape. He protested, he grew his hair long, he was at the edges of the big moments – the Vietnam protest, the festivals – always half observer, half participant. He took that anti-authority spirit to Sussex University, where he organised sit-ins against examinations and helped his friend run a pirate radio station. His radicalism only went so far, as he was always grounded by the everyday aspirations of his suburban upbringing.

My mum was also breaking out of the suffocation of her 1950s childhood, a social life that didn't go beyond the synagogue and her parents' well-meaning attempts to find her a nice Jewish husband. She didn't know what she wanted to do but she knew it was more than the route society had mapped out for her. My mum found her political home in the women's liberation movement and she spent the early 1970s consciousness-raising in feminist book clubs. In their different ways my parents represented the search for self-expression that accompanied rising prosperity. They were breaking free from the roles society had handed down to them and creating their own identity. My mum and women like her wanted more than their mothers' generation.

Young people like my parents were challenging the status quo across Britain; it was a generation straining against pre-war hierarchies. There was a moment in the late 1960s when this young generation seemed to be provoking a crisis in democracy. As their contemporaries in the US and France led campaigns against the Vietnam War, the calm consensus of the post-war period seemed to be shaking under the demands of a new angry generation.

Again for critics it felt like the end of the world. When in 1964, seventy-three coachloads of mainly middle-aged women gathered in a town hall to rally against declining moral media standards and the permissiveness of the young at the first public meeting of Mary Whitehouse's 'Clean Up TV' , they represented an older generation afraid of a changing world. [13]

There was a degree of truth to the concerns – drug taking increased throughout the 1960s and 1970s. In 1960 there were 235 cannabis convictions; by 1970 there were 7520.[14] Crime had been gradually rising since the 1950s.[15] While the majority of young people in the 1960s were not campaigning against Vietnam, living in communes or high on drugs, young people were becoming more liberal about sex and marriage.[16] Young women were starting to demand greater rights. It was also a generation taking consumerism to new heights. While small numbers were leading collectivist actions, the majority were embracing individualism well before Thatcher came along. The new shopping centres were packed with young people wanting some of the action.

In the 1970s the playful experimentation took a harder edge as economic problems began to bite. Half of all sixteen-year-olds left school, but declining manufacturing meant that it was no longer easy to walk into a job.[17] By the end of the 1970s, four out of ten under-twenty-fives were out of work.[18] This hit certain areas hard as deprivation and unemployment spiralled. At the same time the post-war consensus was beginning to crack under the pressure of economic crisis.

For white working-class young men who weren't taking up new opportunities in the service industries, these were unsettling times. They had been brought up with the expectations of a male breadwinner society but were struggling to find the jobs to realise these aspirations. Unlike the generations before who were leading the consumer boom, they had become dole-queue spectators. Out of this growing sense of dislocation came a lot of anger and many people looked for a scapegoat.

There were communities where poverty, unemployment and immigration were colliding. Young people from ethnic-minority backgrounds were facing similar problems with the added barrier of racism. Young black male school-leavers were four times less likely to find jobs than their white counterparts.[19]

Immigration emerged as a convenient explanation for unemployment, housing shortages and the high demand on public services like the National Health Service. The 1970s saw the rise of the National Front, embraced by sections of the skinhead youth movement. This provoked an equally violent counter-movement from left-wing anti-fascist groups and the period was marked by clashes.

Rising youth unemployment was also the backdrop to the growth of Punk, dubbed dole-queue rock 'n' roll by journalist Tony Parsons.[20] These were musicians on a mission to attack everything middle England held dear – queen, country and calm.

Their style was angry and loud, their message anarchic and nihilistic.[21]

For all the talk of the punk movement as an expression of working-class anger, many middle-class young people embraced it in an attempt to express an identity that was different from their parents'. One woman I interviewed for this book described to me her memories of being a teenager in the 1970s: 'I left the country and all my friends were smoking dope and wearing flowing skirts. I came back a year later and they had Mohicans and safety pins in their ears.'

The fears about the punk movement were far more hysterical than the reality. Most young people were busy living their lives as they had been lived in the 1960s and 50s before them. The biggest singles of the 1970s were disco hits, not 'God Save the Queen' by the Sex Pistols.[22] However, for an older generation scared by a changing world, the punk movement – characterised in the public consciousness by swastikas, mindless rage and violence – seemed to represent everything that had gone wrong. For others worried about immigration, groups of young black men clashing with police at the Notting Hill Carnival were emblematic of social breakdown.

Margaret Thatcher not only presented a cure for the winter of discontent and the growing power of trade unions, she was the answer to an out-of-control generation. She represented a return to law and order, family values, patriotism and respect. Like Mary Whitehouse and the coachloads of middle-aged women before her, she placed the blame for social ills on the sexual revolution and liberalism of the 1960s.

At the same time as she attacked social change, she was propelled by it. The aspirational teenagers of the 1950s and 60s now wanted to own their own homes. The young consumers didn't want to be part of austerity Britain, the drabness and conformity of the post-war period.

The aspirations of ordinary people were always Thatcher's powerbase. Right to Buy, where the government subsidised the sale of social housing, was incredibly popular as it talked to people's hopes for their families. The privatisation of nationalised industries like BT weren't marked by public outrage but by a rush to buy shares.[23] People wanted a stake in the new consumer economy.

At the same time many young people were growing richer. The so-called 'yuppies' were making the most of a booming London economy. Suddenly wealth was something to celebrate. And there was plenty of celebrating; the drug of choice for the 1980s teenager was ecstasy, intimately connected with the rise of house music.[24]

However, those at the bottom of society could only watch this growing prosperity from the sidelines. The problems of youth unemployment that had grown in the 1970s worsened in the 80s, bringing with them an increase in social disorder and crime.

In Brixton, half of sixteen- to nineteen-year-olds were unemployed,[25] poverty and poor housing were endemic and crime was spiralling, up by 138 per cent between 1976 and 1980.[26] Toxic relationships existed between the community and the police. This was partially fuelled by the use of so-called 'sus' laws,[27] which allowed police officers to make arrests where they suspected someone might commit a crime. There is no doubt that these powers were disproportionally used to target the black community;[28] they were administered by an almost entirely white police force (286 black and Asian officers out of a force of over a hundred thousand).[29] In April 1981 tensions were heightened by 'Operation Swamp 81' randomly stopping and searching hundreds of people, most of whom turned out to be innocent.[30]

On Monday 6 April 1981 the situation descended into out-and-out chaos when police were thought to have prevented the treatment of a black man suffering stab wounds. Three days of riots commenced: petrol bombs rained, hundreds of buildings and vehicles were destroyed and hundreds injured. Disorder spread across London and to pockets of deprivation around the country, most notably Toxteth in Liverpool but also Manchester, Birmingham, Derby, Cardiff and many other towns and cities.

Although the Brixton riots involved black and white young people, some commentators used the disorder to attack immigration. Others pointed to the rise of youth employment and the rise of consumerism. In *Bang! A History of Britain in the 1980s*, Graham Stewart quotes a report where 'one youth was observed breaking into a sports shop and unhurriedly trying on a succession of trainers until he found a pair that suited him'.[31]

Tensions cooled with the changing seasons and the publication of the Scarman Report. This had been commissioned after the riots in Brixton, and acknowledged that deprivation and discrimination were significant contributing factors to the events. It also called for urgent reform within law-enforcement agencies. However, the wounds were far from healed, and in 1985 further riots erupted.

At the same time football hooliganism, the so-called 'English disease', was on the rise, with police struggling to control the violence. For those looking for an escape, the sudden availability of cheap heroin offered a route out, and by 1984 fifty thousand Britons were estimated to be using the drug.[32]

For Thatcher these events together confirmed her view that personal responsibility had been abandoned during the 1960s: 'The fashionable theories and permissive claptrap set the scene for a society in which the old virtues of discipline and self-restraint were denigrated.'[33] The majority agreed with her.

Globalisation was happening regardless of Thatcherism, and manufacturing was declining before 1979. Coal was a dying industry. It wasn't Thatcher but James Callaghan who announced the death of the post-war consensus when he told the 1976 Labour Party Conference, 'We used to think that you could spend your way out of a recession, and increase employment by cutting taxes and boosting Government spending. I tell you in all candour that that option no longer exists.'[34]

People wanted to see trade union power challenged. In 1979 80 per cent of all adults and 69 per cent of trade union members agreed that 'trade unions have too much power in Britain today'.[35] They were fed up with poorly managed state-run industries that seemed uninterested in offering value to the taxpayer or service to the customer.

The problem was the post-war consensus fell apart and rather than build a new one, what followed was a free-for-all. There was no coherent central vision of what the state owed to its citizens and what citizens owed to each other. Labour offered nothing that spoke to ordinary people and working-class and young voters abandoned them in large numbers.

The fundamental issue was not that coal mining declined but that communities weren't helped to take up other opportunities. The state stepped out in the hope that the market would step in, but it many places it didn't. No breaks were put on rising inequality.

Thatcher may not have actively endorsed greed or uttered the words 'no such thing as society' but her time in office symbolised a put-yourself-first, sink-or-swim brand of individualism that took deep root in our national consciousness. Young people were expected to take up responsibilities but with little support.

Trade unionism wasn't just beaten back; it was kicked a few times just to make sure it was dead. It limped on but has never regained its collective power. The fundamental way unions were diminished contributes to stagnating wages today. The baby went out with the bath water in so many areas of British life.

The problem with the sink-or-swim approach is that it didn't work. In fact, public spending increased: the state spent nearly 13 per cent more at the end of the 1980s than it did at the end of the 70s.[36] A large part of this was the burden of unemployment and the social security budget grew by a third.[37] Ironically, more people became dependent on the state than ever before. Whole communities were abandoned to unemployment and the cost is still being felt today, as I explore in Chapter 5.

Right to Buy was a popular policy but there was little replenishment of the council house stock, meaning that today waiting lists spiral out of control and the government ends up subsidising landlords through housing benefits.

Tony Blair came to power trying to forge a third way between Thatcher's individualism and Labour's social justice. Tax credits and the implementation of the minimum wage helped protect people from blunt market forces. Efforts were made to support communities that had been left behind by Thatcherism through regeneration projects and family support programmes like Sure Start. The success of this approach can be seen in the declining number of young people engaging in crime, as we will see later in the chapter, and the increase in educational attainment.[38]

However, the New Labour government was tackling embedded social issues and global forces. They did a lot more than they are often given credit for to tackle inequality, but it was a struggle just to stop things getting worse.

For many teenagers, the late 1990s and 2000s were an optimistic time, at least in their personal lives. Education rates and university enrolment increased; up to the mid-2000s youth unemployment was reducing. The choice of entertainment and communication tools grew exponentially and kept growing. Hotmail began in 1996, Google in 1998, MySpace in 2003, Facebook in 2004, YouTube in 2005, Twitter in 2006, and the first iPhone was released in 2007. The internet brought with it new opportunities for connection and self-expression. It also brought new fears.

Despite a period of relative optimism, some of today's issues were already evident. The lack of investment in house building meant that young adults were struggling to get on the property ladder and floundering in the private rented sector. The problem of the lack of affordable private housing was put off by a housing benefits policy that saw the state subsidise private landlords.

Traditional employment routes for young men have continued

to decline. For 'working-class' young men without work this identity crisis can alienate them from mainstream society. The 2000s saw race-related riots in Oldham, Bradford, Leeds and Burnley. Nothing could be more symbolic of the changes of the last fifty years than the cities that had once been beacons of an industrial power attracting workers from around the world burning under the frustration of unemployed and hopeless young people.

Antisocial behaviour orders introduced in 1998 protected communities from crime but contributed towards the criminalisation of young people. Despite the number of young people involved in crime decreasing during the Blair years according to government statistics, the media continued to bemoan the yobs, louts, chavs and hooligans.

The 1990s saw the hoodie replace the Edwardian frock coats and leather biker jackets as the symbol of teenage delinquency.

The recession brought things to a head as the overexposure of the economy to the financial industries and service sector became suddenly very clear. As consumer demand reduced so did jobs. Youth unemployment, already increasing, spiked.

A Conservative–Liberal Democrat government came in, applying austerity policies that severely constrained public spending. Young people lost out in the national budgets and in the vast cuts to local councils.

The state of the nation's youth once again swept headlines in August 2011 when rioting broke out in Tottenham and then in town centres across Britain, sparked by the shooting of Mark Duggan.

In an echo of the riots of 1981, these took place in a context of rising youth unemployment, concentrated poverty, anger over 'stop and search' and cuts in youth spending. The debate that followed mirrored the one back in 1981. Some blamed the culture of materialism, some the rise of youth unemployment, but once again many clamoured against the decline in personal responsibility.

Max Hastings of the *Daily Mail* summed up many on the right's response: 'Years of liberal dogma have spawned a generation of amoral, uneducated, welfare-dependent, brutalised youngsters.'[39] He went on, 'They are essentially wild beasts. I use that phrase advisedly, because it seems appropriate to young people bereft of the discipline that might make them employable; of the conscience that distinguishes between right and wrong. They respond only to instinctive animal impulses – to eat and drink, have sex, seize or destroy the accessible property of others.'

The riots were seen as deeply symbolic of a problem with the British young, not a group of young people but a generation. Never mind that it was a tiny minority of young people, that only 27 per cent of the rioters were under the age of seventeen and that the worst criminality came from older organised criminals.[40] The reporting once again focused on consumerism. In a strange echo of the 1981 story, the *Telegraph* picked up on a twenty-two-year-old brazenly trying on training shoes taken from a sports shop in Tottenham, north London, as an illustration of blatant greed.[41]

Research from NatCen, Britain's largest independent social research agency, who conducted interviews across five areas of the country affected by rioting, found that the degree that young people felt they had a stake in their local community and their assessment of their own life chances were key determinants of whether young people took part: 'Hope of a better future through current education and employment or an aspiration to work was seen as the main constituent of having something to lose. Alternatively, some young people felt that their prospects were so bleak that they had little to lose by their involvement.'[42]

A joint study from the *Guardian* and the LSE found that of the rioters not in education, 59 per cent were unemployed. Further analysis by the *Guardian* suggests 59 per cent of rioters came from the most deprived 20 per cent of areas in the UK.[43]

There were some young people who were there out of

genuine anger at the police, who saw the destruction as an act of politics. There were others who saw it as an opportunity.

The reality is that a society that allows young people to grow up in extreme poverty, alienated from their communities and without hope of a better future will see this kind of periodic violence. Many young people I spoke to used the riots as a reference point to sum up their sense of anger; even if they didn't take part it made perfect sense to them that people would lash out.

The challenges facing young people

The obsession with the state of youth over the last sixty years has much more to do with social change than it does with the characteristics of young people.

Globalisation and technological change have driven profound changes in our economy. The backdrop of the welfare state gave the young people of the 1960s new opportunities that they embraced wholeheartedly. The traditional working class has declined and with it a sense of class identity.

Rising prosperity has meant that the politics of empowerment and identity have become increasingly important. The broad collectivism of the 1950s gave way to increasing individualism, which I will explore in Chapter 3.

Through all of this change, young people's aspirations have remained remarkably consistent. In the past the quiet majority have got on with the process of living out these aspirations. Today the quiet majority are hitting a brick wall.

In *Jilted Generation: How Britain has Bankrupted its Youth*, Ed Howker and Shiv Malik showed how young people are doing less well than previous generations in relation to housing, jobs and inheritance, while the Conservative MP David Willetts, in *The Pinch: How the Baby Boomers Took Their Children's Future – And Why They Should Give It Back*, made the case that there had been a breakdown in the social contract between generations. They were both in different ways pointing to the challenges young people face in reaching the same standard of living as their parents.

Home ownership seems a distant dream for most young people. Between 1991 and 2009/10, owner-occupation levels in the sixteen to twenty-four age group fell 61 per cent[44] and the proportion of young people under thirty with a mortgage has reduced from 43 per cent in 1997 to 29 per cent in 2009.[45]

This means the private rented sector is becoming a long-term solution for young people: 51 per cent of eighteen- to thirty-year-olds 'currently renting thought that they would not be able to own in the next ten years'.[46] Yet the British private rented sector is relatively unregulated, offers little security and is beset by rising prices. The move from owning to sustained renting also matters for community formation. An Institute of Public Policy Research (IPPR) report found that 'owning a home increases a person's sense of belonging to a neighbourhood as much as simply living there without owning for fourteen years'.[47]

This also impedes social mobility, as more young people than ever are reliant on their parents. In 2009 it was reported that 80 per cent of first-time buyers under thirty needed help from their parents.[48] The Resolution Foundation, a non-partisan think tank focusing research on low to middle earners, found that 'In 2010, it would have taken the average low- to middle-income household thirty-one years to accumulate a deposit for the average first home if they saved 5 per cent of their income each year and had no access to the "bank of Mum and Dad".'[49] Furthermore, the IPPR found that 'there are now half a million more young people (aged 20–30) living with their parents than in 1997, and three million in total'.[50] This means where your parents live becomes even more important in determining your life chances. A disjointed economy means much of the employment growth, especially in the professions, is in London, yet prices are increasingly unaffordable for those who can't stay with family. Council housing is increasingly not an option as waiting lists spiral. For the many young people who don't have family support to fall back on their options are limited, with Citizens Advice reporting a 57 per cent increase in the number of homeless seventeen- to twenty-four-year-old clients they met between 2008/9 and 2012/13.[51]

Looking forward these problems look set to escalate: at current rates housing demand will outstrip supply by 750,000 by 2025.[52] This is disastrous for young people, as housing represents stability; it gives young people a stake in society and a base to pursue their dreams of career and family.[53]

At the same time as facing a housing crisis, many young people are increasingly facing an employment one.[54] Young people were hit hardest by the recession, with youth unemployment rates hitting a peak of over one million in 2011. In 2014 more than seven hundred thousand young people were still unemployed, with two hundred thousand unemployed for more than a year.[55] Underpinning this is a long-term structural problem with youth unemployment. Even when the economy was booming, 7 to 9 per cent of young people were headed for long-term worklessness at the age of sixteen.[56]

While youth unemployment has been higher in other parts of Europe, in Britain it is young people who have been disproportionately affected. According to research published by Demos in 2011, 'one in three unemployed people were aged fifteen to twenty-four in the UK, compared with one in four in France and the USA, and one in six in Germany.'[57] In the first quarter of 2014 young people were still three and a half times more likely to be unemployed than older adults.[58]

Things don't necessarily look much better for those going into work. The UK's 'work first' approach to tackling youth unemployment means that those entering work are most likely to be going in to low-skilled jobs without the support or qualifications to build a sustainable career.[59] Research into the characteristics of low-skilled young workers show many drift in and out of employment. Young people are more likely to be working part-time or on temporary contracts out of necessity rather than choice than older generations.[60] In 2013 the Chartered Institute of Personnel and Development found that those employed on zero-hour contracts are twice as likely to be under twenty-five or over fifty-five as other age groups.[61]

Wages have been stagnating from a combination of flexible and open labour markets and the decline in trade unionism. This has disproportionately hit younger workers: a joint report by the Resolution Foundation and the IPPR found that, 'Younger workers face a severe risk of low pay with 76 per cent of under-twenties paid below the living wage.'[62] Young people are more likely to be working for low pay than at any time in the last thirty years. At the same time many young people are struggling to find full-time hours, compounding the issue of low pay.

Things aren't going to improve, as this is a generation with some big bills to pay in the future. They are reaching maturity in a time of declining public spending, yet they are also looking at a large, ageing population set for a long retirement. They will have to work longer to support the kind of pensions they will never see.

It is possible today for young people to work hard, do the right thing, fulfil their obligations as good citizens and still be struggling. This makes a mockery of the social contract and helps explain why many young people feel deeply frustrated.

It is time to end the myth of a problem generation

The starting point for understanding the contemporary debate about young people is to understand what our fears are as a society.

There are fears that individualism has gone too far, that the market influences every element of our lives and that we are starting to treat people like commodities. A 2012 YouGov poll commissioned by the Mental Health Foundation found that

76 per cent of people feel that others in society are more selfish and materialistic than they were ten years ago.[63] Many are worried that Britain can no longer compete in a global world.[64] People fear the impact the internet is having on how we relate to each other, how we work and how we live. Some are concerned about the opening up of Britain to other cultures.[65] Many have a sense that our traditional notions of community are under threat and that 'moral values' have been forgotten. A 2007 Comres poll for the BBC found that 83 per cent of people believed that Britain was in 'moral decline'.[66] Mostly we are afraid of losing control, of things descending into chaos.

These fears find a tangible manifestation in our young, as they have for the last fifty years. Today's commentators hark back to the 'grit' of the 1950s youth – the same young people that back in the 1950s another generation of commentators were busy labelling 'louts'.

There are real debates to be had on some of these issues but young people should be active partners in these discussions rather than scapegoats.

Why does it matter? As we have seen, young people have always been deemed the problem until they grow up and start seeing the next generation as the problem.

It matters more today for three reasons. These stereotypes are pervasive and the media climate is all-consuming. They leave young people, especially those that resemble media stereotypes, feeling increasingly alienated.[67] Firstly, the decline of forums where the generations meet means that outside of the family and the workplace, media fears become the lens through which people view younger generations.

Research commissioned by the organisation Women in Journalism in 2009 found that out of over eight thousand articles written about young men, half were about crime and the most commonly used words were 'yobs', 'thugs', 'sick' and 'feral'.[68]

It has got to the point that young people feel that they can't

walk in to a shop and talk to their friends without arousing suspicion. A fourteen-year-old from Glasgow told me how it feels to
be constantly viewed as a problem: 'It's bad classing anyone as a
NED. NED actually stands for Non-educated Delinquent. It isn't
true. You'll be sitting at shops, talking to friends, or going on a
walk, or going to do something fun or going to a youth club even
and you are tagged as a NED.' He looked bemused for a second.
'I don't really understand it; everyone has to go to school.'

Young people like Franklyn carry the weight of people's prejudices for doing nothing but looking like the media's portrayal
of a criminal. It isn't just boys; different stereotypes abound
about working-class girls. Vicky Pollard appears to be a harm-
less caricature until you read that a 2006 YouGov poll found that
70 per cent of TV industry professionals think this is an accu-
rate reflection of white working-class girls.[69]

Secondly, young people are increasingly disengaged from traditional communities, institutions and politics. There is a lot to
value in our institutions and the pre-war generation and baby
boomers are the engine that drives them. They need to have
someone to hand over to. We can't be complacent that young
people will buy into institutions that do nothing for them.

Thirdly, we need young people more than ever. The technological revolution is bringing about change at a pace unknown to
previous generations. It is enabling completely different ways of
living, working and doing business. It is sweeping through and
transforming whole industries. Yet many of those in power across
business and especially across politics and social institutions are
suspicious, ambivalent or uninformed. Gen Y and especially Gen
Z have grown up in an age of technological dynamism; they are
comfortable with the flux and creative destruction the internet
brings with it. Their voices cannot be ignored as society seeks to
mobilise the power of the internet for social transformation. The
world of the 1950s, where children were there to listen and adults
to teach, is turned on its head when a six-year-old is more

technologically proficient than their parents.[70] Young people have the most experience in the most vital engine of change in the modern world, so continuing to cast them as a problem is not just counterproductive, it is suicidal.

The 'youth as a problem' narrative has never been a successful platform on which to build a cohesive society. We can't build a common agenda if we continue to harbour negative myths about younger generations. As I show in Chapter 3, the decline of mass-membership political and religious organisations means that generations are less likely to come into contact with each other, allowing these myths to proliferate.

Myth 1: young people are apathetic

The debate about engaging young people in politics is too often about binding them into existing institutions. I have met young people who are angry, cynical, frustrated, hopeful and idealistic but I have yet to meet one that is apathetic. The vast majority of young people are highly opinionated about political issues and want to have more of a say over political decision-making. However, they are equally disdainful about formal politics from parties to parliament. They are often less enthusiastic about trade unions and religious institutions. They have given up on the traditional levers of power, but this is an active choice not passive apathy. To rebuild our political institutions we need to break down the apathy myth and start taking seriously young people's critique, which I lay out in Chapter 2.

Myth 2: young people have no values

'It seems everywhere I turn, I see evidence of the monstrous "me" generation, 20-something despots like Sam, who care only about themselves, and blame everyone else when things don't go their way.'[71]

Today's youth are seen as 'the spoilt generation', 'the Big Brother generation', 'the get-rich-quick generation', valuing fame, looks and money before hard work and moral fibre. In fact, most young people don't want to be footballers or Page 3 models. The 'Nothing in Common' report from the Education and Employers Taskforce found that seventeen- and eighteen-year-olds' top-five preferred career options were teacher, psychologist, accountant, police officer and lawyer.[72] CelebYouth, an empirical study of fourteen- to nineteen-year-olds, found that far from uncritically following celebrity culture, young people use celebrities as a means of testing and developing moral ideas. They distinguish between good and bad role models and they are critical of excessive wealth.[73] Youth attitudes to work and consumption actually tend to be more concerned with ethics than previous generations, as I show in Chapter 9.

Myth 3: young people are lazy and entitled

Businessman Luke Johnson summed up the prevailing viewpoint in the *Daily Mail*: 'In the hospitality trade, which I know well, there is a high proportion of foreign-born workers because of their greater diligence, skills and enterprise compared to many British workers. This negative outlook, or lack of "grit" to use Hurd's phrase, has been created by a number of factors. One is the unfortunate sense of entitlement too many young people possess, fuelled by the belief that some jobs are beneath them, particularly if they involve manual labour. A lot of teens and twenty-somethings I meet have very high expectations in terms of salary and holidays, but a limited appetite to put in the hours or carry out unpleasant, boring tasks. That mentality was epitomised by the recent case of Cait Reilly, an unemployed university geology graduate, who successfully sued the Government because she was asked to work in discount store Poundland as part of a work experience scheme. Her rarefied dignity seemed to be offended. But

I could tell her that any kind of work can be beneficial. When I was growing up, I worked during vacations and weekends in factories, as a postman, in a hospital and in a hotel. All those experiences taught me a great deal about the realities of life.'[74]

The problem with these hard-work tales is that they existed in a very different economic climate. If Mr Johnson tried doing the same thing today, he would probably be handing out his own CV rather than delivering other people's mail. More young people work for free and for lower wages than in previous generations.

The view of an entitled generation doesn't reflect the young people I have met: the eighteen-year-old boy who had been putting on a suit every day for months to walk round Birmingham City Centre handing out his CV; or the twenty-one-year-old girl I spoke to in Glasgow who has applied for three hundred jobs and never heard back from any of them so volunteers every day at a youth centre; the thousands of young people who are desperate to get any job at all or are working for free in unpaid internships to get a foothold on their chosen career ladder. In 2011 26 per cent of UK graduates aged between twenty-four and twenty-nine were in jobs that didn't require a degree.[75] Cait Reilly, who garnered media attention for refusing to take up unpaid work, wasn't sitting at home doing nothing when she was asked to stack shelves in Poundland for no money. She was volunteering at a museum, gaining valuable work experience in the career she wanted to pursue.[76]

If young people want to do work they love, explore new opportunities or start their own businesses, why are we telling them to lower their expectations? If they are demanding a better future shouldn't we be trying to support their demands rather than belittling them?

If there is a problem with skills it is because we have allowed inequality to become entrenched in our education system and have failed to invest in the 50 per cent of school leavers who don't go to university. A quarter of young people born in 1958 acquired an apprenticeship; in 2009 only 6 per cent of employers recruited any sixteen-year-olds and 11 per cent any eighteen-year-olds.[77] Young people can't even get work-ready with a paper round because such jobs just aren't available to them any more.

If young people's aspirations are not matching the reality of the labour market that is because they have been let down by poor advice and inadequate support. A report conducted by the CBI revealed that only 5 per cent of employers in the UK think our careers advice is good enough.[78] If some young people do not want to accept certain jobs it is because far too many are poorly paid with low progression routes. A sixteen-year-old who has watched his parent work long hours in a job for little reward won't want to take on a job with similar prospects. We are feeling the consequences of allowing wages to stagnate for low-paid workers. We talk about how previous generations worked their way up from the bottom and ignore the fact that social mobility has halted.

This is not only a British issue: the same trends are evident in the US and across Europe. Studies show that 'routinisation' – the notion that human capital is replaced by technology for routine tasks – is driving polarisation across Europe.[79] Rising youth unemployment throughout the Continent should put paid to claims from those who think that young people in the UK are particularly lazy, entitled or deficient.

Myth 5: young people are selfish

'With their blithely recalcitrant, "the world owes me a living" attitude and lack of a hard work ethos, they have imbibed and been corroded by the materialistic hedonism of short-term bling culture and its penchant for easy money and fast living, heedless of the consequences. Often, they are neither industrious nor motivated.'[80]

I will show in Chapter 4 that while young people have lost touch with traditional notions of community this does not make them selfish. They are just as likely to volunteer as older generations and more likely to informally volunteer.[81] They are using the internet to find new ways to share, collaborate and connect. It is young people pioneering the sharing economy, creating new community groups built on empathy and experimenting with collective structures at work.

Myth 6: young people are out of control and large numbers are criminals

'The nation is in the grip of an epidemic of deadly youth violence. Teenagers are having lives that are full of potential snuffed out by mindless stabbings, shootings and mob beatings. The toll is mounting almost daily.'[82]

There are, of course, some young people who commit crimes; however, this is a small and decreasing minority of young people. In 2012/13, there were 27,854 first-time entrants (FTEs) to the Youth Justice System. The number of FTEs fell by 67 per cent from 2002/03 to 2012/13 and has fallen by 25 per cent in the last year.[83] However, youth crime is vastly over-reported and sensationalised in the media so adults end up overestimating the amount of crime committed by young people by a factor of 100 per cent.[84] As many as 75 per cent of adults assume youth crime is rising, when the actual rate has been falling year on year.[85] This perception of the breakdown of public order is so deep in the public consciousness that the idea of 'youth' is synonymous with 'delinquency'. It divides communities, stigmatises young people and prevents intergenerational dialogue.

Trends in first time entrants, 2002/03 to 2012/13

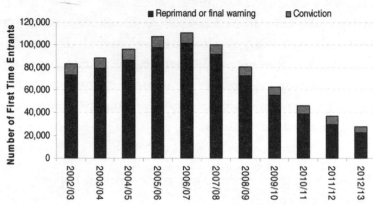

Source: 'Youth Justice Statistics 2012/13', Youth Justice Board/Ministry of Justice Statistics bulletin (2014)

Myth 7: young people are irresponsible

'The furious cop said: "We have gangs of young people hanging around on street corners being abusive, swearing, intimidating and causing trouble. They are feral, have no parental control or respect for anybody and are often fuelled by alcohol. They don't give a damn about the police or the criminal justice system.

"Intimidation is a part of life for these people and the criminal justice system holds no fear for them."'[86]

The general view that we are bringing up a generation without a sense of personal responsibility is deeply entrenched. This is supported by endless headlines about 'binge drinking', 'drunken louts' and 'feral youths', and further corroborated by the trend in television broadcasting that brings together young people and large quantities of alcohol in various settings and films the results (*Geordie Shore*, *The Valleys*, *What Happens in Kavos*). Despite being colourfully displayed to us at every opportunity, drug taking and alcohol consumption among young people are both going down. The number of sixteen- to twenty-four-year-old men drinking more than eight units on at least one day reduced from 39 per cent to 22 per cent between 1998 and 2011.[87] In fact, a survey in 2012 found that 49 per cent of sixteen- to twenty-four-year-olds had drunk nothing the week before, the least likely of all age groups.[88] 15 per cent of sixteen- to nineteen-year-olds smoked in 2012 compared to 31 per cent in 1998.[89] Teenage pregnancy rates are going down (see graph below), though Ipsos MORI polling shows that in the UK we think teenage pregnancy is twenty-five times higher than official estimates. As we saw above, youth crime is going down. The hysterical headlines bear little relation to the reality. Young people are taking more responsibility for themselves and their behaviour.

Under 18 conception rates 1992–2012

England and Wales

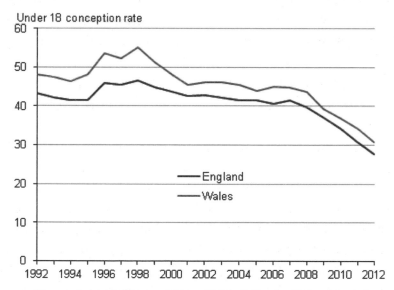

Source: 'Conception in England and Wales, 2012', Office for National Statistics Statistical bulletin (2014)

Myth 8: young people are all the same

There are so many diverse tribes of young people that to even divide them into subcultures would take for ever. Our increasingly diverse and global society allows young people to choose their identity, their style and their music tastes from an ever-widening range of options. Throughout this book we will see how different young people are responding to the modern world in very different ways. We will see huge differences based on socio-economic status, with some young people embracing a global world and others feeling left behind by it.

The problem with these stereotypes is that they influence how young people view themselves. Young people who are treated as apathetic become more turned off from political decision-making that seems to forget them. The teenagers who hear themselves condemned in the media and watched by fearful eyes in their communities become increasingly angry and alienated from mainstream values.

There was a moment where it seemed that David Cameron was opening up a different debate about young people. His 'hug a hoodie' speech in 2006 spoke about the circumstances that blight young lives. It was a speech that acknowledged personal responsibility but also the context underlying many of the choices made by young offenders. It was a speech that called for compassion, understanding and even love.[90]

In government the narrative of personal responsibility has stayed loud and clear – earn or learn, automatic sentencing for young people carrying knives and proposed cuts to housing benefits for under-twenty-fives.[91] The compassion has all but disappeared. When the London riots happened there was little nuance or understanding, it was tougher policing, tougher sentences and back to the language of personal responsibility. Commenting on the riots, David Cameron said, 'Do we have the determination to confront the slow-motion moral collapse that has taken place in parts of our country these past few generations? Irresponsibility. Selfishness. Behaving as if your choices have no consequences. Children without fathers. Schools without discipline. Reward without effort. Crime without punishment. Rights without responsibilities. Communities without control.'[92]

A narrative of responsibility can get us so far. But this is a generation that is showing itself prepared to take responsibility, to work hard and to do the right thing. However, we have to ask: What is our responsibility to this generation?

Our institutions are no longer providing young people with answers to the challenges that face them. For many young people such institutions seem set up against them or at best simply irrelevant. None more so than political institutions that should be helping to solve the challenges young people face but in fact end up alienating them further.

Chapter 2

The Problem with Politics

Searching for a voice – Natalie Robinson, 19, Nottingham

Like most of her generation, Natalie grew up feeling disconnected from national politics. Westminster felt a long way from her estate in Nottingham. 'I was seeing all of my friends going through struggles. And these guys who are sitting in parliament are just having a nice time and sorting out problems for people who are just complaining about stuff that's not life-endangering.'

After witnessing one too many instances of youth violence, Natalie decided to try to do something about it and at twelve she became a youth councillor, and at fourteen she ran to be the Youth MP for Nottingham. She has been championing young people in her community ever since. She spends every spare hour outside of her job and education representing young people. No one pays her; she does it because she feels compelled to give a voice to the people she grew up with. The fact that she is such a strong representative is all the more remarkable because she never really had anyone to champion her. 'When I was growing up I didn't know sometimes when I was going to eat next. Like many other young people I've experienced sitting in the cold for days with no electricity.' When we met she was experiencing first-hand the challenges of homelessness. 'I can feel the pressure that is on a young person when they have nowhere to go, you just feel, Oh my God, what am I going to do?' She says that living the problems faced by young people gives her a fresh perspective.

Yet she has hit institutional barriers when she has tried to get that perspective heard. 'I went to a homelessness strategy drafting the other day at Nottingham council on behalf of the many young people I know who are facing homelessness. All they had to say was mediation: we'll mediate young people back into their families. They just don't understand that some young people don't have a choice, it isn't always as easy as going home and giving your mum a hug. All they had to say was, "But mediation is really good." I know it is good. It is good for young people who can mediate back to their families – they have run away or there is a communication barrier – but for some older young people they've gone past that.'

Despite the struggle to get her voice heard, Natalie has kept going, trying to be the bridge between the young people she grew up with and the political institutions that are meant to serve them.

She tells me, 'I feel like I'm an eagle that carries all of these views on my back. Like they are quite heavy but I'll still deliver them to the right leaders. I'm not looking to change the world but if I can maybe influence a decision with a tangible outcome that was from someone else's perspective then I'd be happy.'

Too often she delivers the message but finds it doesn't get heard. 'I go to meetings about local budgets and ask, "What about young people? Will there still be activities to keep them off the street?" They look at me as if I was a kid asking, "Are we still going to have our toys?" Too often they follow the minimal responsibility on the statute.'

She wants more from politics: 'We should have a duty of care. We should have a sense of responsibility as people and institutions.'

Yet she tells me she feels like a ghost whisperer, her head full of voices that only she seems to hear.

Natalie is exceptional in many ways, and one is that she is channelling her frustration into an attempt to influence formal political institutions. The majority of young people I meet have given up. It isn't that they don't care – they are in fact deeply political, as we will see later on in the chapter – but it is difficult to engage with a process that makes them feel invisible.[1]

Young and ignored

The dictionary definition of apathy is: 'showing or feeling no interest, enthusiasm or concern'. This is a far better description of our collective attitude to youth disengagement than it is of young people themselves. Why a generation is rejecting politics should be the driving political question of our times and a rallying call for reform. It is not young people's apathy but our failure to listen to them that is the real threat to our democratic future.

Engagement in politics has been slowly declining across every generation and today young people have all but given up on formal political institutions. It is a fundamental mismatch between political leadership and the demands and outlook of the citizens it seeks to serve, creating a dangerous democratic deficit. Young people are trapped in a downward spiral – they don't vote because they feel alienated from politics, politicians don't take their concerns seriously, thus entrenching their alienation.

The numbers speak for themselves. In 1964 76.4 per cent of those under twenty-five are reported to have voted, the same number as those aged over sixty-four.[2] By 2005 only 38.2 per cent of young people under the age of twenty-five voted, compared with 74.3 per cent of over-sixty-fours.[3] Even in 2010, which was an incredibly competitive election (and historically more likely to engage young people), an Ipsos MORI poll showed that only 44 per cent of eighteen- to twenty-four-year-olds voted, compared with 76 per cent of those aged sixty-five and over.[4] This marks a profound change in the nature of our democracy, where the voices of one section of society dwarf those of another.

Turnout has declined for all voters but the declines were unprecedented for younger voters, falling by 29.1 per cent and 29.6 per cent for eighteen- to twenty-four- and twenty-five- to thirty-four-year-olds respectively.[5] All other indicators of engagement show the same pattern. Likewise, the decline in party affiliation is most stark for the young. In 1991, 29 per cent of fifteen- to twenty-four-year-olds supported a political party; in 2011 it was 15.8 per cent compared with 57.8 per cent of over-seventy-fives.[6]

This is a long-term trend and nothing from historic experience or academic research suggests that they are going to grow out of it. While life-cycle explanations (where we become more interested in politics as we get older and settle down) explain modest differences in turnout during the 1960s, 1970s and 1980s, they cannot explain the huge gaps that have opened up between generations in the 1990s and 2000s. Research shows that voting patterns in early adulthood determine lifetime attitudes. As one study of the trends put it, these declines are unprecedented at this magnitude.[7]

Almost half young people aren't even registered to vote,[8] and the introduction of individual voter registration will likely only exacerbate this. In 2014 only 24 per cent of eighteen- to twenty-four-year-olds said they were definitely planning to vote at the next election.[9]

While some young people are engaging in political activity, it is only a minority who do so in a way that directly reaches representatives, such as turning up to a public meeting or going to the ballot box. There is little evidence that the young voters who are abstaining from voting are engaging in other forms of traditional civic participation. While there has been an increase in political protest like petition signing, this is predominately among voters.[10]

This is not a blip or an anomaly; it is the end of a long-term trend that threatens the future of our democratic institutions. We cannot have effective, fair government when so many voices are outside the democratic process.

Young people end up as the discussion point of political debate, important only in how they affect older voters on issues from antisocial behaviour to the tax bill. There is little incentive to spend time tracking down students or visiting schools, and when they do young people like Natalie who do take part feel that they are consulted but not listened to. Youth engagement is too often an end in itself, a box ticked.

Politicians are increasingly dealing with depleted resources and facing tough decisions about how to distribute those resources throughout society. The interests and values of young people are not just different, they can be in direct conflict with those of older voters.[11] Take the planning system where the dominant voices tend to be home-owning middle-aged residents protesting against new housing that will threaten the value of their homes and the amenity of their neighbourhoods. Meanwhile young people struggle to get on the housing ladder. When forced to choose, political leaders are more likely to go with their most powerful stakeholders, with the voices they hear at their surgeries, at their public meetings,[12] in their media and most importantly at the ballots.[13] In the 2010 spending review, the IPPR calculated that sixteen- to twenty-four-year-olds faced cuts to services worth 28 per cent of their annual household income, compared with just 10 per cent for those aged fifty-five to seventy-four.[14] The cuts have fallen disproportionately on the young, from tuition fees through to youth services.[15] Or, as it looks through the eyes of Reuben, who is a seventeen-year-old college student in Birmingham, 'Youth are the future but they've just stopped everything. No explanation. No support, no financial support, no support of any kind, it is all slowly disappearing into the darkness.' He is reflecting wider attitudes among his generation: only 15 per cent of young people believe the government generally treats young people fairly.[16]

At the same time there is also a growing gap between rich and poor, in turnout and consequently in political decision-making. Young people from disadvantaged backgrounds, living in insecure housing or private rented accommodation,[17] are the least likely to vote out of a generation already staying away from the polls.[18] As a result, focus groups too often ignore them and party strategists, who pore over the results of such discussions, are left in the dark about what young people from poorer backgrounds really think. Their concerns get lost under the clamour of the voices of those who determine elections. They have become politically invisible. As Camila Batmanghelidjh, founder and director of Kids Company, a charity supporting vulnerable children in London and Bristol, put it to me, 'The journalists ask [politicians] about the economy, the NHS, they never ask them about vulnerable children. It's not there in the national debate, no one prioritises these children.' It is the pressure of these forces that pushed Cameron away from compassionate conservatism and 'hug a hoodie' to dispassionate conservatism and 'jail a hoodie'.

This entrenches youth disengagement as young people legitimately ask, What do politicians ever do for me?

As a society we blame the 'troublesome' young. As political sociologist Rys Farthing puts it, 'Older people define what a good citizen is, and young people, unsurprisingly, emerge as troubled and troublesome yet again. Proponents of this paradigm view young people's rejection of traditional political forms (such as elections and the media) as a "fault"' of young people, blind to the possibility that this may be a legitimate response to faulty institutions themselves.'[19]

Or, in the words of eighteen-year-old Jake from Birmingham,

'They portray the youth as the problem for what has happened to the UK but it is not us that are the problem it is them, it is the people in control.'

The misdiagnosis of apathy means politicians prescribe the wrong cures. We put forward policies to teach young people to be good citizens without recognising how much they can teach us. Natalie Robinson doesn't need a role model. She is a role model.

The debate about youth disengagement so far predominately focused on citizenship education, votes at sixteen and online voting. Of course, anything that can make it easier to engage in democratic processes is a no-brainer. Votes at sixteen will force politicians into schools where there is a captive youth audience with a lot to contribute. It will also put some faith in young people. The experience of the Scottish referendum shows that sixteen-year-olds are more than capable of taking on the responsibility. However, we can't expect it to solve everything. Many young people don't even support votes at sixteen[20] – why would they be passionate about extending a process that they have no faith in? We need to recognise that they are often staying away from the ballots as an act of protest, not apathy.

We could ignore this protest and watch our political institutions slowly fade into irrelevance or suddenly collapse. Nobody would be able to say the signs hadn't been there. Or we could listen to what young people like Natalie have to say and make the broader institutional changes they are looking for. In the process we would improve politics for everyone.

How did we get here?

Voter turnout has been reducing across all age groups. Between 1992 and 2001 levels fell by more than 16.3 per cent among all voters.[21]

It is not just young people that are frustrated with politics and politicians. The whole of society has become less likely to engage in formal politics. It is just that young people are the most visible in their rejection.

This is a long-term trend and first became a topic of political debate in the 1960s and 70s when the baby boomers came of age, shook off deference and began to challenge the status quo through mass protests and political mobilisation, leading many theorists to point to a 'crisis of democracy'.[22] Despite the predictions of some academics at the time, democracy did not flounder and continued on but with ever-decreasing active participants.

The decline in democratic involvement is often put down to declining trust. Commentators point to the expenses scandal as destroying faith in our public representatives. The scandal that rocked Westminster actually had relatively little effect on the public trust in politicians. This is not because the public were in any way forgiving, rather that their trust levels didn't have much further to fall. It confirmed what they already believed: politicians are out for themselves, not the public. This is nothing new – politicians have never been trusted.[23] It also isn't a particular feature of youth;[24] research shows trust in politicians actually declines with age.[25]

If trust levels have remained statically low, we have to look elsewhere to explain patterns of disengagement. What has declined across the board is satisfaction with political institutions, belief in their relevance and people's belief that they can influence them.[26]

The world has changed and political institutions have stayed static. Change is fast-paced. The news cycle supports short-termism when many challenges require long-term thinking. Citizens and their leaders are suffering from an information overload. People are more demanding, with higher expectations just when the capacity of governments is reducing.

In the West we are dealing with depleted resources and a changing global power balance, with much of the economic dynamism and growth coming from the developing world. As the global middle class grows, the pressure on resources will only increase and the energy we consume will have to radically change or reduce. Many challenges – terrorism, tax evasion, climate change – can only be solved by global institutions and governance. National leaders are left with the façade of power but limited room for manoeuvre. Populations look to political leaders for answers and they exaggerate how far they can influence the course of events.

In Britain we have specific challenges – particularly low levels of party affiliation,[27] an often cynical media, highly centralised political institutions and an adversarial political debate.

First, the decline in party affiliation and trade union membership means politics feels ever more disconnected from people's lives. As parties shrink in size they become harder to access and more remote from people's lives. This is particularly true for the working class who traditionally found routes into politics through Labour politics and trade unions based on the collective power of class solidarity.

As these bridging institutions fade away, politics increasingly becomes something people view on television rather than act on in their communities. If the only politics you ever see is snatches of Prime Minister's Question Time then it is not surprising that it feels alien, remote and highly unattractive.

The British media can be a toxic environment in which to conduct political debates. The media appointed themselves as the official opposition during the Blair years as the Conservatives floundered in internal hand-wringing. Of course, fair media scrutiny of politics is important. It prevents corruption, encourages debate and exposes genuine hypocrisy. Problems arise when cynicism becomes the lens through which all news is filtered, when the default assumption built into coverage is that all politicians must be lying. Online media often perpetuates rather than challenges this culture.

The constrained language of many politicians is partly the product of an environment where any comment can be taken out of context. Chloe Smith's *Newsnight* interview where she was publicly mocked (*Daily Mail*: Is this the most humiliating political interview ever?) for being unable to offer a straight answer to Jeremy Paxman's questions is just an extreme example of this move towards conformity.[28] The tolerance given to 'mavericks' like Boris Johnson is not extended to the majority. Politicians are given neither the freedom to experiment nor the liberty to make mistakes. One off-the-cuff comment can mean the end of a career. An ill-thought-through video can be played back to you in a thousand internet parodies. Media outlets pour scorn over these terrible 'gaffes' but in the same breath accuse politicians of being robots.

One of my oldest friends is a journalist and while he was studying journalism and I was studying politics we would have a circular debate about who was at fault for the terrible representation of politicians in the media. His argument was that the media only reflects the mess they are presented with. I would say too many journalists go out of their way to run down Britain and put a negative spin on every political act. The truth is we were both right.

As the BBC's Nick Robinson put it in a similar debate with Rachel Reeves, a member of Labour's Shadow Cabinet, 'I've seen a crisis in trust, first in politics and then in the media. It's a vicious circle where everyone involved thinks if they do down the other they'll be better off. So the media have a go at politicians, politicians have a go at the media – just try to make the other person look more corrupt than you are.'[29]

The culture they are both attacking is the third issue, the nature of our adversarial politics. While the battle for headlines is being so passionately fought in the halls of Westminster and both sides are keeping a close watch on who is up and who is down, the public is long gone and young people, who are facing

so many challenges, only have to see glimpses of it to be convinced that none of the answers they seek can be found in our
political institutions.

Even our politicians feel uncomfortable with modern politics.
In 2009 David Cameron described what he called our broken
politics: 'Politicians who can't bring themselves to recognise any
good in their opponents and refuse to work together to get things
done. Politicians who never admit they're wrong and never
acknowledge that they've made a mistake . . . These are some of
the reasons that politics is broken.'[30]

He is not a million miles away from the unemployed young
person who told me, 'They just bicker . . . you just hear them
taking the piss out of each other. All they try and do is get pub-
licity off each other's failings.'

Yet somehow David Cameron never got round to trying to
change politics; his good intentions got lost in the day-to-day
battle for headlines and one-upmanship. The immediacy and the
clamour of Westminster is a powerful force. The echoes are all
the louder because they are being heard in a bubble.

Local politics has some of the same problems. Every month I
go to council meetings and I sit in a room with a group of
people who I know are there because they care deeply about
Camden and at a community level are intimately involved with
local issues. Yet too often we engage in a debate that is just a
parody of the national one. There is an element of theatre but
it is not really clear who we are performing for because the
public galleries are generally empty. The emphasis ends up being
on rallying the troops, nailing your party colours to the mast,
because the people listening are your colleagues. The format of
formal political decision-making at a local and national level
doesn't give enough opportunities for the public to initiate or
lead discussions and so they stop tuning in. As the most visible
political forums, our parliamentary and council debates have to
reflect a more open and collaborative kind of politics.

Too often in politics the most fiercely fought elections are the internal ones. Much of the most passionate political debate ends up happening within closed party-political forums. The problem today is that most of the public never see these political discussions because the majority of them have never been near a party meeting. They assume that the dull dance of party-political lines is all there is.

They would rather see some give-and-take between parties or a passionate debate. Division without debate is unwatchable.

A big part of the problem is the highly centralised nature of Westminster politics. Devolution has to happen not to centralised mini-Whitehalls but empowering local structures, as I describe in Chapter 11.

The institutions as they are make it hard for individuals to find a new way of engaging with young people. I am as guilty as anyone of making boring speeches, sticking to a bland party line and giving too much time to archaic process rather than engagement. It is easy to do, whether you are an MP, a councillor or secretary of a local party branch. You can spend a lot of time trying to win over the ten people in the room rather than asking why no one has turned up. You are so preoccupied with the processes of how things have always been that you never get round to asking how they could be different.

Young people, like the rest of the population, find all of this really unattractive. We have to work harder to show young people that political institutions can give them the power they are looking for.

Youth disengagement is not an inevitable factor of modern politics. While youth turnout has declined in some countries, it stayed steady over time in parts of Europe (Sweden, Italy, Netherlands and Germany).[31] There is evidence to show that sustained focus on youth engagement in political decision-making has made a difference in these countries. While these are global trends it is important to remember that the scale of youth disengagement from formal politics we face in the UK is not a forgone conclusion.

The cost of youth disengagement

There have been some who asked me, does it matter? Youth disengagement shows things are stable, it was ever thus, the system works, why rock the boat?

It is my view that we can no longer take for granted the sustainability of our democratic institutions. There is a burning anger among many young people that has to be addressed. There is also a wealth of energy and reforming zeal that can form part of the solution. Ignoring the problem means we end up losing the contribution of a huge section of our population, which in turn leads to disjointed decision-making and narrows the pool of political candidates. It should matter to all political persuasions because as we saw in Chapter 1, there are some serious challenges facing this generation, challenges they want to help solve. In 2008 75 per cent of eighteen- to twenty-four-year-olds said it was important to influence decisions in their local area, enthusiasm that could be harnessed.[32]

As political parties become dominated by fewer people from older generations it promotes factionalism and inward-looking debates. If young people are only engaging in politics outside of formal processes it will create a vacuum between citizens and their representatives. The end result is that young people feel as though they are shouting but no one is listening. Politicians feel exactly the same way. There are few places where the two meet, and even when they do they struggle to find the language to communicate.

This leaves young people feeling powerless. It pushes them to seek alternative outlets – from angry protest through to conspiracy – and pulls us deeper into a vortex of democratic decline.

There are some who are actively encouraged by youth disengagement from democratic institutions, seeing it as the start of a new revolutionary politics. In 2013 Russell Brand struck a chord when he called for those disengaged from politics to stop voting altogether. While the attention on voter disengagement is welcome, any narrative that calls on young people to further reject politics rather than try to reform it in my view only ends up entrenching their powerlessness.

Our democratic institutions are creaking but they are by no means impotent. At its best democratic politics can be a forum where trade-offs are negotiated, diversity is represented, brave decisions are made and society is improved. It was a political movement of trade unions and Labour politicians that created the NHS and the post-war consensus. It was Tony Blair's political vision that introduced the minimum wage, a campaign with a hundred-year history. It was David Cameron's political courage that means one day my cousin will be able to marry her female partner in the synagogue she grew up in. It is only in a democracy that it is possible to hand down the power that young people are looking for.

The gradual evolution of our democratic institutions created entrenched democratic norms that no hastily drafted constitution could ever emulate. Their greatest strength is also a weakness, as they have not proved flexible in a changing world, nor responded to a new generation.

While the majority of young people still support democracy, this is not unconditional. We can't take it for granted that young people will continue to put their faith in a system that isn't delivering for them. They are already less inclined than older generations to support parliamentary institutions. 50 per cent of eighteen- to twenty-four-year-olds see Parliament as essential for democracy, as compared to 67 per cent on average.[33] The longer this continues the stronger the calls for alternatives will become. Anger and alienation are always going to be breeding grounds for system overthrow. This is especially true of young people from disadvantaged backgrounds feeling the full force of the democratic deficit.[34] Reforming our democratic institutions is the only way to save them, as I show in Chapter 8. We have a collective obligation to the next generation to create a politics they can believe in. We need a political revolution, not the politics of revolution.

We have to take account of their critique of our institutions and recognise the myriad ways they are actively participating in politics.

The youth revolution

If you approach a group of young people and open with the statement 'I want to talk to you about politics', the general response is likely to be a mix of horror, disgust and boredom. For many it's like a light switches off. A young person who two minutes before has been passionately advocating what the government should do on youth employment will tell you that they don't know anything about politics. Or that politics is boring. Or that politicians are all the same. Or we're better off without them. Or nothing ever changes.

Politicians, teachers and party members can be forgiven for feeling that they are embarking on a thankless task or that young people just don't care, because many will tell you exactly that. They just don't do politics. Politics as a brand is toxic. However, if you rephrase your opening gambit – what would you like to see change in your local area? What are the issues that affect your life? – you will get a very different response.

We are asking young people the wrong questions and then making the wrong assumptions. In different ways the examples we see here and in the next chapter show how young people are increasingly concerned with the politics of self-expression, and political issues that impact their daily lives and the lifestyle choices they make. It doesn't sound political because it is so personal.

The German sociologist Ulrich Beck puts forward the view that 'freedom's children' have internalised democracy to such an extent that what we are witnessing is a 'highly political disavowal of politicians'.[35] Rys Farthing characterises this as young people living their politics, 'they do not vote for change; they do change.' He says, 'For young people, a politics that requires the delegation of power to nation-state experts simply will not tackle their agenda; rather, they need to actualize their politics.'[36] They express their politics 'as "micro-political" actions or as "cause-oriented" actions'.[37] For example the act of story-telling, choosing a job on the basis of the impact it makes, setting up an online campaign or volunteering are how they express the change they want to make in the world.

Those who are often seen as most apathetic and unpolitical are young people from working-class backgrounds. However, I found some of the greatest passion, anger and desire for change in focus groups with young people from DE backgrounds (semi- or unskilled manual workers, casual workers and unemployed). This demographic group is most neglected in public discourse because it is furthest away from mainstream political institutions.

Self-expression as activism

Research by the Youth Citizenship Commission categorised 15 per cent of young people as 'willing but disconnected', who were most likely to be older (nineteen to twenty-five), unemployed, BME and from C2DE social grade.[38] These are young people who are feeling under attack, stereotyped and alienated. Talking to young people from this background they often use the 2011 riots as a reference point, not to justify the criminality but as an indication of the level of dissatisfaction and anger at the status quo.

Steve Anderson produced both *Question Time* and its youth version *BBC Free Speech*. He told me how different the two shows were during the week of the riots. 'The BBC1 programme ... it was very much middle England feeling threatened ... The BBC 3 show was very much ... well, this has been coming for a long time, there's a lot of trouble out there, you don't realise how much tension there is. We get treated badly by the police, we've got no jobs ... they were very, very different.'

Many are using music and spoken-word poetry as a means of expressing rage or pain, a cry of distress at a society that seems to be leaving young people behind. Subjects include violence, racism, capitalism, abuse, poverty. Too often, however, the audience is other young people. So they are creating works of political expression that give others a sense of solidarity but this doesn't translate into concrete action.

United Northern Development is a Bradford-based music collective of sixteen young men in their late teens and early twenties ranging from artists to graphic designers, from camera men to directors. They all have a common experience of disadvantage and frustration at the stereotypes people throw at them. They try to give a voice to the kind of frustrations they feel. 'We address everything that goes on in our personal lives. If it affects us we address it. If you're just speaking about something you've read it's not got the ownership ... we just try to speak from what we've experienced personally. The more authentic [it is], the more you're going to have a unique selling point, and that's really what we're trying to own up north. We're all just people from similar backgrounds, with similar views about where we want to go.'

Their music, their politics and their self-expression are all tied up together. Authenticity is more than a goal; it is at the heart of how they approach their work. They address politics in how it relates to their lives. They act politically in how they live.

This can coincide with a rejection of formal politics and structures. Zaneta, a writer and spoken-word poet, tells me, 'A lot of spoken-word poets don't want to play the game ... actually form a party and do things in a formal manner. I think it is more revolutionary, "let's rise up", change everything rather than reformist.'

But this doesn't mean these young people are unreachable. *I Am Hip-Hop* magazine is a youth publication that 'seeks to go back to the fundamental roots of hip-hop music, exposing the powerful discourse of the genre'. It was from reading *I Am Hip-Hop* that I found myself at Whitechapel one Tuesday evening watching a debate about whether or not hash was destroying our communities. What ensued was informal, and slightly disorganised, but it was also one of the most passionate political exchanges I've ever seen. There was a full range of perspectives: the medical marijuana lobby, the Rastafarian who felt it was linked to the criminalisation of young black men and a young Somali woman who felt that tolerance of khat (a now-banned drug popular among some Somalian communities) was oppressing women – 'If it was white middle-class kids taking it, they would pay attention.' As the organisers called time there were heckles from young people who hadn't had a chance to speak, demonstrating that young people from all backgrounds will engage on issues that lace the fabric of their daily lives.

Straight to the issue

There is one generalisation that holds true for the majority of younger generations: they are much more comfortable engaging with politics as issue debates than through the prism of party politics or ideology.[39] Over 94 per cent of young people said they were concerned about at least one political issue.[40] Most in-depth studies of young people's political attitudes find a great deal of openness towards the idea of engaging over specific issues, as one qualitative study concluded, 'non-activists had strong convictions over a number of issues (whether they defined them as political or not) and appeared surprisingly open to the prospect of political mobilisation'.[41]

These tend to be issues that affect their lives, whether it is drug policy, racism, homophobia, mental health, youth unemployment, education, youth provision or housing. Sometimes these issue-based campaigns translate into large-scale demonstrations like the Iraq war or the student fees protests.[42]

The high turnout and passionate debate exercised by young people during the Scotland referendum shows that an issue that has meaning to them can mobilise them in large numbers. There was no 'youth view': polling showed a mixed picture, with Ipsos MORI putting the 'yes' of sixteen/seventeen-year-old voters at between 55 and 60 per cent, and YouGov having 51 per cent of sixteen- to twenty-four-year-olds as 'no' voters.[43] This split shows how live the debate was for young people. A 2014 Economic and Social Research Council poll of 1006 fourteen- to seventeen-year-olds conducted by the University of Edinburgh's School of Social and Political Science department showed that more than 70 per cent had discussed the referendum with their classmates, parents and friends and 64 per cent had followed the debate on social media.[44] There were many reasons for this high level of engagement – the stakes were high and school-age pupils were enfranchised – but the debate gave voice to some of the under-lying frustration they felt with politics in general and allowed them to engage in an issue that was wrapped up in their identity.

While young people are engaging with issues, relatively few convert this interest into a political platform or make connections with specific issues and broader power imbalances. Young women are far more comfortable talking about sexual exploitation and tweeting about everyday sexism than they are defining themselves as feminists or discussing gendered power dynamics. Equally, a young person might be angry about their perception that the police base stop and search on racial profiling, however they may not see the connection with the Greater London Authority elections or local safer neighbourhood panels where police are held to account. Much of young people's political energy remains un-channelled into political decision-making, as the institutional mechanisms to engage in specific debates outside of parties are limited.

While an approach that only views politics in terms of disjointed issues is not sustainable, opening with relevant political issues rather than with party politics or ideology can help unlock young people's latent political passion. This is what Michael Sani found as a twenty-seven-year-old business studies teacher at a comprehensive school in Dartford. Like the sixth-formers he was teaching, Michael had never voted and was disillusioned with politics, but having witnessed the gap between his students' enthusiasm for debate and their profound disillusionment with politics he began to question both himself and them. He set his students a challenge: go out and speak to other young people about politics. 'It became clear that young people are passionate about issues but politics puts them off.' He helped found Bite the Ballot, a not-for-profit organisation modelled on Rock the Vote in the US, which seeks to register and mobilise young voters. He has toured the country with a band of young volunteers and he never fails to engage his young audience in lively debates. They have created a youth manifesto combining insights from thousands of young people around the country and have persuaded party leaders to engage directly with young people through live-streamed question-and-answer sessions. Their methods are not revolutionary, they just start with a question: What do you care about?

Online petition sites like Change.org are also providing opportunities for young people to engage directly over political issues. Brie Rogers Lowery, UK Director at Change.org, believes that this is helping to challenge apathy myths, especially among young people. 'People are taking action on a huge number of issues; it's just on those issues rather than political ideologies.'

The success of Rock the Vote in the US is proof of the power of an umbrella organisation to mobilise millennials by engaging with them on their terms. It emerged out of similar levels of youth disengagement and has become a powerful political force, registering six million young Americans and literally earning young people a seat at the table – they meet a representative from

the Obama administration regularly. Rock the Vote's Chairwoman Heather Smith tells me they try to take young people on
a path to political engagement, starting quite literally where they
are, by turning up at music festivals and concerts to register young
people and ask them what they care about. As an organisation
they embody young people's desire for openness and empowerment. They are there to provide an umbrella and training but
then hand over the reins to young people. Heather tells me that
being 'open with their brand' and letting young people take the
lead is essential to their success.

Online activism

Young people are beginning to reformulate politics online.
However, this is not mirroring back to traditional politics. When
you consider that only 7 per cent of sixteen- to twenty-four-
year-olds have ever contacted an MP or councillor online,[45] while
the majority of politicians do have websites and social media
accounts, these aren't necessarily reaching young people.

However, between 10 and 20 per cent of young people have
signed an online petition[46] and 36 per cent have looked at a political campaign or an issue website online.[47] These efforts have
often been belittled as 'clicktivism'. Author and prominent internet critic Evgeny Morozov refers to it as 'slacktivism'. He sees it
'as the ideal type of activism for a lazy generation: why bother
with sit-ins and the risk of arrest, police brutality or torture if one
can be as loud campaigning in the virtual space?'[48]

It's an unfair characterisation of how campaigns are evolving
online. It isn't that online petitions replace physical protests; they
can provide a gateway into offline action for young people who
wouldn't necessarily know how to start. The debate about the
trade-off between offline and online activity is a red herring;
young people intrinsically understand that the two reinforce each
other. Take the Facebook page Ben Lyons created highlighting

the issue of unpaid internships. He started it sitting in his bed-room after a conversation with a friend at Bristol University – a classic example of slacktivism, a lazy generation's activism. Except it wasn't. Within a week he had thousands of people signing up and two years later they have paid staff, office space, they've got companies like Harrods and Sony to make pay-outs to unpaid interns and the leaders of all political parties have come out in support of their campaign. In another example, seventeen-year-old Yas Necati and two school friends were so worried about the effect of online pornography on their generation that they set up 'Campaign 4 Consent', demanding better sex education. The topic was later taken up by the *Telegraph* and together they ran a successful campaign to change the way sex education is taught to deal with the effect of online pornography.

For young people like Yas, the internet is changing the power balance in favour of citizens: 'It's a place where grassroots activists can have their voices heard. It's not just about big organisations; anyone can start a petition or set up an account in relation to a certain issue. It's a great way for people to get their voices heard and for people to come together.' Brie from Change.org tells me that the site records eight victories per week.

In many ways the format of politics online is not yet fixed and young people are experimenting on different platforms. There is still a disjuncture between how networked they are and their capacity to channel this into political change. Young people like Yas and Ben are the exception not the rule (only 2 per cent of sixteen- to twenty-four-year-olds have helped organise a petition)[49] and both would qualify as activists (see below). However, as they continue to succeed in setting the debate and winning arguments, they open up online campaigning to more and more young people. The point is not to deride young people signing petitions but to encourage them to start their own and take online politics into their communities.

Mainstream politics in the UK is trying to catch up with

young people, but Brie from Change.org told me she thinks the UK is at least one election cycle behind America and Australia in terms of the way politicians are using online tools. Petition-based campaigns do not match the geographical remit of MPs and councillors. May Gabriel, 17, who blogs and campaigns about mental health issues, told me that she thinks this will start to change when younger people take on more powerful positions. 'Our generation is completely involved in the internet,' she says. 'We see things on the internet and then we make changes. I think when we are all older and there are a few people from my generation in power making those changes then the internet will have more of an influence.'

Jamal Edwards, at twenty-three years old, is one young person who has already taken up a powerful leadership position in the media. He was fifteen when he founded SBTV, now the UK's biggest youth media platform with over 250 million hits on YouTube. He believes there is a huge amount of untapped potential for youth political engagement, pointing to the political nature of a lot of the music on SBTV.

For Jamal it's not that young people don't care about politics, and he points to the political nature of a lot of the music on SBTV as proof of that. As he says, it's 'because I don't think it's put out to them in the right way ... they look at the language and they think, This looks proper long. I think if it was put out in a cool way a lot more young people would get involved.' He thinks young people also need to believe that their intervention can change things. 'They don't know they can shape their future as well. They're like: They won't listen to me so what's the point? They just have to overcome that aspect of it.'

He is taking up his own challenge to help reformat the language of politics for his generation. 'I think I can add a certain kind of spice,' he tells me, laughing. I asked him if politicians should be scared. 'Yes, definitely,' he replies.

In 'The Future of Democracy', a TEDx talk Jamal gave at the

Houses of Parliament, he imagined where this could lead: 'YouTubers could be political, political with massive followings, followings of millions of young people who know, like and trust their brand. That brand could be famous for what they stand for. That YouTuber could become a global political figure. They could use the YouTube arena to engage people in social issues, political actions, campaigns and causes. They could influence change. Imagine that YouTuber on a mission to Number 10, the self-made YouTuber with global links, transparent and open beliefs, a connection with their audience interacting with them daily.'

While some young people are using the internet as a tool for mass mobilisation, others are engaging in politics at the personal, grassroots and community level.

Community politics and direct action

Some young people are taking direct action. There is no set format to this. In the Welsh Valleys, Donna and her sister Gemma were studying media at Merthyr Tydfil College, living in a community where unemployment and poverty blights the lives of the majority. Listening to the Work and Pensions Secretary Iain Duncan Smith tell Merthyr's unemployed to get on a bus to Cardiff to find work, they decided to take him up on his challenge. They created a film showing the human face of benefit claimants and the relentless rejection they face. On their journey to Cardiff they found the bus from Merthyr didn't get them to Cardiff for a 9 a.m. start and employer after employer told them that they were unlikely to find work as they were competing against large numbers of job seekers in Cardiff who could offer greater reliability and flexibility. The video was featured on BBC Wales and received a huge amount of attention. These two sisters weren't political activists, but they were able to have a political influence through sharing their story.

Other young people are engaging within youth structures as youth MPs and mayors. There are six hundred young MPs across Britain and 620 youth councils, and in 2014 865,000 eleven- to eighteen-year-olds voted in 'Make Your Mark', the British Youth Parliament's annual ballot on the issues most important to young people.[50] These roles appeal to them because they are independent and about direct representation of young people. While there is a huge variety in the effort local councils put in to supporting these structures and reaching out to diverse groups, where it is done well it has provided a platform for young people to politicise and explore different models of engaging with young people. Jacob Sakil was sixteen when he became Youth Mayor of Lewisham in 2009 in an election where over 50 per cent of young people voted, a higher youth turnout than at the general election. He put his success down to the fact that he had a similar background to the young people who voted for him. 'Outside of politics, I knew young people who were involved in gangs ... I'm in the same boat as many of these young people ... So it wasn't hard to get those young people interested because they had a connection with me as an individual.'

It can also be easier to engage young people at a local level because young people have 'higher levels of trust for those groups and institutions they engage with daily in their near environment'.[51]

Throughout this book we will meet young people who are creating community-based campaigns and movements totally outside of any formal structures.

There is a common thread that links these young people: they are actively engaged in politics, but it is a non-partisan politics that is strongly rooted in transforming their communities or solving specific problems. They are generally willing to engage in formal institutions but find them remote and hard to access.

Outsider and insider activism

A small number of young people are consciously seeking to work within or transform political institutions. These young people are overtly and consciously political, often highly educated, knowledgeable and committed. The complexity of power structures, the professionalisation of politics and advocacy means trying to influence political change has become a minority pursuit. There is an all-or-nothing approach, either it consumes you or you stay well clear of it. Young activists connect online, by forming their own networks, language and norms. They are their own tribe.

One qualitative study conducted by Dr James Sloam, senior lecturer in Politics and International Relations at Royal Holloway, found that in relation to young people 'young activists were not just far more politically active, but were totally different social animals'.[52] Other academics have pointed to 'a new breed of "super-activists"', as the number of people of all ages 'who say they have undertaken three or more [protest] actions has doubled since 1986'.[53] While most people are showing declining political participation, this group is becoming more active. I distinguish between outsider activists who are working or campaigning through NGOs, coalitions, grassroots organisations or loose coalitions often supported by the internet, and insider activists who are working through existing political institutions. The former tend to be campaigning on issues around social justice and environmental change, often with a broad international focus; the latter on party platforms.

There is strong evidence that activists tend to be highly educated.[54] In fact, much youth activism actually begins on university campuses. Analysis by a New York college of the US Occupy Wall Street protest found that 76 per cent of protesters had a college education, over two-thirds were employed professionals and one-third lived in households earning more than a hundred thousand dollars per year.[55]

Many of these outsider activists are not ideological in the traditional sense but are trying to carve out new ideologies that fit their perspective on the modern world, combining elements of environmentalism, anarchism, socialism and international justice. They are distinct from the majority of their generation because they see politics not as isolated issues but as interconnected power structures. As one young activist, Guppi Bola, put it to me, 'Now I look at things through understanding where power is held in society and where it is not. Who makes the decisions, why and where . . . ? It's something systematic and procedural. They transcend issues.' While there are shades of grey across political activists – some wanting to influence existing structures and some to replace them – they are aligned in seeing change as coming from beyond party structures. As Guppi says, party politics is 'just setting yourself up for disappointment because you know those same power structures are upheld within them'.

The issues they are raising are about inequality globally and nationally, but they are also about taking power more directly. I visited Sussex soon after hundreds of students had finished their month-long occupation of the university. Maybe because I'd been brought up on my parents' stories of Sussex in the 1970s – mass walk-outs, pirate radio and an air of rebellion – I felt as though I was stepping back in time. There was a carnival atmosphere in the student common room and I quickly found myself with my face painted and on my way to an LGBT choir to learn the Occupy Sussex protest song. Speaking to two of the organisers later on, they said that while the issue they were protesting was outsourcing of staff, they felt they had been pushed to occupy by the university leadership's refusal to take them seriously: 'We're just dismissed as lefty students, that's not fair; we want a seat at the table.'

Youth-led campaigns from Occupy through to the climate-change campaign 10:10 have had a huge influence in setting the debate and in some cases even changing policy. However, they have not sparked a generational mass movement.

Many young people are focused on getting through their day-to-day lives, and don't have the time or the energy to devote to broader issues, whether that be finding a job or looking for somewhere to live. As one twenty-three-year-old from a white working-class background put it, 'it is the desperation of now'. While many activists are increasingly feeling a sense of global solidarity, young people from lower socio-economic backgrounds are more likely to be concerned about cutting international aid – 'we need the money here' – and stopping immigration, feeling they are competing for limited jobs and services.

These new movements are also based on a sense of collective endeavour. This runs counter to the individualistic political upbringing of this generation. While they face common problems, they do not feel a common sense of identity around class or as a generation to rally around.

Finally, the diversity of campaigns and causes is a barrier to the establishment of a mass movement. By their nature these campaigns are fluid and often limited in time and loose in focus. This makes such activity hard to embed in long-term institutional structures.

Young activists are aware of these challenges and constantly seeking new ways to organise. Twenty-eight-year-old Daniel Vockins, co-founder of environmental campaign 10:10, now leads NEON, a New Organisers Network that seeks to bring together young campaigners tackling structural issues around a shared agenda. He also co-founded Campaign Bootcamp, a non-party-political campaign training camp for young campaigners, and Campaign Lab, a six-month training programme for 'economic justice campaigners'.

While outsider activists are engaging in a variety of campaigns parallel to parties, there is a small group of young people seeking to achieve change from within party structures. The pull factor to get involved in party politics varies. For some I spoke to it is their parents, for others a passionate politics or history teacher, or just a connection with a set of ideas.

The young people I know and work with who are involved in party politics are deeply committed to political change, however many feel just as frustrated with political institutions as those watching from the outside.

One twenty-six-year-old councillor told me how she had joined the Labour Party when she was sixteen because she was fed up by how her single mother was treated by society. Her mum was a Liberal Democrat and her dad switched between the Conservatives and the BNP, but she felt Labour was the right way to achieve the change she wanted to see. However, she had to fight hard to get involved as she found her local branch 'unwelcoming to young people. The culture was if you are grey and old that's fantastic, because you know everything. Age was seen as equivalent to experience and competence.' She wanted to stand as a councillor but was discouraged, then eventually put into an unwinnable ward. Moving to London she found people who supported her, but it was still hard to be taken seriously.

Now she is an elected councillor but struggling to change the things she didn't like about local politics: 'We ourselves become insiders at some point – having fought so hard to get in and learnt how to work the system, I feel like I end up reinforcing it.' It is easy to do: you make friends, find a strong sense of camaraderie and forget.

A green activist told me there were lots of moments when he thought about giving up because he was looking for open discussions about ideas, but he found too many of the young people attracted to politics overly competitive and tribal. Another young councillor agreed: 'They become all about their career, it all becomes about progression within the party, meeting MPs, walking around the place talking on BlackBerrys pretending to be on an episode of *The West Wing*. It just doesn't speak to ordinary young people.'

A parliamentary researcher aged twenty-three, tells me he is frustrated by the daily briefs laying out a 'party line' and prescribing language, which constrains individuality. He understands that is what is required to win, but he feels he is perpetuating something that ultimately turns the public off politics. Another researcher said she constantly considered leaving because she felt like she was pushing against a system that was never going to change. It can be hard to convert ideals into practical political change even for those engaged in trying on a daily basis.

Once you are involved in any political network, whether it is the Young Conservatives or the 'No More Page 3' campaign, then the ties of friendship and shared purpose deepen engagement. Many young people described how activism changed their social circle, introducing them to some of their best friends. Ultimately relationships entrench these networks. However the force that gives them so much power and shared cause can prevent them reaching out in the way they want, so we have an increasing divergence between the super-activists and everyone else.

What do young people want?

Youth activism is a diverse and messy picture. There is no 'youth view'; there are huge differences in the way some of these groups think society should be organised. However there are some common themes that come up in the way young people critique our political institutions.

Youth representation

Young people look at politics and they don't see people that look like them, they don't see people that understand them and they don't see people that put them first. They see an abstract, alien political class. They often don't distinguish between Labour and the Conservatives. Politicians 'are all the same', cut off and distant from their lives, in what they say, how they behave and the decisions they make. As one seventeen-year-old put it, 'You often associate politics with older men ... they've been to Eton or they've been to Oxford ... you don't really see working-class people or people from ethnic backgrounds.'

Politics is too often still a middle-class, older white male pursuit.[56] As trade unions have diminished, some of the pathways to political life have closed off. The same forces that hold back working-class young people from entering the professions hold them back from political life.

While representation of women is improving,[57] the House of Commons does not reflect back to young people a mirror of their generation in age or diversity. Likewise, local councils are not providing enough opportunities for young people to take on leadership positions. The average age of a councillor in 2013 was sixty; 88 per cent are over forty-five.[58]

For Jacob Sakil, Lewisham's former Youth Mayor, lack of youth representation – especially working-class youth representation – influences the issues on the political agenda. 'I think the people who are our main figures in the political system don't come from the same background ... The interests that those politicians have are not the same as those that the young people have ... When they do talk about the real issues that need to be addressed it's always tokenism.'

It is crucial that we create pathways through to political leadership for young people. It isn't easy to do. Even highly political young people are nervous about taking the next step. Despite the leadership roles they've taken on, party structures are still a shadowy world and they have little idea about how to navigate them. More importantly they are reluctant to sign up to a party in the first place, feeling they will be sacrificing their independence and even their credibility. Natalie Robinson told me she would like to be a councillor, 'to show them a brown working-class girl can become councillor. I can actually represent people; I know where they're coming from.' Even though she leans towards Labour she is reluctant to join the party because as she says: 'People don't want to badge themselves to a political party. There is a stigma attached when you label yourself. I don't want people from my area thinking, Just another Labour person. You lose quite a lot of interest, people who you would have got interest from before.'

Party politics has become a dirty word for many young people. It is associated with bickering, point scoring, putting personal and party interest before representation. They are nervous about subsuming their political identity under a party banner, toeing a party line. They feel they will inevitably have to sacrifice their integrity.

There are opportunities for enterprising independent candidates to reach out to young voters. If political parties are to remain relevant, and attract the next generation of young people, they will have to open up, become more fluid, dissolve some of the hierarchy.

Young people are also nervous about coming up against a hostile media, and this is by no means an irrational fear. I remember interviewing a brilliant young man about his work as a social entrepreneur and encouraging him to stand as a councillor. I later looked at his Twitter feed and immediately saw so much there that would get him into trouble. If an ordinary young person has been documenting their life in public, viewing Twitter as a channel to communicate among friends, then they are incredibly vulnerable to press intrusion. In 2011 the *Daily Mail* ran a story with the headline: 'And the Tory councillor for the wild party is . . . 23-year-old Tory politician slammed for her boozy photos on Facebook'. The accompanying photos were a typical set of university pictures, but they became a political issue with a disapproving comment from her Labour opposition.[59] Young people who have grown up documenting their lives online are an easy target. If we don't have some leniency as a society we will exclude some of the creative leadership our politics needs.

It goes without saying that diversity makes for more informed decision-making. Any debate that includes Natalie or Jacob will be enriched by what they have to contribute.

Authentic and inspirational leaders

'Honesty, sheer honesty,' a group in Glasgow tell me when I ask them what they are looking for from politicians. 'Even if it was "we tried this and it didn't work", at least then you know they are being honest.'

When young people were asked what quality they most admire in politicians, the majority (61 per cent) chose honesty and trustworthiness.[60]

I heard it time and time again in different guises from the young people I spoke to: 'to be truthful', 'no lies', 'the ability to go through with what they actually say'.

It is a quality they think is lacking: 71 per cent of young people believe politicians lie to the public and the media.[61]

They talk about honesty in a direct sense, as an approach to electioneering that doesn't promise the undeliverable. Doing what you say you will. It is why for young people Nick Clegg's turn-around on tuition fees was so problematic, as evidenced by the decline in youth support for the Liberal Democrats.

There is honesty in admitting mistakes. As Jacob puts it, 'If we're really going to have a solution to the problems in our community, that means people who are in power need to actually own up that they've done things wrong, and it's not a lot of times that we actually see public apologies from officials unless they've been caught red-handed.'

But there is also a more intangible quality of 'authenticity'. It is living your values. It is no longer possible to say one thing and do another. Authenticity in politics is linked to conviction, it is about passion. Young people listen to politicians evade questions or repeat a scripted line and they get the sense that they are watching a carefully constructed mirage, not a real person.

This further explains the 'Boris Effect'. People as far from London as the Welsh valleys were more likely to talk warmly about Boris Johnson than about many other politicians. He breaks out of the conventional mould of politician and as a result gets an easier ride in the press. His humour works for a generation that according to MTV sees 'smart and funny' as the new rock 'n' roll. However, there is also an institutional reason for his ability to transcend. It's easier for Boris to be a maverick because he is in a position of some independence. As a city mayor he is able to talk pragmatically about London's interests and sometimes to speak out against his own party. To some extent he transcends left and right to focus on London, at least in public perception.

It is hard for politicians to be honest because they will more than likely be forced to say things people don't want to hear. On almost every issue there are contradictory viewpoints where the public want to have it all. It's not an easy task to convince people to accept the tough trade-offs we face. People would much prefer to blame politicians for not being hard-working enough or not caring enough to find a solution that helps everybody. Some of the dissatisfaction with politics is dissatisfaction at the dilemmas we face as a country. There are no easy answers. Taking a position ultimately loses favour. Politicians struggle to find the language to explain the problems, let alone the solutions.

People are more willing to accept hard truths if they are presented as part of a vision about how things could be. The thin line between honesty about challenges and optimism about overcoming them is hard to find.

Young people's frustration is all the more powerful because they have high expectations. They are looking for vision, hope, inspiration and mission.

Matthew Taylor, Chief Executive of the Royal Society for the encouragement of Arts, Manufactures and Commerce, writes about the need for 'normative leadership' for the modern world, combining a focus on 'substantive mission not procedural means, a willingness to accept the risk of public failure, leadership through exemplary action not mere exhortation'.[62] He gives the example of the Mayor of Oklahoma who, seeing statistics on his city's obesity crisis, didn't start an obesity policy unit: he got up and announced he was going on a diet and invited the town to join him and lose a million pounds together. I'm fat, you're fat, we're all fat. They did it and policy supported the objective but the leadership came first.

Conviction doesn't have to be divisive. Young people want to see more consensus and less ideology. As one young man put it, 'I think it should be a case of them all coming together and deciding what is best rather than coming up with something new all the time.' Another fifteen-year-old youth MP said, 'I wish parliament could be more like youth parliament, working together to focus on issues rather than bickering.'

Finally, they want to feel that politicians are passionate about the issues they face. Language is very important to young people. The language of blame and sanction may appease older voters but it further alienates younger ones.

Power to the people

I was in Bradford speaking to a group of white working-class unemployed eighteen- to twenty-four-year-olds who had never voted and never planned to. They are the invisible voters, all on benefits, on the edge of society. The government would call them NEETs – Not in Education, Employment or Training. When I ask them about politics, they immediately start: 'Why do we need politicians? We have Facebook, why can't we all make decisions together?'; 'The people need to take control like in Egypt'; 'We want to be more involved in decision-making. Because then we'd actually know what's happening in our country'.

Young people's activism is diverse and covers much ideological ground, from environmentalism through to free-market capitalism. However, one thread that connects all of it is the desire to 'have a voice'. Sometimes, when I would push this while conducting interviews for the book, young people weren't clear what they wanted to say. It was an end in itself, to be heard, to be recognised and valued.

According to research by Matt Henn and Nick Foard, the number-one response when asked what would make them trust politicians more was simply 'listen to us'.[63] 61 per cent of young people think there aren't enough opportunities for people like us to influence political parties.[64]

Whether young people are talking about honesty, representation or conviction, it all comes down to this. They don't feel that they are valued or listened to. They can't see access points to influence decision-making.

This can't just be for the sake of young people. It has to be because we recognise the value of those voices, that our institutions will work better if we include them.

As Marc Kidson, the twenty-four-year-old Chair of Trustees for the British Youth Council, which tries to encourage and support youth participation, put it to me, 'You have to see [young people] as both having an interest in what you are trying to achieve and also having the capacity to improve it because they are experts in their own experience, and for so much youth policy it doesn't work because it is not based very fundamentally on the lived experiences of being a young person.'

The scale of participation demands varies – from a group in Woking who wanted youth-focused meetings with politicians at their local community centre through to a group of young Somali men in Camden who told me that they thought politicians should have to go to people with a direct vote before they implemented legislation affecting them.

For many young people who are cut out of decision-making,

they are calling for direct power. As an eighteen-year-old in Birmingham who had been chucked out of school put it to me, 'Change is through the people not through politics. Change is through protest and other forms of people making their voices heard. Politicians can't make a change; only the people can make a change.'

Path to change

Finding that their problems went unsolved and their protests ignored, many of the young people I met could only conclude that their political leaders either didn't care or were actively corrupt. While my experience is that the vast majority of politicians of all ages want to make a difference,[65] the fact that most young people believe the opposite[66] indicates that something has gone seriously wrong.

Politicians are trapped in institutions that aren't fit for purpose. They are making decisions at the wrong level in forums that highlight divisions rather than enable compromise. Much of the problem comes with the culture of political debate and the centralised nature of institutions. Where politicians have to take responsibility is for not doing more to challenge and reform these institutions. Young people are also dissatisfied with the outcomes of political decision-making, and in Chapter 10 I look at how to address some of these demands.

However, there are no easy answers to these questions for elected representatives. Reforming the political system demands that every person involved in modern political debate think about their responsibility to the next generation. Politicians need to remember that they ultimately lose when they go to score an easy point against their opposition. The media also needs to think about the consequences of creating a storyline where politicians are always the villains. Older voters who care about our institutions, who do turn out and vote, have to consider the needs of young people. The demographics are in their favour and in many ways the future of our institutions falls on their relationship with younger voters.

Young leaders have to challenge their peers to put the energy and enthusiasm into changing politics rather than simply rejecting it. Politicians have to stop trying to engage young people in the institutions as they are, and instead work with them to improve them. The starting point is understanding how young people view the world.

Chapter 3

Project Me

Doing well for myself and others – Edwin Broni-Mensah, 27, London

I met Edwin at the Olympic Excel Centre. It was an appropriate venue as Edwin's approach to life is all about pushing his own boundaries and demanding excellence. At twenty-seven, he has his own business, a degree in Mathematics, and Computer Science, a Ph.D. in Applied Mathematics, and was recently named the 'Most Outstanding Black Student in the UK' by *Future Leaders* magazine.

He is also on a mission to make clean water accessible to every person in the world through his social enterprise, Give Me Tap. Customers purchase a Give Me Tap bottle that they can fill up for free at participating restaurants and cafes. It's a win–win, he tells me: you save money, shops get new customers and landfills get fewer plastic bottles. It also saves lives, as a proportion of the profit from each bottle is used to build water infrastructure in Africa.

It's a business with a strong social purpose. So when I asked him what his inspiration was the last thing I expected him to say was his six-pack. Three years ago Edwin was in the middle of his Ph.D. He had just wound up a business and suddenly found he had a lot more time on his hands for reflection. 'I was thinking a lot about life. I was twenty-four and I thought if I don't start looking after myself before I'm twenty-five I never will.' He worked out his priorities: 'Ok, so let me get a six-pack, if I have a six-pack I can attract all these beautiful women.'

He began a ninety-day intensive programme in which he had to drink five litres of water a day, and from here came the inspiration for Give Me Tap. 'Just being caught too many times not having my bottle filled up. Going into a cafe, asking to get it filled and then being told no. It was ridiculous. I can see that you have clean water, right behind you.'

This struck a chord with Edwin. His studies were taking him more and more into the world of water deprivation and poverty bonds. And underlying it all were his parents' stories of growing up in Ghana without access to clean water. Give Me Tap was a vehicle to connect it all together. It was more than just a business, it was a personal mission weaving together his past and present.

An image-conscious twenty-something, yes. A philanthropist with a deep sense of purpose, definitely. He's given a TED talk on the topic 'How being selfish can help others' and tells me, 'If you love yourself you can more easily love and help others.'

He doesn't want to choose between doing well and making a contribution: 'I want to have it all, I want to have it both ways.' Even if that means making a little less money.

He sees himself as an engine of change. 'I create the value and impact I want to have on the world.'

He adds, 'It's a great thing to wake up in the morning and know that I have a purpose.'

Through his search for purpose Edwin is expressing the promise of an empathetic individualism where young people, anxious to have their autonomy protected, respect and promote the autonomy of others. While individualism is a progressive force here, in the wrong conditions it can turn into the pursuit of personal goals above all else. Whether Edwin's empathetic individualism will win out against a harsh individualism for young people depends on the support they are given. What is certain is that individualism is here to stay.

DIY Generation

When *Time* magazine ran a cover story in May 2013 naming millennials around the word 'The Me Me Me Generation' it summed up some of the popular clichés about young people. They were presented as a 'lazy, entitled, selfish' generation. This is the same language and tone used in the UK to blame young people for their own unemployment because of a misguided belief in what is seen as 'young people's unfortunate sense of entitlement'.

Younger generations are always going to be more focused on themselves than older ones. They are still working out their identity and they are burdened by fewer responsibilities. Young people today have grown up in an increasingly empowered consumer culture. The internet is a space where they can express their individuality, build up an audience and hold others to account. Online they are increasingly able to create a reality based on their preferences. They can literally map the world around themselves. This has consequences on the way they react to all areas of their life. They have bought into the idea of self as the area of *their* responsibility, *their* personal engine of growth. It is their ideology and their refuge. When you ask young people about their identity or class, you're most likely to hear the response: 'I'm just me' or 'I don't like to be labelled'.

This doesn't make a whole generation selfish any more than Edwin's search for a six-pack devalued his commitment to helping others. It can encourage them to take responsibility for their lives and to try to make a positive impact on the world. As I will show in Chapter 4, young people are pioneering new forms of collective action and community organisation but on their own terms.

However, it does mean they view themselves first and foremost as individuals. They are one more generation away from class-based politics, from majority-organised religion and mass-membership trade unions. Talking to young people today, these concepts are all hazy, like digging through someone else's memories. Their world is more diverse and they've adapted to it.

It is also true that millennials, compared with previous generations, are much more likely to feel that they have to rely on themselves. They don't have much of a choice. The capacity of government has diminished, the bedrocks of the post-war consensus – a job for life, free education, independent housing – have ebbed away. Now doing it for yourself isn't a choice, it is a fact of life.

For some, like Edwin, it can be liberating. The world is his oyster. But it can also be exhausting and, when it doesn't work out, demoralising. If you subscribe to the mindset of self-reliance then when you fail the first person to rail against will be yourself. The pressure can be overwhelming. It also prevents collective action as one's own failure is experienced as individual and specific, not based on common experience with others.

Subscribing to the ideology of individualism does not mean young people are all individuals. In fact, their tastes and preferences are more socialised than ever. But this is the prism through which they see the world and policy solutions must understand this.

Individualism can be a force for progress but if it is unconnected to communal values it can stoke division and competition. We will see in this book that some young people are flourishing and see limitless opportunities while others feel trapped in a Darwinian race where only a few can succeed.

Understanding the nature of young people's individualism is key to every part of this book. It is in many ways the heart of

society's fears about the next generation. If we do not do our
duty by the young and harness their potential, these fears could
be realised. Young people could slip into a survival mode that
will kill their compassion and drive division. Some are already
there.

This is by no means inevitable. The young people I met have
convinced me that their individualism is at root an exciting,
empowering, progressive and transformative force, which is not
just compatible with solidarity but intimately connected to a collective purpose.

All the young people I have met want to live in a society
where everyone gets the opportunity to seek self-actualisation but
they also want to be part of communities that allow them to
express their differences and they want to be part of institutions
that give them a voice.

In many ways we have an aspirational, optimistic, demanding,
forward-looking and lively generation on our hands. We need to
play to their strengths.

The search for self-actualisation

In order to respond to young people's individualism we need first
to understand it. This is not a fad or a reaction to the internet but
a more profound shift in our society that has been taking place
across generations.

Sociologist Anthony Giddens sees this as all part of moving to
late modernity where identity isn't fixed but a reflexive project. We
no longer live the social roles others have created for us. Instead,
we choose what to believe based on a vast amount of contested
knowledge and choose how to live after considering myriad
lifestyle options. Our identity becomes an ongoing and changing
narrative, written by us. Giddens writes, 'In modern social life, the
notion of lifestyle takes on a particular significance. The more
tradition loses its hold and the more daily life is reconstituted in

terms of the dialectical interplay of the local and global, the more individuals are forced to negotiate lifestyle choices among a diversity of options.'[1]

In other words, in the modern world we choose who to be and how to live. As we move away from traditional roles defined by gender, class and religion, we have many more options available to us. Or as Edwin puts it, 'I'm just me. I have a reluctance to label anyone and I don't want anyone to label me. I don't have to be one thing for ever or have a sense of loyalty to a brand, a company or a party.'

Identity becomes a continuously revising project rather than a fixed entity. We ask ourselves, 'Who do I want to be?'

Unlike previous generations, today's young have access to the internet as they start to explore their own identity. It allows young people to engage even more deeply in this reflexive project of self by carving out their own identities online.

One social media expert described to me the increase in young people understanding themselves as brands: 'Everything is so on show that your Facebook feed, Twitter feed, YouTube channel is an extension of you. It's not just about having a Facebook page, it's about having a Facebook brand. These young people are discussing their brands ... some of them are sixteen or seventeen and they're saying, My identity is my brand. It's very important for me to get my branding right.'

Nineteen-year-old Talisha 'Tee' Johnson's personal website reads, 'Talisha Johnson is a Journalist, Author, Public Speaker, Singer and Song-Writer'.

'I'm Talisha,' she tells me when we meet at a Starbucks in Birmingham city centre, 'before my race, my faith and what I wear.' Through the internet she is forging a career out of being Talisha.

She is a journalist because she has created her own magazine, an author because she self-published her own book at sixteen and a popular public speaker because she directs the Celebrating Youth Excellence Awards to celebrate the academic, artistic, sporting and business success of Birmingham and the West Midlands' young citizens, parents and organisations. When I meet her she's in the process of setting up Skool Girl, an online lifestyle magazine for teen girls to talk about topics from business and entrepreneurship through to style, health and relationships.

Young, empowered individuals like Talisha and Edwin are increasingly shaping their own destiny. They are not then content to be passive when it comes to their work, their identity or their political engagement.

Edwin tells me, 'Where I am currently positioned and where I want to be positioned is to be an organisation of influence so that we can start dictating what sort of policies come out ... I want to be involved in policy creation rather than just saying whether I agree with a policy or not.'

The American academic Ronald Inglehart argues that this focus on empowerment and self-expression are features of post-materialism. He traces this back to the post-war generation who were the first to enjoy a higher standard of living wrought by industrialisation combined with a welfare state that could ameliorate the inequalities it produced. According to his scarcity hypothesis, 'virtually everyone aspires to freedom and autonomy but people tend to place the highest value on the most pressing needs'.[2] Therefore, as people become more secure in the knowledge that their basic needs will be met, post-materialist goals emerge, such as 'belonging, esteem and aesthetic and intellectual satisfaction'.

Giddens similarly writes about the move from the politics of left and right to 'life politics' concerned with personal choice and ethics. This means individuals can express their politics not just in how they vote but in how they live. This doesn't entirely replace emancipatory politics, as in some ways the gap widens between those able to focus on self-expression and those struggling with material needs. Giddens acknowledges that, 'In late modernity access to means of self-actualisation becomes itself one of the dominant forces of class division and the distribution of inequalities more generally.'[3]

We will see later on in this chapter that these divisions have materialised, with some young people increasingly concerned with self-expression and emancipation and others feeling alienated by the knowledge that self-expression and emancipation aren't even an option. We even see the divide in the two prominent characterisations of young people – the entitled and overindulged frame and the yob/lout frame. A theory of change and progress based on the idea of individual action, in a world where not everyone has the capacity to act, is as problematic today as it was in the era of Samuel Smiles.

The politics of individualism

To understand the nature of young people's individualism we must look at how political projects in the UK have responded to, and in some ways shaped, these trends.

Leaders try to direct society, to change culture and set agendas. They also try to respond to changing electorates. It is a cyclical process without a definite start or end and it marches forward to its own rhythm. No one is really in control; it is the coming together of millions of individual choices. Ideas are a product of a society but they also transform a society.

Often change follows generational lines – a group brought up in different circumstances have new assumptions and in turn grow up to take on leadership roles. A dialectic relationship is established whereby each generation creates the conditions that a new generation responds to.

Some ideas fail. History is full of forgotten speeches. But sometimes an idea meets the national mood, it captures a moment and becomes part of the zeitgeist.

Thatcherism was one such moment. It was a consequence of a generation throwing off tradition and hierarchy, looking for personalisation and choice. The rhetoric and the policies won over an aspirational country. The left failed to understand the direction society was moving and were out of power for a generation. Thatcher was on a mission to liberate the individual from the claws of the state and socialism and to unlock a new wave of society; however, she never quite got round to creating the society.

The legacy of Thatcherism can be found throughout this book. The individualism she promoted entered our national sub-conscious and I've heard it repeated back to me from young people around the country. You can hear it in the attitudes of Right to Buy, the steady and unwavering aspirations of home ownership. You can hear it in the belief in the 'self-made man' (or woman). You can hear it in the desire for wealth creation. You find it in the attitudes to welfare and in the belief that unem-ployment equals laziness.

But the young people I'm talking about in this book aren't really Thatcher's children at all, they are Tony Blair's. The aver-age was eight years old in 1997, the youngest hadn't been born.

Young people in Britain today are by no means unrecon-structed Thatcherites.

Some of the messages of New Labour also seem to have influenced this generation. As I explore later in this chapter, they are more liberal in their attitude to race, gender and homo-sexuality than previous generations. Politically, much of the evidence shows that they tend to the centre,[4] they believe in equality of opportunity and they want to be part of a compas-sionate society.

We have some understanding of the trends in young people's views and the differences between generations from the National Centre for Social Research's annual British Social Attitudes (BSA) survey. Each year a different but representative group of more than three thousand people in Britain are asked many of the same questions exploring political and social attitudes.

The results show that the young don't fear the state but have very different relationships with state institutions, ranging from proud to suspicious.

On some issues they want less state involvement, on others they want more. In the conversations I have had I found no sense of a state crushing and oppressing the individual spirit. Those arguments belong to a different era on both sides. It's why there is more traction in defending the NHS (popular) or bashing welfare (unpopular) than defending the state or decrying big government. It comes down to how far a service makes people feel dependent and respects their individuality rather than whether the state delivers it or not.

Despite this, New Labour lost some of the big arguments for this generation around social justice, collectivism and equality. As Ipsos MORI's Social Research Institute's analysis of BSA data on generations drew out, young people tend to be less proud of the welfare state, less supportive of redistribution and harsher on benefit claimants than previous generations (see later on in this chapter: 'Responsibility and fairness in a "dog-eat-dog" world' for more detailed discussion of these trends).

Partly it was because these young children and teenagers weren't the political audience of New Labour. In 1997 it was taken as a given that Labour was for the poor and for a more just allocation of society's resources; but they weren't perceived as being for people who wanted to get on, for business and aspiration. It was in some ways a given that the Conservatives had gone too far in their relentless pursuit of individualism – this wasn't the argument the Labour Party had to win. The audience was made up of those who remembered and rejected the pre-1994 Labour Party. The mission for New Labour was to convince them that the left had changed.

Labour's dominant narrative was aspiration, choice, social mobility, equality of opportunity not outcomes. This was a response to the changing nature of the electorate. The politics of solidarity were not the loudest.

This generation has never heard mainstream politicians advocate redistribution or champion the welfare state. Labour did a lot to redistribute but they didn't shout about it. Older generations could remember both sides of the argument; they witnessed the post-war consensus as well as its breakdown. But those born after 1979 have only ever heard one side of the argument.

They didn't have people on the television advocating collectivism. The majority don't go to a place of worship each week to be reminded of a collective moral obligation. They grew up in an atomised society and as such it can be no surprise that they are a product of that society.

Like the generation growing up in the 1950s and 60s they have had access to the post-war welfare state, but unlike the baby boomers they did not have parents of a different generation pressing ideas of gratefulness and contrasting it to their experience. It's very different when my grandmother says, 'You've never had it so good.' She's from a world I can barely understand. It's less present. The welfare state is part of the fabric of society, so all you see are its flaws.

For all that New Labour did do – establishing Sure Start centres, investing in public services and redistributing through tax credits – there was a lot they didn't do, including failing to build enough homes, paying too little attention to vocational education or focusing on diversifying the economy.

Young people have grown up with a welfare state that is crumbling, creaking under the pressures of years of underinvestment. When members of this generation were old enough to need it, it didn't give them the personalised support they wanted. It didn't help them fulfil their aspirations. It made those of them that needed it feel like dependent failures and encouraged everyone else to resent them. The attitudes we see throughout this chapter are rooted in that experience.

They also grew up in a boom. The dominant political narrative was optimistic about growth, jobs and expanding opportunities. Globalisation was how everyone got rich. We didn't have to choose between left and right, compassion and responsibility, individualism and community. We could have it all. This attitude lingers on. Despite constricting opportunities, something of that early optimism remains in this generation. Despite the difficult labour market they face, they still want to have it all.

Young people are a product of this political and social context. It helps explain the contradictions we see in some of the views: on the one hand yearning for self-expression, purpose and meaning; on the other turning on each other or themselves when this doesn't materialise. It is only by understanding the magnitude of young people's ambitions that we can fully comprehend their alienation when they aren't able to realise them. Too often young people's optimism and aspiration hits a brick wall of hard realities and stagnant politics. Instead of harnessing this potent and highly positive force we are letting it slowly fade away.

The Dreamers

'I believe I was put on this earth to do something important, to change something even if it's the tiniest thing. I want to represent young Asian women and show the younger generations it doesn't matter what background, what gender, how many disadvantages you think you have, if you work hard enough you will get there in the end. I try and work as hard as possible and put as many hours in as I can. I want to do directing and act, experience everything. I know this sounds like a big ask but take every opportunity as it comes and hopefully I'll find my task.'

Sarah, 17, Birmingham

David Cameron wants an 'Aspiration Nation'.[5] He's got one.
If young people are the lost generation no one has told them.
Young people like Sarah believe they can have it all.

76 per cent of teenagers want to achieve more than their parents.[6] 78 per cent of young people surveyed, including those from
both well-off and disadvantaged backgrounds, agreed that finding a good job was their key priority for the future.[7] Young
people from disadvantaged backgrounds do not lack aspiration.
A Prince's Trust survey highlighted the gap between the 95 per
cent of young people from affluent backgrounds who believe
their life goals are achievable and the 77 per cent from disadvantaged backgrounds who share this belief.[8] In Chapter 5 I look
at the problem this gap represents, but looking at these statistics
it is remarkable that the vast majority of young people from all
backgrounds believe this despite the challenges they face.

A Joseph Rowntree Foundation study commissioned to look
at intergenerational worklessness struggled even to find any families where there were three generations of worklessness. They
did find a middle generation between thirty and fifty who had
been long-term unemployed, and of whom some had given up
on finding work, but across the board they had high aspirations
for their children. The report found that 'these parents were
unanimous in not wanting their children to end up in the same
situation' and were actively supporting their children to look for
work.[9] Equally, they found young people had normal aspirations:
'Younger interviewees emphasised how they wanted to avoid the
worklessness and poverty of their parents' lives. They expressed
conventional aspirations about wanting a job, and most were very
active in seeking work.'

Many have bought into a British Dream, and despite often
facing enormous challenges, they believe that for them it can and
will be different. You often get a more positive response if you ask
young people about their own future compared with the future
of the country. The simple reason for this is that they are far more

likely to be positive about *their own* life chances because they are in the hands of someone they trust – themselves.

This affects the way they approach politics. Right to Buy, for example, was a big issue on one of my trips to Scotland in June 2013, as the Scottish National Party had just announced an end to the policy. The group of eighteen- to twenty-five-year-olds from working-class backgrounds I spoke to felt this was an attack on social mobility: 'If people have invested their time and money and the opportunity comes up to buy their home, of course that's a good thing, it lets people feel good about themselves, proud, a bit more social mobility.' Another agreed: 'That's the way people have managed to better themselves.'

There is a strong feeling that hard work should be rewarded, that the Alan Sugars of this world deserve their good fortune. Linked up in this is the thought that it could be them that makes it. As a young woman from a non-working home in the Valleys told me, 'If they earnt their money I don't think we should take it off them. I know if I earnt money and I worked hard for it I wouldn't want that money to be taken off me.'

The rise of entrepreneurialism

Who do young people admire? The most common responses that I get are: Richard Branson, Alan Sugar and, from some groups of young people, Jamal Edwards. This is a generation that more than ever before admires the 'self-made' man or woman.

Research consistently finds that young people are much more likely than the rest of the population to want to start their own business. 49 per cent of young people said they would like to start their own business or enterprise compared with just 37 per cent of the general population.[10]

I will explore in more detail some of the diverse ways young people are using the internet to carve out their own companies and portfolio careers in Chapter 4.

First I would like to focus on why young people are drawn to entrepreneurialism. Partly it is as a result of lack of other options. 24 per cent of unemployed young people 'would rather try to set up their own business than continue to job-seek in today's competitive market'.[11] It is also as a result of new opportunities; the internet means barriers of entry are lower than ever before.

However, the overwhelming response from the young people I spoke to is that they want to be the authors of their own lives. The answers were similar around the country: 'freedom to make my own choices', 'work when you want', 'you don't have to answer to other people', 'It's your own ideas so I'd feel more accomplished in my goals'. They all liked the idea of taking charge of yourself, being able to control your hours and tangibly seeing the fruits of your labour.

Edwin started Give Me Tap after realising he could directly take on the problems he saw around him: 'I thought you had to work for someone to solve problems, but actually you can just look at the world and do it yourself.'

It was a huge unmet demand for alternative career paths that convinced Rajeeb Dey, who was twenty-seven when we met, to set up Enternships, linking graduates to entrepreneurial opportunities. He tells me the advantage of entrepreneurialism for young people is that 'you can see the impact of your work rather than being part of a massive thing where it's really difficult to see the difference you're making'.

This desire to see the impact they are making extends to the majority of young people entering the labour market. Daniel Pink writes about the three career drivers for the modern world – autonomy, mastery and purpose. Autonomy is the desire to direct your own life; mastery is the urge to get better and better at something that matters; purpose is the yearning to do what we do in the service of something larger than ourselves.[12] It is this issue of purpose that plays such a crucial role in how young people see themselves as individuals and in relation to the world around them.

As young people carve out their own identity, what they do becomes increasingly important as a shorthand for who they are. Careers become more important in this context – not just a job but an expression of self. This is especially true as many young people invest more in their education and push back having families. In Chapter 9, I will explore how this search for purpose at work can be a powerful force in transforming the public and private sector.

Live and let live

Young people value self-expression and independence in their own lives and they increasingly respect individual freedom and choice in others. As a generation they are more liberal and tolerant than older generations on a whole range of issues – homosexuality, dress, race and gender roles. If you look at data on most social issues you are likely to see successive cohorts becoming more liberal.

Research from the British Social Attitudes Survey shows successive generations of young people becoming more tolerant towards same-sex couples. In 1983 only 17.2 per cent of fifteen- to twenty-four-year-olds believed that 'sexual relation between two adults of the same sex' was not at all wrong; by 2013 it was 78.3 per cent of fifteen- to twenty-four-year-olds.[13]

According to research into public attitudes carried out for British Future by pollsters BritainThinks, 'one in four of the over 65s still say that they would be uncomfortable about a child or grandchild marrying somebody from a different race, but that falls to one in twenty of those under 25'.[14]

This doesn't mean homophobia, sexism or racism can't be found among the younger generations. Of course they exist. I met young women campaigning on university campuses against horrific sexism perpetuated by fellow students and young men who had experienced homophobic bullying at school; and some young people hold racist views. There are a thousand shades of grey in young people's view and they respond differently based on their socio-economic background, faith and gender. However, this doesn't take away from the fact that the general movement over generations is towards more liberal and open attitudes.

One conversation sums up the generational change. I was speaking to a group expressing some tough anti-immigration rhetoric and a sense that British culture was under threat. But when I asked them what the difference was between their generation and their parents', the first thing they said was 'we're less racist'.

While 41 per cent of fifteen- to twenty-four-year-olds still disagree that immigrants are good for our economy, the number agreeing has risen from 14 per cent in 2001 to 36 per cent in 2010.[15] For this reason UKIP has struggled to break through with this generation: in a recent poll 9 per cent of young people said they would be voting for UKIP compared with 20 per cent of over-sixties.[16] Nigel Farage has a lot of the attributes young people look for in a politician – authenticity, conversational style, the fact that he doesn't sound like a typical politician – but he is still the kind of guy their granddad would want to go for a drink with, not them.

The Britain we celebrated at the Olympics was not a mirage, it exists within communities of young people increasingly accepting and even celebrating diversity.

In the US, 'lifestyle' issues have become a generational rallying point as many millennials mobilise around a right-based agenda. This hasn't happened in the UK in the same way because there is now a broad, liberal consensus on many of these issues. There are different political perspectives but they tend to be more nuanced, inspiring activists but not the majority.

The gap between dreams and reality

While some young people like Talisha, Matt and Edwin are well on their way to self-actualisation, defining their own purpose and creating opportunities, others are struggling to get started.

We have brought up a generation believing that if you work hard and take responsibility for yourself then you will be rewarded. It is the British version of the American Dream, the belief that wherever you come from you can get to the top. The Pew Research Center, a non-partisan American fact tank, asked adults in Europe and the US if they agreed with the statement 'success in life is pretty much determined by forces outside our control'. In Europe the balance was weighted towards factors that were outside an individual's control. For example, in Germany 72 per cent of respondents believed that the power of outside forces was more powerful than that of individual drive in determining success. The number stood at France 57 per cent and Spain 50 per cent. However, in Britain only 41 per cent believed that success was based on external factors – closer to the 36 per cent of US citizens.[17] Here in the UK we are much closer to American-style individual responsibility than to European collective responsibility.

As we've seen throughout this chapter young people have internalised this. 61 per cent of teenagers surveyed in 2013 'believe that getting on in life is more about hard work', compared with only 31 per cent who 'believe it is more about luck'.[18] I heard it around the country from young people in interviews: 'People are responsible for themselves as much as the government is responsible for you'; 'You have to do the best that you can for yourself ... don't let yourself have something on a plate, just work.'

And young people are more than prepared to shoulder their share of responsibility. 65 per cent of teenagers 'would prefer to work even if it paid them less than they could get on benefits'.[19]

The breakdown in our social contract comes when, as we saw in the previous chapter, young people are never given that opportunity. Every young person can't expect to become Richard Branson but they all deserve the chance of housing security and a career that can meet their basic living expenses. However, it is currently possible to work hard, be responsible and not achieve this.

As I explore in more detail in Chapter 5, your education, background and family support network matter more than they did in the past in deciding whether you get to fulfil your aspirations. Some young people are being left behind before they even get to school, others have all the talent in the world but they can't afford to take a risk on a new business or support an unpaid internship. They are caught between their desire to branch out and their fear of losing what they have, even if what they have is not a lot. Failure is more daunting when there is no safety net.

It is the difference between wanting something and believing it can happen. It is the gap between the 49 per cent of eighteen-to thirty-year-olds who want to start their own business and the 7 per cent who are actually in the process of doing so.[20] It's the 64 per cent who say fear of failure holds them back.[21]

It is within the gaping hole between some young people's aspirations and the reality they are faced with that 'doing well for myself and others' turns into 'looking after number one'. The British dream without a level playing field breeds resentment, anger and conflict. This is where the openness and tolerance of this generation get tested.

When young people fail, they turn on each other, and if that fails then they turn on themselves. Research by academics David Bell and David Blanchflower linked youth unemployment to low self-esteem and depression.[22] 40 per cent of unemployed young people 'have faced symptoms of mental illness – including panic attacks, suicidal thoughts and feelings of self-loathing – as a direct result of being unemployed', whilst one in three long-term unemployed young people said that they have felt suicidal.[23] In a world where individual responsibility isn't moderated by our collective responsibility, just as success is a mark of your individual talent, failure means there is something wrong with you.

*

In a pub overlooking the Welsh valleys a group of young people tell me that their earliest memories of politics are of 'Margaret Thatcher, milk snatcher'. They talk about her as a looming presence in their childhood, brought to life through the stories they heard over the dinner table and in their classrooms. They felt her growing up through the scars of their parents' unemployment and their own limited opportunities.

When we meet they are either out of work or in poorly paid jobs. They all have a vision of where they want their lives to go, the businesses they want to start or the courses they want to do. They also all have a reason why it isn't happening for them. I ask them about joining a trade union: a few don't know what I mean; others don't think it would help because 'unions stop people working'. One twenty-two-year-old who minutes before had been describing how he was brought up on his dad's tales of the miners' strike replies, 'The only person who can help is yourself.' They all agree. I ask them if they wouldn't have more power together. They look at me as though I'm mad. As one twenty-one-year-old puts it, 'What happens if everyone turn up, we're all together and there is only one job available, everyone's against each other again.' They see themselves in a race for limited opportunities – 'We're all fighting against each other for jobs.' In one generation they have moved from the power of the collective to the dislocation of competition. Rather than pulling together, limited opportunities are forcing them apart. They really are Thatcher's children, but not in the way their fathers or their teachers taught them.

Responsibility and fairness in a 'dog-eat-dog' world

The debate between individual and collective responsibility is played out in young people's attitudes to welfare and redistribution.

Support for redistribution and caps on wealth is lowest among the young. In a YouGov poll for British Future, eighteen- to

twenty-four-year-olds were asked whether they would support a
legal maximum earnings level of one million pounds a year
including bonuses; 30 per cent agreed compared with 49 per cent
of adults of all ages.[24]

In another YouGov poll, 66 per cent of eighteen- to thirty-
four-year-olds agreed that it is the job of government to give
everyone an equal opportunity to achieve on their own merits,
similar to older generations polled. However only 14 per cent
agreed it is the job of government to narrow the gap between
rich and poor, compared with 21 per cent of those fifty-five and
over.[25]

In Guildford one young man summed it up when he said,
'That's just capitalism. It gives you the motivation to think I
could be a millionaire.' Or as one unemployed boy from Bradford put it, 'If someone's worked, self-employed, then fucking
nice one.'

Research from the British Social Attitudes survey shows the
general trend away from supporting redistribution. In 1990 55.8
per cent of fifteen- to twenty-four-year-olds supported redistribution, in 2011 it was down to 37 per cent.[26] Digging deeper in
focus groups I found that it is not simply hostility to redistribution – young people's attitudes are far more nuanced, especially
when it comes to distinguishing between earnt and unearnt
wealth.

I found that the young people I spoke to were more supportive of inheritance tax than redistribution but it is still very mixed.
Again it comes down to a belief that if people have worked hard
for their children they deserve the money. They personalise it: 'If
my gran died and left me fifty thousand pounds, I wouldn't want
to give any to the state.' However, they will support increases if
the threshold is high enough.

Part of the negative attitude stems from their perception of
welfare and the stereotypes attached to the 'undeserving poor'
compared with the 'hard-working' rich.

Young people's faith in individual responsibility means they are far harsher about benefits than older generations, as many see claiming from the state as a failure of that responsibility.

Research from Ipsos MORI analysing British Social Attitudes data on pride in the welfare state across generations found that 'seven in ten of the pre-war generation say they are proud of it, a figure that is virtually unchanged in the last eleven years. Baby boomers are not far behind, particularly in more recent years. But then there is a large gap to Generation X and an even larger gap to Generation Y: just 25 per cent of our youngest generation said they are proud of the welfare state in 2011.'

Part of this is the degree to which they associate welfare with a 'benefits culture'. Responses to the British Social Attitudes Survey highlight the changing attitudes of fifteen- to twenty-four-year-olds over the last thirty years. It was from 1997 and 1998 that, for the first time, more fifteen- to twenty-four-year-olds thought that benefits were too high rather than too low. This is the cohort born between 1973 and 1979, now between thirty-four and forty years old. They are the first generation not to remember the post-war consensus. They grew up with Margaret Thatcher and 'dog-eat-dog' individualism, which has subsequently shaped their social attitudes.

Two focus groups in Guildford, with eighteen- to twenty-four-year-olds, summed up the arguments I heard around the country when talking about unemployment benefits: 'If it was cut back it would motivate more people to find more jobs.' I pressed them with some of the stories of young people struggling to find work in areas without jobs. The response: 'They should use their initiative and move somewhere.' They have no time for empathy because they are too caught up in their own frustrated ambitions. One member of this group explained that he had gone to college on the advice of his career adviser because he wanted to be a police officer. A year after completing his course he is working as a cleaner at a fire station, the closest he can get to his dream job as a police officer. It took him months even to get this job but he refused to go on benefits. I asked him why not? 'Stigma,' he replied. 'I didn't want to laze around all day and get paid for it.' Young people like this, who have invested in their education and feel they have compromised on their aspirations, end up asking, Why should I work for low pay in a job I dislike to fund others to do nothing?

This view isn't restricted to young people in work. Those on benefits are as harsh if not harsher than their employed peers and just as likely to demand cuts in benefits. When I asked a group of unemployed eighteen- to twenty-four-year-olds from Bradford living on benefits what class they identified as, they reflected back society's perceptions: 'People think we're scum'; 'we're just above smackheads, just below working class'. One young mum responded, 'Right now I feel like a piece of shit. I feel like I'm at the mercy of social. I'm trying to do my best for my daughter but at any moment it could all go tits up.' In 2011 'half of young people seeking work say that visiting the job centre makes them feel ashamed'.[27]

While they want to see cuts in benefits, when it came down to it they didn't want to see cuts in welfare for people like them. They believed they were losing out because others were getting the opportunities. There was widespread support in the same Bradford group for one young man's idea to use the money to fund unemployed 'British' young people to start their own businesses so they could employ 'immigrants'. He went on, 'They're cutting it in stupid areas and if you come from Afghanistan with eight kids you can get forty thousand pounds a year.' Others agreed: 'We're too soft on Asians'; 'It's always funding extra things for them . . . where's our extra?'

And so on. Them and us.

Rather than feeling part of an open, inclusive society where there is enough to go round, some are left feeling that there are finite resources, limited opportunities and someone else is getting them. One twenty two year-old boy from Glasgow looking for work summed it up: 'It's just dog-eat-dog . . . the apprenticeships aren't there.'

It's not that they have no compassion. Many young people I met had an idea of a 'deserving poor' – the elderly, the sick, the disabled and those who've contributed and fallen on hard times. They have a huge affection for the pre-war generation who are seen as having contributed all their lives and defended the country during the Second World War. Far from an intergenerational divide, young people are more likely to support spending on the elderly. 32 per cent of eighteen- to twenty-four-year-olds agree that the government 'should stop paying the state pension and winter fuel allowance to pensioners paying higher-rate tax, and use the money instead to provide more help to people who need the money more', compared with 43 per cent of all adults.[28] As one young woman in Glasgow put it, 'Old people are losing out because of the people who are claiming but shouldn't be claiming.'

One person's 'deserving poor' is another's 'scrounger', but common recipients of the title 'undeserving' are those who've never worked but could, immigrants, the long-term unemployed, 'the lazy' and 'single mums'.

Wherever you go and start these conversations you hear back a sense that the wrong people are being rewarded. As one young woman in Glasgow put it, 'It's a joke. Every day we pay people who don't deserve the money and can't pay people who do.'

Young people talk about wanting to see those who 'do the right thing' supported. They think the incentives are wrong and push people to exploit the system. One twenty-one-year-old woman in Woking struggling to get on the housing ladder with her young family told me she believed she was being punished for having a partner. Her friend felt the same way about having a job: 'The cost of childcare means it's better for me to stay home on benefits than go out to work, the incentives are all wrong.'

They have a view of fairness that is based on contribution. If
you work hard, do the right thing, you should be rewarded. For
those living on benefits they want the opportunity to work hard.
They want a system where hard work is rewarded and freeload-
ers are punished.

A twenty-one-year-old second-generation Somali who grew
up in social housing told me, 'The Conservatives, as much as I
hate them, do get people off their backsides. Labour are too
wishy-washy. They are too lenient. The Conservatives are ruth-
less.'

Another young woman living on benefits put it to me, 'Do
you know why Labour is in charge for most cities? Because they
are dole bosses. I'd vote Conservative.'

It's not that they have rejected the state. Data from the British
Social Attitudes Survey shows that 92.7 per cent of fifteen- to
twenty-four-year-olds would either retain or increase current tax
and spending on health and education.[29] They are just as proud
of the NHS as their parents and grandparents, and they welcome
the idea of an enabling state that supports those aspirations. I
found strong support for intervention in the private rented sector
or to support grants for young people who want to start a business and train. The problem comes down to unemployment
benefits that are seen as exactly that: a benefit rather than social
insurance. In Chapter 10 I look at how a focus on reciprocity can
help re-frame the debate about benefits.

Individualism is here to stay. The battle for this generation is
whether this amounts to competitive individualism, or if we can
find a way to channel that energy towards creating the conditions
where more stand to succeed. How we respond to inequality,
stalling social mobility and youth unemployment is key to determining which wins out.

There is nothing wrong with young people having high aspirations; in fact, we should celebrate their aspirations. We will
need big, creative ideas for the future.

There is also nothing wrong with young people wanting a greater sense of purpose, meaning and fulfilment from work. It will increase productivity and reduce the health burden of an unhappy and stressed population. The problem comes when they don't have the skills or opportunities to realise those aspirations. Individualism turns sour when it loses touch with solidarity and empathy, when young people feel they are in a zero-sum game where only some can succeed. This is when they bunker down and retreat to a politics of blame.

The answer is not to try to push them back into traditional collective identities but to help them to forge new communities that celebrate, promote and harness, rather than suppress their individuality.

Chapter 4

Searching for Community

The community revolutionary – MC Angel

MC Angel is a hugely talented poet, MC and rapper who built her career after leaving school at fifteen. When we meet, it turns out she grew up just down the road from me.

She is now busy leading a revolution. It has nothing to do 'with the powers that be' and everything to do with how we relate to each other.

At the heart of her revolution is Lyrically Challenged, the spoken word event that is all about collaboration and sharing: 'A whole ethos of inclusion, encouragement, love and support and community, which is what we're lacking these days.'

She sees this as intimately tied to self-expression. She describes how people come to her events and 'bare their heart and soul on a microphone'. 'People talk about sexual abuse and stuff like that on the mic' and everyone gets a hug afterwards; 'to me that's a revolution and that's freedom'.

She goes on: 'It is a community where people can be open and raw and honest about who they are. We have, like, LGBT, we have disabled people, we have rude boys, hippies, everything at our events. It's a big collection of people together uniting.'

She sees honesty and authentic dialogue as key to empathy and change. 'Everyone's wearing a mask; we need to just take them off and be raw and be vulnerable, because when your heart is fully open and you're open to others and their hearts are fully open to yours then we can have a whole different dialogue.'

She understands in a tangible way the importance of relationships in binding young people because she grew up with troubled ones. 'I felt like there was nothing, absolutely nothing. In my house my mum would just start smashing up the house and ripping my things and being violent to me and throwing my clothes out on the street at night before I had to go to school the next day with scratches on my face and shit.' Growing up, she never felt part of her school community or neighbourhood. She certainly doesn't feel connected to any traditional political institutions.

The turning point for her was being introduced to Jennie Matthias, who was running a charity to help give young people self-esteem through the arts. Jennie became her mentor. That one positive connection started to open up other connections. 'We all need that one person,' she says. 'I wouldn't have done it without Jennie. We all need that person to give us that little bit of encouragement.'

Things were still tough but everything had changed. 'I was living in my hostel, crackheads banging on my door all night, you know. I just kept my head down and went to college and did my thing.' She applied for five thousand pounds from the Prince's Trust and put on a massive community show with all the kids from the estate she grew up on. She began doing poetry workshops with young people and started doing poetry gigs and 'it just started a snowball effect'.

At the same time one of her friends introduced her to Buddhism, which was the start of a new journey. 'I got into Buddhism because it was like the only place where I felt a bit of calm within myself.' She credits it with her own personal revolution. 'My parents are both drug addicts and I don't take drugs or drink, so I've managed to break the pattern of addictive cycles in my life. So that's my human revolution.'

She is deeply religious but not in any kind of traditional sense. In fact, she sees traditional religious language and hierarchy as letting down young people and providing a barrier to spiritual enlightenment.

Yet she feels what is lacking in society is a sense of the spiritual: 'You know, so we are like disconnected in that sense of learning the spiritual importance of human connection.' She says she sees this in the work she does with young people in prison. 'We are not taught how powerful we are. We feel powerless and that is why them young people can hold them knives and guns and think nothing's gonna happen until they see the blood on the floor. She told me about a young woman she worked with who had a knife pulled on her and ended up in a fight: 'Next thing she just saw the blood pouring out of her. She's just like, "What the fuck have I done?" She said she was just crying her eyes out, she just couldn't believe she'd stabbed someone.' MC Angel things that split-second decision was possible 'because you're not taught about the power that one has, how powerful we are and how fragile life is. And how precious it is, [the] consequences of actions.'

The answer, she says, is education that appeals to the spirit and not just the mind.

'We should be waking every morning, coming into school, sitting having a five-minute meditation and talking about how thankful we are for our lives, our first-world problems, like, kids would be killing for this education, but, we're not taught gratitude, we're taught that we need these fucking trainers so I'm gonna stab you for that shit.'

Her life now is all about passing on the spark of self-worth that Jennie Matthias gave her to young people and rebuilding community links.

'What I'd like to see happen is people working to become very successful and for us to regain the money and regain the power and pump it back into our communities and to live, eat and breathe community.'

And regardless of what formal institutions do she will be busy with her own community revolution.

For MC Angel, a strong community has provided her with an anchor and a liberating sense of purpose. Not all young people have been as lucky. I found that every young person I met was in some way searching for connection and meaning in their lives but far too many were struggling to find this beyond close friends and family.

Have we lost a sense of community?

Every so often something will happen that provokes my gran to rue the breakdown of community: someone doesn't get up for her on the bus, she reads about a mugging, anything she hears about the internet. She'll sigh, a wistful look will come over her, and she will start to tell me about the Blitz. 'I was less scared walking down the street then than I am today,' she'll say. 'In those days people had respect, neighbours spoke to each other and we looked out for each other.'

During my research when I asked about 'community' I heard so many young people echoing their grandparents' nostalgia. As one young woman in Lewisham put it, 'The community spirit is broken down. Before when you lived on a street you knew everyone's name ... Now we live in a society where everyone is so closed. Everyone gets up, goes to work, comes home, shuts the door. OK, we're neighbours, but could I go to them if I needed help?' There is a feeling that we have let something go, a sense of collective endeavour, of mutual trust and shared identity. The Conservative idea of 'Big Society' and Labour's 'One Nation' mantra both, in different ways, point to something lost.

Community is a difficult concept. It can be a byword for other values – compassion, friendship, fraternity and solidarity. It can be a descriptive term for a group of people in a shared locality, network or interest group and it can also be a political project. A community can be a nation or a neighbourhood. The notion of a decline in community is a constant companion of social and technological change. It is so contested that some academics have concluded that it has no value as a concept at all and purely focus on social networks.

The community life that my gran refers to was her synagogue, her father's involvement in the Labour Party and her mother's informal networks in her working-class neighbourhood. It was underpinned by homogeneity and strict social norms and gender roles as well as religious and class identity. While she is right that it generated stronger social trust, that came at a price.

The tug-of-war between the power of entrenched local community ties and respect for individual difference still plays out today. A couple of years ago I spent some time in Newcastle as my dad was receiving medical treatment there. I loved everything about it. The sense of solidarity, the way the cab driver taking me to the hospital would tell me with a sense of pride that Geordies are friendly people and how quickly I was on first-name terms with everyone from the newsagent to the fellow patients. At a breakfast for everyone who'd been treated by my dad's amazing surgeon Mike Griffin, I sat talking to a table full of middle-aged cancer sufferers and their partners from South Shields. They told me about how they formed local associations for oesophageal cancer sufferers, helping each other with advice, cooking and house-sitting. It was a close-knit group who'd formed strong ties of trust and friendship based on their shared location and experience. The talk turned to London and the group started to say things like: 'I don't know about London, I went there once and there were so many different people', 'it's scary, it's not really British'. Everything I loved about London, the complexity, the surprising diversity and vibrancy, the fact that you could be crushed between an ageing punk and a Nigerian pastor on your weekly commute was a threat to their way of life. There can be a trade-off between community and individualism, diversity and solidarity.

As we saw in the last chapter, in the battle for the values of the majority of the next generation, individualism has won out. It is a natural response to difference, a consequence of social change and the dominant political ideas.

The question remains, is my gran right? Has something been lost along the way and if so what is it? The answer is yes, there has been a decline in social trust and solidarity at local and national level. However, the solution is not to try to return to the past and re-create the communities of the 1950s. We have to find new forms of solidarity that take account of increasing diversity and individualism and give room to self-expression and differ- ence. Some young people like MC Angel are already doing this, and they show what is possible. But this new world is still an aspi- ration for many young people. Too often they feel isolated from their local neighbourhood and formal community associations and they don't have access to groups that connect to how they view the world. The twilight zone between the death of defer- ence and the birth of emphatic individualism can be a harsh, lonely individualism. In this chapter I look at the challenges of this twilight zone, and some of the ways in which enterprising young people are responding.

Measuring community

What has happened to community depends on how you define it. For the purposes of this chapter a community is a group of people that voluntarily recognise a sense of mutual obligation to each other. The idea of 'social capital', defined by sociologist and Harvard professor Robert Putnam as the 'social networks and the

norms of reciprocity and trustworthiness that arise from them'
allow us to measure this nebulous concept.

In *Bowling Alone: The Collapse and Revival of American
Community*, Putnam used evidence from political groups, professional associations, religious bodies, clubs and community
organisations to make the case that in the US social networks,
which underpin strong communities, had been in decline since
the 1970s. He argued that 'without at first noticing we have been
pulled apart from one another and from communities over the
last third century'.[1] The evidence he drew on was American but
the argument he put forward had traction across the Western
world.

It provides some hard evidence to my gran's nostalgia. As we
saw in Chapter 2, similar trends exist in the UK with the decline
in civic participation, in membership of political parties and in
trade union engagement. We see the same patterns across a host
of other forms of community life. Take, for example, membership of social organisations. Looking at people born in 1946,
around 60 per cent of men and 50 per cent of women belonged
to at least one organisation when they were in their thirties, such
as a trade union, traditional women's organisation or service
organisation; for those born in 1958, the numbers were 15 per
cent and 25 per cent, and of those in their thirties born in the
1970s the numbers fall to 10 per cent and 15 per cent. Most
tellingly, World Values Survey data showed 'social trust' – the
belief that most others could be trusted – declined from 56 per
cent in 1959 to 30 per cent in 1996.[2]

This is not, however, a linear process of decline, as there were
several indicators such as social trust that either increased slightly
or plateaued after 1996, suggesting that the political efforts made
to stimulate a sense of community by Tony Blair's government
may have had some effect. However, the long-term pattern has
been a decline in community associations.

Digging deeper into the data shows there are big differences between social classes. Social capital is holding up and even increasing among higher socio-economic groups and reducing within lower socio-economic ones.[3]

There are also distinct intergenerational differences. These trends are most pronounced for younger generations. In fact, Putnam ascribes a great deal of the general decline in social capital to a younger more atomised generation replacing an unusually civically minded pre-war generation. We know young people are least likely to join a trade union or religious organisation or to attend a public meeting. In 2010 65 per cent of young people between eighteen and twenty-four did not belong to a religion compared with 24 per cent of those over seventy-five.[4] A 2009 survey found that 41 per cent of people over fifty actively practised their religious faith compared with 29 per cent of sixteen- to twenty-nine-year-olds.[5] An Office for National Statistics study found that eighteen- to twenty-four-year-olds 'were the least likely to speak to their neighbours regularly, know or trust the people in their neighbourhood, have done or received a practical favour from a neighbour and were more likely to report that their neighbours did not look out for one another'. Fewer younger people also had high levels of reciprocity (measured in this instance by trust in people who are like you/ not like you, confidence in institutions and perception of shared values): 26 per cent of sixteen- to twenty-four-year-olds had a high reciprocity score compared with 53 per cent of those aged twenty-five and over.[6]

The problem in the UK is that social capital is increasingly enjoyed only by older and wealthier members of society. The data could be interpreted as young people rejecting notions of community but that would be a mistake. It is often the other way round, with young people feeling excluded and rejected.

Qualitative research for the Youth Citizenship Commission, set up by the government in 2008 to explore what citizenship meant to young people and how to engage young people in politics, helps to shed some light on this. It separated the different ways that most of us engage with the world. First as individuals in isolation from others (me), second with friends and family (we), third by engaging with the community (us) and forth by engaging with formal institutions (them). The community provides the bridge between the 'we' of friends and family and the 'them' of civic institutions, giving individuals a sense of collective power and belonging. However, for most young people (thirteen to twenty-five years old) the 'us' of community didn't exist. Indeed, their view of community was just as abstract as formal institutions. For the majority of young people their dominant form of interaction was within the 'we' of friends and family. Many young people from disadvantaged backgrounds hadn't got past the 'me' stage of engagement. This meant that they were engaging with the world in a purely individualistic mindset.[7]

The patterns we see here of declining social capital (connections between individuals – social networks and the norms of reciprocity and trustworthiness that arise from them)[8] are not simple. They are messy across generations and classes. The same is also true of religious belief. While religion has declined in general,[9] some communities are engaging as enthusiastically as ever.[10] The same holds for politics and community associations. The passion of the true believer has replaced the power of numbers across so many walks of life.

As a local councillor in a diverse London ward I am at the intersection of the many parallel communities that coexist. Although people live side by side this doesn't mean they are neighbours in any meaningful sense. In other cities in the UK communities are not so much running in parallel but often existing in isolation and sometimes conflict, such as in Oldham, Bradford and Burnley.

How can we explain this diverse and fragmented picture? Again Putnam helps by introducing the concept of 'bridging and bonding social capital'. 'Bridging social capital' are networks that are 'outward looking and encompass people across diverse social cleavages'. 'Bonding social capital' are tight, dense networks that 'tend to reinforce exclusive identities and homogenous groups'.[11] As our world becomes more globalised many groups have sought refuge in the intense ties of bonding social capital, strengthening the relationships with people who share similar life experiences. As such there is a proliferation of micro-communities and a reduction in the values that unite people across them.

In my view three major sources of bridging social capital are missing – the bridge between generations, the bridge between social classes and in some cases the bridge between different cultures.

The bridge between generations

Part of the reason why many young people see traditional neigh-bourhood communities as abstract and removed compared with their parents and grandparents – who see them as a more impor-tant part of how they engage in the world ('us') – has a lot to do with the breakdown between generations. Beyond the tight ties of families the relationship between generations is too often char-acterised by fear, misunderstanding and misrepresentation.

I was at a selection meeting recently for local election candi-dates and when each candidate (all of whom were over thirty) was asked the main problems in the local area, alongside problems such as housing, transport and health inequalities, they all iden-tified 'young people' as an issue. No one batted an eyelid because there is a shared assumption in this country that there's something wrong with our young. When asked to rate how positively people in Britain felt about people in their twenties, respondents in the UK gave our young the lowest score of any country in Europe.[12] The relentlessly negative portrayal of young people in the media deepens and perpetuates these misconceptions,[13] as we saw in Chapter 1.

This unwarranted criminalisation of a generation has real consequences within our communities, breeding fear and preventing the casual conversations and acts of random kindness that build a community. An anecdote from a teenager in Glasgow is just one example of the way friendliness can be lost in translation between generations. He described an incident where he ran over to help an elderly lady burdened by shopping to cross the road, only to find himself being sworn at and hit by her walking stick. The chances are that the next time he sees an old lady trying to cross the road he'll give her a wide berth, and like my gran she might go home and tell her grandchildren that these days young people have no respect.

Some young people start to internalise the attitudes they are shown. Eyes that follow them with suspicion when they sit on a bus or enter a shop, curtain-twitchers who call the police when they are mucking around with friends and officers that stop them on the way to work are part of their day-to-day story. Is it any surprise if some begin to feel that maybe there is something wrong with them and lose the inclination to show respect to a society that judges them before they have done anything wrong?

It's not the fault of the vulnerable and scared woman who seeing a young man in a hoodie reacted with fear or the old man living on his own who wonders what the group outside his house are capable of. They are often just reflecting back society's prejudices.

The broken relationship between generations is in many ways a consequence of the erosion of other kinds of community associations such as religious groups that forced generations firstly to interact but secondly to negotiate their difference within a shared cause.

Outside of the family, opportunities for generations to spend time together are limited. As an Ipsos MORI report that examined intergenerational perceptions put it, 'Beyond the context of the family and friends, the two generations seem to coexist in almost parallel universes, with very few opportunities of establishing real contact.'[14]

This is backed up by research from the Prince's Trust that finds, 'More than half of young people (54 per cent) "rarely" or "never" speak to people over the age of forty in their local community; while more than two-thirds (68 per cent) "rarely" or "never" speak to those over sixty.'[15]

The internet deepens these divisions. Evidence shows increasing divergence between where young and older adults live and work.[16] The new wave of tech start-ups populated by twenty-somethings clasping MacBooks are entire ecosystems dominated by the young. In the past, the majority communicated using the same medium, whether it was letter-writing or the telephone. That is no longer the case; many older adults do not use the communication apps that young people live on. A generation brought up on email are less likely to send Christmas cards.

This lack of contact between generations is all the more tragic because of the growing problem of loneliness in old age and the associated health risks. Individuals who are socially isolated have between two and five times the risk of dying early from all causes compared with those who have strong social ties.[17] Research conducted by the charity Age UK found 41 per cent of elderly people reporting that their TV or pet was their main source of company.[18] Fear stands between a generational dialogue that could ease the loneliness of the old and the sense of alienation of the young.

Intergenerational differences are accentuated by the fact that older adults are the dominant force in our communities. In the 1960s we had a younger country, young adults set the agenda, they changed the terms of debate and created their own movements and communities. While many young people are straining to create their own language of community and new community associations they find that the dominant power in all our communities is older adults.

Intergenerational breakdown can't however explain every-thing. The full weight of negative stereotypes is reserved for young people growing up in poverty. The biggest differences in terms of social trust are actually found between young people from different socio-economic backgrounds.

The bridge between classes

Over the last half-century we have seen the gradual ebbing away of class identity. This wasn't a dramatic shift. It went hand in hand with the slow unravelling of an industrial economy. Today British Social Attitudes research shows if you ask most people what social class they belong to, the answer will be 'I don't know'. However, if you push them, around six in ten will tell you they are work-ing class and three in ten middle class.[19] For many this is a nod to their parents or a vague link to their work: it is not the primary force they use to identify themselves, it isn't bolstered by a sense of solidarity or shared purpose and often bears little relation to their objective social class. British Social Attitudes analysis shows very little correlation between social class and values; rather, edu-cation levels, gender, race, religious belief and age are all more significant in determining how we think.[20]

But whether you acknowledge it or not, the social class you are born into is still a powerful determinant of your outcomes in education and employment (as we will see in the next chapter) and your propensity to vote (as we saw in Chapter 2). Today it is also a strong indicator of your likelihood to engage in com-munity life.

So we have one group becoming more connected and pow-erful relative to others as they feel the full benefit of a sense of belonging and assert themselves in community groups and civic decision-making.

This is exacerbated by the fact that social classes come into contact with each other even less than they did in the past.

Research from the Institute for Public Policy Research, IPPR, shows that in the past, marriage across different social classes was common, especially for women. In fact, only 39 per cent of women in 1958 had married a partner in the same social class as themselves; but of the latest cohort (born in 1976–81) 56 per cent have married a partner in the same social class. As more middle-class women entered university, graduates became more likely to marry other graduates, thereby entrenching and cementing their social networks. ONS research showed that degree-educated professionals are five times more likely to have a large support network compared with people with no formal qualifications.

The rich and poor increasingly live in different areas and attend different schools. Beyond the 7 per cent of young people who go to private schools,[21] research conducted for education think tank the Sutton Trust found that middle-class children are disproportionately clustered around certain state schools. They found that while at the least-deprived comprehensive only 4.2 per cent of children came from families in receipt of housing benefits, this went up to 68.6 per cent for the most deprived.[22] This can't all be explained by differences in communities. The same research found that, 'In the hundred most socially selective comprehensive schools in England an average 8.6 per cent of children are from income deprived households, despite being situated in localities where 20.1 per cent of children are income deprived.'

One twenty-six-year-old young management consultant and Oxford graduate told me, 'One thing that has struck me in the past year or so is that my view of what real life is is just so obscured. I live in this weird little bubble. You go to Oxford, which is already limiting the type of person you get to know, then you then go into consulting, which tends to be a certain type of person. Everyone you work with went to Durham, Oxford or Cambridge, and it's like everyone's friends all know each other. It gets to a point that everyone you meet through friends is just the same type of person.' The kind of people he meets tend to be highly connected, widening his networks and reinforcing his privilege. The opposite effect occurs if you grow up in a community beset by unemployment.

Unfortunately, Britain today is made up of too many bubbles that exist in isolation from each other. It is a matter of luck whether you grow up in a bubble of privilege or a bubble of poverty.

We have seen on the one hand that people are less likely to strongly identify with a class but on the other hand their class (objectively defined by researchers) is a strong predictor of their outcomes. Professor Mike Savage, sociologist at the LSE, has drawn attention to this 'paradox of class' where the structural importance of class in people's lives is not recognised by them. The two are linked. Class is all the more pervasive because of its lack of visibility. There have always been differences in the social networks of the rich and poor, the address books of the wealthy being more likely to include those in positions of power and influence. However, both groups enjoyed strong social networks. Working-class men especially were likely to be engaged in labour unions and working men's clubs and women in more informal networks. However, during the 1960s and 1970s as the fabric of the economy has changed and white-collar jobs expanded we became a more middle-class country on a wave of aspirational individualism.

This massive structural upward mobility drastically improved the quality of life of many. However, it left some communities stripped of the solidarity and the sense of collective power offered by the trade union movement and strong working-class identity. As religious identities have also declined, people have lost the hope that things might be better in the afterlife and the promise of equality before God. They are left with just the poverty. For all that the decline of these shared identities may be liberating for some, it is disorientating and alienating for others.

The lack of strong social ties can have significant consequences for young people's sense of well-being. Research by the Prince's Trust shows that young people growing up in poverty are 'six times more likely to feel that "everyone puts them down"'.[23]

There is a knock-on effect on their propensity to volunteer, to engage in informal activities and to feel like they belong.[24] 22 per cent of sixteen- to twenty-four-year-olds 'feel isolated "most of the time"' while 11 per cent report feeling 'like an outcast'.[25]

Young people who are brought up in these neighbourhoods grow up feeling trapped and alienated. In some environments the dominant social currency is fear. A nineteen-year-old Londoner told me how it felt being sent to her local authority's Pupil Referral Unit – an establishment that provides education for children who are classified as being unable to attend a mainstream school. 'Some people are involved in gangs and getting arrested, you don't know who is sitting next to you. You don't know everyone properly, everyone is wary of each other unless you've know them a while. There is a big trust thing.' Another fifteen-year-old in Birmingham told me that he kept his head down and didn't talk to the other young people on his estate.

Some young people don't have enough confidence in each other to build bonds; others have never learnt how to make connections. Gangs can be a response to distrust and fear, a grasping for protection, acceptance and belonging where nothing more constructive is offered.[26]

In a further tragic paradox, while class solidarity has broken down, class prejudice is still alive and well, as I show in the next chapter.

These perceptions of themselves also impact the way that they see others in times of disadvantage and struggle. We know that rising inequality has an impact on community. Unfortunately, today there is not just inequality of income but also inequality of belonging and of friendship. The increasing diversity of our communities can help explain why the common experience of disadvantage hasn't translated into a renewed sense of solidarity and collective purpose for working-class voters.

The bridge between different cultures

I remember one evening sitting in a tenants' hall with a majority white tenants group trying to convince them to agree to a scheme to build family-sized council houses on their estate. I thought the scheme would be popular as we were giving priority to residents of the estate, but tenants were united in their opposition. I stayed behind to sort out a bit of casework and could hear a few of the tenants discussing the meeting. 'You know what family-sized housing means, it means Somali and Bangladeshi families. I don't want to look out the window of my cramped flat and see their kids enjoying a massive garden.' There was general agreement. However much we may want it to be different, the reality is that among many working-class communities there is not a sense of shared solidarity across some racial and religious lines. There is a sense of competition for scarce resources. Those families would rather all lose out than risk giving another an advantage.

Evidence from the US shows that the higher the level of ethnic mixing, the lower the level of social trust, associational activity and informal sociability.[27] This is an issue in diverse societies where people have to negotiate difference and helps explain some of the difficulties Britain has had in comparison with other more homogenous nations in terms of declining social trust. Here in the UK new analysis from British Social Attitudes supports these findings by showing that ethnicity rather than socio-economic status is a better predictor of attitudes to a whole range of social and political questions. This means that we are going to have to work harder to find shared values in mixed neighbourhoods.

Any question of diversity quickly turns to a discussion of

immigration. Immigration is an issue for most voters, and young people are no exception. 71 per cent of eighteen- to twenty-four-year-olds across Britain would like to see immigration reduced, less than older adults but still highly significant.[28] Analysis by Ipsos MORI shows that these attitudes harden among white Britons living in 'northern manufacturing and industrial towns', 'areas of low migration' and 'asylum dispersal areas characterised by high worklessness and high social housing levels'. Attitudes towards immigration are more relaxed in 'cosmopolitan London', high-turnover student towns and prosperous small towns.[29]

This is nothing new. Immigration was the biggest issue ten years ago when I first started to go to focus groups with my dad. However, the nature of the debate has changed; people in the early 2000s would talk about their fear of overloaded public services and cultural decline. Speaking to young people around the country today, it is competition for jobs not competition for benefits and services that they focus on. The argument I kept hearing went something like this: immigrants will work for less and live in more overcrowded accommodation, they undercut young British workers in the jobs market and send most of the money home, which doesn't contribute to the economy. As one young man in Bradford put it, 'All these Europeans, they all send money back to their countries, they don't pay taxes like we pay our taxes on everything we spend. They send it all home, buy houses there then leave.' This sense of competition for limited opportunities deepens divides. It is not just young people from working-class backgrounds that are worried about this. A Department of Education study of local cohesion (how far young people feel those of different racial, religious and ethnic backgrounds mixed well together) found that those with parents from the intermediate/supervisory group (commonly thought of as lower middle class) were twice as likely as the children of the high professional/managerial group to have low cohesion scores.[30] I look in more detail at this in the next chapter but there are real concerns about low wages, housing costs and lack of opportunities that are wrapped up in the immigration debate.

There are some cities where a mix of poor job opportunities and high levels of immigration has turned these differences into deep divides. Bradford was one such city. Young people there described the layers of prejudice and hatred that characterised social relations: 'You still have your areas where the majority are black people, white people, Asian people. But now the Polish are coming across, that's where everyone's turning their hate to them. They don't like each other but they'll come together just to hate them.'

It was while speaking to young people from white, disadvantaged backgrounds that attitudes were harshest. Immigration and race issues dominated their worldview; it was how they framed every question. Immigration is the lens through which they see their city. It's the reason why there are no jobs, why job centre staff are stretched, why they can't get a council house, why wages are low. They frame this through harking back to their grandparents' generation: 'They fought to keep this country alive. Now look what's happening. They are letting people invade in.' There is a sense of cultural erosion: 'Culture's gone, innit? Walk through Bradford town now and it's like spot the English person, eight out of ten might be from Europe or Pakistan; where's the English?' This all affects their view of community, of reciprocity and of giving back. When talking to them about work, one boy said, 'Back in the day it used to be helping people, making a difference whatever job you're in, customer satisfaction. Now it's just getting money. Nowadays there's no point making a contribution because the system is fucked anyway.'

While these views are on the extreme end of a marginalised group (many were considering support for the English Defence League), I heard softer versions of this culture-threat narrative as I travelled the country talking to white young people about immigration. 39 per cent of eighteen- to twenty-four-year-olds surveyed by British Social Attitudes believe that culture is undermined by immigration – this is less than the 53 per cent of those aged 65-plus, but still a sizeable minority.

This sense of a cultural threat is most powerful around religious differences. According to British Future only 5 per cent of eighteen- to twenty-four-year-olds are uncomfortable with relationships across different races, but this goes up to 17 per cent for religion. And Islamophobia is the most potent of all religious prejudice. A poll of eighteen- to twenty-four-year-olds found that a quarter of young people don't trust Muslims compared with the 16 per cent for Hindus or Sikhs, 15 per cent for Jewish people, 13 per cent for Buddhists and 12 per cent who don't trust Christians.[31] In the same poll 44 per cent of young people said they didn't think Muslims had the same values as the rest of the population. These views are often formed through the media rather than personal relationships. A study by the University of Leeds found that 70 per cent of articles about Muslims across four major newspapers were negative. Another study analysing the representation of British Muslims in national print media from 2000 to 2008 found that, 'Four of the five most common discourses used about Muslims in the British press associate Islam/Muslims with threats, problems or in opposition to dominant British values. So, for example, the idea that Islam is dangerous, backward or irrational is present in 26 per cent of stories. By contrast, only 2 per cent of stories contained the proposition that Muslims supported dominant moral values.'[32] This has a knock-on effect in communities. I recently attended a workshop about the issues Somali women face on public transport and they all reported an upturn in verbal and physical abuse in relation to global events. As one sixteen-year-old Muslim girl put it to me, 'Muslims are portrayed as terrorists; white people are portrayed as EDL [English Defence League] nutters. They should focus on the good people of the white community and the Asian community.' Media reports are all a lot of young people have to go on as only 33 per cent of non-Muslims have a Muslim friend according to a Populus poll in

2006. This matters because young people with friends across different races are much more likely to have higher levels of cohesion.

There are young Muslims who have been radicalised and a full discussion of the complex factors that lead to this is outside the scope of this book. However, the young Muslims I talk about here are the majority getting on with their daily lives who feel hemmed in by stereotypes that don't represent the faith they practise or the values they hold.

Of course all value differences are not imagined. There are differences on some questions between an increasingly secular white British community and many ethnic minorities who maintain an active faith. Some religious communities choose to keep themselves apart to protect their culture and religious values. While this can foster a shared sense of belonging there are real drawbacks in terms of opportunities for social mixing, both at school and beyond. Speaking to a group of young Muslim women from a secular girls' comprehensive with a predominately Muslim intake, they told me they were struggling to convince their parents to let them leave Bradford for university.

For young people it doesn't have to be a binary choice between two cultures. Bonding social capital can in some instances support bridging social capital by giving members of a closely bonded group the confidence and security to engage more broadly.[33] While the girls in Bradford all took their faith seriously as a source of identity and values, they all talked about wanting to be part of mixed communities. They were frustrated by this sense that their faith made them somehow alien to non-Muslims: 'People see me in a headscarf and they think she must be so holy. I'm exactly the same as you, I still watch TV, I still listen to music, I just wear something different.' It isn't just the tabloid press; they also find the attitudes of some of the liberal media frustrating, such as the coverage of FEMEN (Ukrainian feminists): 'We don't need to be liberated by them. We can liberate ourselves. There's so many Muslim feminists but they're not being spotlighted.'

Young people in Bradford may not have solved cohesion issues but they agree they are more adept than older generations. Nadeem* puts it, 'I know Asian people in their fifties who are as racist as fuck. My best friend for thirteen years has been a white person. At first everyone was like, What's that about? Now everyone is just getting along and no one cares any more.' And there is similar evidence of intergenerational change among the white working-class young people I spoke to; as one girl matter-of-factly put it, 'My nan was very racist but unfortunate for her, her first grandchild was black.' In Oldham, a community very similar to Bradford with a history of racial violence, '82 per cent of those under twenty-five were optimistic that people from different ethnic backgrounds could get on well together, compared with 52 per cent of those aged seventy-five and older.'[34]

We have to find ways to bridge the real divides that exist. Integration is not a choice for young people growing up in Britain today, it is a living reality. Those who can't deal with diversity risk alienation and unemployability. We cannot abandon whole communities to poverty and unemployment because those are the conditions that fan division and conflict. The more young people are left without opportunities, the harder they will search for someone to blame and the more cohesion suffers.

The cost of segregation

If you look at these trends together and focus on young people you are left with distinct groups: the children of professionals, rich with opportunities and strong social networks; the children of parents from a strong religious or cultural community benefiting from the sense of belonging even if it doesn't come with material resources, and the children of parents who themselves are alienated from any sense of community.

* Not his real name.

The decline of bridging organisations like mass-membership political parties and religious congregations that bring young people together with each other and with older generations means they exist in totally different worlds. When I speak to young people on some of the estates in Camden, they've rarely left the boundary of their estate; they have never even been to central London. They live within walking distance of the British Library, the Google offices, the British Museum, University College London and the London School of Economics, but they might as well live in a different country. I remember at a council surgery a woman came to see me about a housing issue and started to shout at me about how the immigrants were taking all the opportunities. 'My daughter's fucked,' she shouted, pointing at her twelve-year-old busy spinning round on the chair next to her. I left feeling depressed for this woman but mainly for the girl who couldn't help but believe she didn't have a future. Waiting for a bus home two boys in their late teens came out of one of the houses next to the estate, chatting about their summer internships. One was going to the UN and the other was going to a friend of the family's law firm. They'd grown up two minutes away from the twelve-year-old I'd just met, maybe they'd passed each other on the street or sat on the same bus, maybe they even went to the same school, but their worldview, their opportunities, their support structure were a million miles away from each other. This is particularly stark in London where inequality is proximate and high but there are similar issues in cities around the UK.

This matters. The segregation between generations, between different ethnic groups and classes is highly problematic for everyone. It claws away at solidarity and erodes compassion. When young people live totally parallel lives, they are left with 'them' and 'us'. It is a lot easier to dehumanise from a distance. They never get the opportunity for the kind of 'equal status' contact that research shows diffuses prejudice.[35] Those from disadvantaged backgrounds lack the networks to find employment, the role models to broaden their horizons and the sense of trust and belonging to feel safe, whilst for young people from more privileged backgrounds, their isolation narrows their perspective and clouds their judgement. Ultimately society loses out, as our welfare state is underpinned by social solidarity. The weak and the vulnerable rely on it. Allowing any group to become marginalised and disconnected sows the seeds of social breakdown. Eventually those groups will show their frustration, whether it is through protest or simply through refusing to accept the rule of law.

Furthermore, community involvement is a gateway to political engagement. If community seems distant, then there is nothing to bridge young people to formal institutions; they end up in a political vacuum. They don't see how their involvement is part of anything broader, therefore disengagement from physical communities also affects broader political participation.

This is not an inevitable trend; while individualism is in some sense a consequence of modernity, the nature of that individualism is by no means fixed. In the Netherlands, Japan and Sweden people have become more trusting of each other and analysis of the World Values Survey shows little relationship between levels of self-interested values and social trust.[36] David Halpern concluded, 'In some places such as Sweden, people seem to be finding a way of expressing their growing individuality within a lifestyle that maintains and enhances the connections between them – what Rothstein calls "solidaristic individualism". But in the USA it is manifested in a more fragmenting form of what we might call "egoistic individualism".'[37] This is the difference we saw in the last chapter between out for 'yourself' individualism and individualism that links personal success to a sense of social purpose.

I'm not suggesting we go backwards to my gran's Britain. I wouldn't sacrifice the upward mobility, the huge gains for women or the acceptance of diversity, but we do have to work harder to find shared values and build communities. We need to create the time and space to form relationships and we need to build those with people from different backgrounds from ourselves. It is a different kind of solidarity, more messy but also more exciting. Luckily there are many enterprising young people showing us how this might be possible.

What does connection look like for young people?

The analysis above provides a bleak picture of decline.

While it is true that concepts like class solidarity have little meaning for the younger generation, ideas like connectivity, networks, collaboration, empathy and sharing are part of their approach to life.

The majority of young people get their primary sense of belonging from strong ties of family and friendship where they hold a deep sense of reciprocity. 92 per cent of teenagers feel their opinions are taken into account by their family.[38] Friendship networks are also important. As young people find it harder to transition to independence, their peer networks becomes increasingly important. It is why the *Friends* format has become so popular. *How I Met Your Mother*, *Girls*, *The Big Bang Theory*, *London Irish*, *Youngers*, *The Inbetweeners* and *Glee* are all about young people and their mates. It's no surprise that most teenagers spend every day with their friends, but almost 50 per cent of young people continue this pattern throughout their twenties and early thirties.[39]

As well as being just as likely to formally volunteer, young people are more likely than older generations to informally volunteer;[40] activities include giving advice (48 per cent), keeping in touch with someone who has difficulty getting about (39 per cent), transporting or escorting someone (35 per cent), looking after a property or pet when someone is away (32 per cent), babysitting or caring for children (30 per cent).[41] This kind of dense trust doesn't show up in generalised surveys of social trust and reciprocity but it demonstrates that these values are very much alive and well.

Schools are not perfect but they are an important place in society where people from different backgrounds come together, and many young people have started to come to terms with difference in mixed schools and youth centres. For most ethnic minority young people in mixed schools, roughly half or more than half of their friends are white.[42] Communities based on homogeneity are not possible in the modern world so harking back to them is unproductive. Young people are best placed to carve out trust within diversity and they are doing so even in our most divided cities.

Many young people are comfortable holding multiple identities, choosing in different contexts to assert one over the other. While nationality is one identity it is not necessarily their primary one. The young Somali group I spoke to saw themselves as Muslim, Somali, 'Camden' and British – in that order. They hold simultaneous and overlapping obligations to these different communities. 'Love your neighbour as yourself' means something different for Savan, a Jain brought up in Kenya and living in multicultural Harrow. A cosmopolitan outlook is part of his life story and the story of his multicultural community: 'We're all in the same world. Wherever you are you can make a difference.' Others find that a shared passion pushes them to engage in a global community or increased exposure to global issues broadens their horizons. The reality of young people's community life means that for some their primary identities are global. All of this challenges the idea that our obligations and rights end at our national borders. It is therefore no surprise that there is a 33 per cent generation gap between eighteen- to twenty-four-year-olds and over-sixty-fives on the issue of staying in Europe.[43] Young people are more likely to have a global outlook. They are more likely to conceive of citizenship as cross-border, and when they consider their future they are more likely to consider working abroad as a real option.

In the section below, I explore what this looks like in practice. I start by looking at three young people who are pioneering new forms of community associations that use empathy to bridge some of the differences they face.

I go on to show how young people are building real communities online that are spilling into offline relationships. Whether the common starting point is love for Harry Styles or veganism, the internet is allowing global communities of interest to build genuine ties of reciprocity. These ties can be powerful even amongst small groups of young people.

And finally I explore how some young people are translating these values into a new sharing economy.

Bridging difference

Eliza (19), Adam (27) and Savan (22) are from totally different backgrounds. Eliza was kicked out of school when she was twelve and experienced first-hand how fear and violence can tear apart youth communities; Adam is from a self-confessed 'elite background', attending private school and then Oxford University, and Savan grew up in Kenya in a Jain household, moving to the UK when he was eleven years old.

Despite their different backgrounds they share a common purpose. At some point all three of them began to question the way they were living and the way their peers related to each other, asking 'Is there a better way?'

For Adam O'Boyle it was arriving at Oxford University and feeling let down. The majority seemed to be blindly treading the same path – a 'big five' firm in corporate law, management consultancy, accountancy or banking, offering clear career progression and good pay in return for long hours. Adam was left wondering where were the visionaries, the social entrepreneurs, the people seeking to change the world. He decided to do something about it. He saw university as a chance to catch students before they were tied down by long hours, mortgages and family commitments, to break out of the bubble and get involved in social change by creating the Oxford Hub. He told me, 'The kernel of the Oxford Hub's existence is about inspiring and supporting students to get involved in making a difference in the world around them so eventually they go on and do that in their future life.' Their model was to 'bring together everything that happens on campus around charities, social action and volunteering, whether it's the Amnesty group or the group working with kids at the local secondary school, and try to promote that and increase the profile of that, in a sense to transform the culture of the university so it's about what you give back to the world not only during your time at university but then beyond.' And it has been incredibly successful. When we met it was in Oxford Hub's thriving café in the heart of Oxford. Their sister social enterprise turns over £1.4 million, they have a staff of fifty and last year alone they had 1300 volunteer placements. Most importantly they have created a momentum and buzz around social change that is spreading well beyond committed activists.

Like Adam, Eliza was feeling trapped by a pervasive culture as she was moved around different pupil referral units. 'Through that whole time it was a regular occurrence to see people arrested, stabbed, killed or in jail. I thought it was normal, just how life was.' She says now she sees things differently but people were afraid to. 'It's not always a supportive lifestyle. Friends don't support you if you're thinking about a better future. It would be really difficult to say you wanted to be a lawyer or a policeman. It is a strange lifestyle where everything illegal is right.' Her own behaviour began to change and she was getting into more and more trouble. It was only when her mum sat her down and told her that life didn't have to be like this that she began to see a way out. She knew she had a powerful voice, so armed with her mum's promise that life could

be different she set out to change the culture of fear that had
gripped so many of her school mates. It started with a T-shirt bear-
ing a simple message – 'Lives not Knives' – and it turned into a
movement. At the heart of what her organisation does is peer-to-
peer mentoring with young people who have been touched by
gang culture. It builds relationships with young people and encourages them to take a different route. She tells me her purpose is
'helping others achieve the things they want to and to help make
people happy. A lot of the young people I work with are really
unhappy. They have a terrible self-perception; they've been told
they're bad for so long they start to believe it themselves . . . to see
that turn around and for them to start to believe in themselves is
the best thing about what I do.'

Like Eliza, Savan was starting to get into trouble at school and
his life looked like it was going nowhere fast, but then he found
dance and it changed his whole perspective. Doing one thing
well convinced him that maybe he could achieve in other areas
of his life. He began to ask why so many of his peers were falling
behind – was it, like him, a result of self-confidence? He created
Inspire4Justice, with the dual aim of helping young people to
fulfil their potential and supporting charitable issues, bringing to
life the idea that by helping others you help yourself. His flagship
programme EPIC, standing for Every Person Is Capable, is all
about inspiring young people to do well in their own lives and
give back.

The Oxford Hub, Lives not Knives, and Inspire4Justice are all
very different organisations, but there are a few principles that
they share that give an insight into how some young people are
rebuilding community life.

They are open and democratic in structure

None of these organisations is prescriptive. They are broad
churches that morph to fit the passions of their members rather

than force members to fit with a tight central goal. There are no membership cards, they are flexible in how people choose to engage, people can flow in and out.

Savan tells me he doesn't see Inspire4Justice as an organisation, it is more like a movement or a lifestyle. Likewise, Oxford Hub has broad principles of fighting for social justice but members have a great deal of independence. Both have a loose central purpose that allows members to make their own choices, while retaining links to a central core.

They both also span micro-community work and global projects. The solidarity they draw on to connect isn't based on class or race or religion, it is based on shared humanity. They use the local community as a shared reference point but then they seamlessly interact globally.

They are practising empowering leadership

Permission to lead has to be earnt. Effective leaders are those that can shift things not just for themselves but also for others. Eliza, Adam and Savan all created movements out of nothing more than their ability to unlock the leadership capabilities of their peers.

For Adam the desire to inspire action in others is very overt. He tells me that their theory of change aims to support students up a ladder of engagement, 'from doing one hour volunteering in a school to realising educational disadvantage is a problem so you go and do loads of reading about it, setting up your own project'. He sees Oxford Hub's role as the catalyst, motivating and energising but ultimately handing over power. He tells me staff are there to connect and support, not to direct. 'We try all the time to shed the identity of staff and push responsibility onto students.'

Eliza thinks the mentors at Lives not Knives are able to break through barriers and change behaviour by honest dialogue: 'The main thing is all the mentors who work with schools have been affected in some way by gangs or knife crime. At the end of each session we give a personal testimonial, we're very open and they can ask any questions. I think they enjoy getting an authentic point of view and we can connect to them.' It is authenticity that is allowing her and the mentors she partners with to connect with their audience and change behaviour.

They have a dual purpose

All these organisations want to do good in their communities but their primary purpose is actually to inspire and motivate their peers. They are as focused on the effect on the 'volunteer' as on those they are setting out to help. The community work these organisations do is based on a dialogue between equals, a two-way exchange. It is not about sympathy or charity but justice and empathy. The activists get as much if not more out of it as the recipients.

For Savan and Eliza it's as much about the confidence and well-being young people get from helping others as it is those they help. Eliza tells me about mentoring: 'You learn more from them than they do from you, it's like we're doing it together.'

For Adam, the central purpose of Oxford Hub is about what volunteers will learn from breaking out of their bubble and about making them think about what it takes to be a good citizen. 'I'd like to shake up people's lives so they don't go off on that easy life path that leads them to misery but great riches, but actually do something deeply fulfilling for themselves and society around them and perhaps fulfil their potential.'

Research shows that this principle of doing good for yourself and others is central to encouraging young people to volunteer. 56 per cent of sixteen- to twenty-four-year-olds volunteer because they want to improve things and help people; however,

46 per cent also say it is because they want to learn new skills, far more than the 19 per cent of all adults.[44]

They focus on breaking down barriers and building solidarity through empathy and personal relationships

This is important because all three recognise and are concerned that individuals have become too separate from each other. For Adam it is an educated elite too removed from poverty. For Savan it is the link between ordinary citizens and those in powerful positions: 'Sometimes I get the feeling that the people at the top never really look at the people at the bottom. And the people at the bottom feel that no one's listening to their views and what they want to say.' For Eliza it is people from the same background who can't find the language to connect.

Empathy is a crucial tool for a generation dealing with difference. The way they broaden horizons is through equal relationships that allow young people to put themselves in someone else's shoes.

When it comes to their ultimate purpose, these three young leaders don't measure it in terms of a grand vision but in the individual hearts of those they work with. As Savan put it, 'If I can inspire one person, then I'll have been a success.' They focus so much on the individual because this is the only way to find solidarity in diversity, creating a thread of empathy and shared responsibility person to person. Collective action that emerges through relationships – from the interplay of one person's connection with another – is the clarion cry of a generation who value their individual identity.

There are hundreds of youth-led organisations I could have chosen. I lost count of the young people who echoed Savan's words and told me that if through their blog/campaign/organisation/music/poetry they could influence just one person they would be happy. The very same impulse to change the world through empathy inspired MC Angel to set up Lyrically Challenged. Chances are there is a young person like MC Angel, Adam, Eliza or Savan in your community. Young leaders are taking their generation's individualism and weaving into it a balancing force, whether we call it community, fraternity or solidarity. They start with where young people are. They don't demand that they engage with 'them', a community they don't identify with, but gradually broaden the meaning of 'we' beyond the perimeters of friends and family. They help align young people's aspirations for themselves and their aspirations for society.

When an exceptional young person lights a spark, they often find they set off a chain reaction beyond anything they ever expected. Adam found other universities started to approach him about sharing the model; Eliza found that one T-shirt started a movement. They are able to tap into the desire for belonging and meaning that too often lies dormant and unlock invisible resources within our communities until individual change becomes cultural change.

This is sometimes a deliberate effort, sometimes it happens organically. The Bradford-based music collective of young disadvantaged men we met in Chapter 2 are a mix of Asian, black and white artists. They tell me how forming a collective has forced their diverse fan bases to come into contact with each other. Music, used in this context, forms a common point of connection for them and their fans. 'At the end of the day you got to look at the music. It's an escape, and once you get into that escape, it don't matter what colour skin you've got, just how good your track is, because you've both got that in common. I guess you could call it a bridge.'

Whether it is Oxford students understanding disadvantage or a white working-class fan recognising the common humanity of a fellow music lover who happens to be Asian, new bridges are being built by enterprising young people every day.

One of the ways that young people are building these bridges is through online expression, enabling vast differences of culture and geography to be overcome. This dialogue, although physically distant, is no less personal – it remains a human-to-human experience.

Connectivity

Some teenagers and young adults are using the internet to form identity communities with likeminded individuals. These identity communities can produce real ties of friendship, reciprocity and belonging. They are not exclusive and young people holding several identities can simultaneously coexist in several thin communities of interest. Young people are attracted to communities that give them the space to express their individuality, where relationships are nurtured and connection happens over the things they care about. These tend to be peer-led. Community isn't locked into the place they live but follows them into how they work and how they socialise online.

Nowhere demonstrates the potential of online community formation as powerfully as YouTube. Since its launch in 2006, YouTube has become the gateway to entertainment online for young people, and was voted the UK's top youth brand by Voxburner in both 2012 and 2013.

The impact of YouTube is now seriously felt among advertisers, media companies and even politicians. Not many people still think it's all cat videos and kids falling off their skateboards. It has become a major force in content creation, business and entertainment.

Key to its success with young people is ownership over the content. As one social media expert put it to me, 'YouTube for a lot of these guys is their stamping ground; it's their home, it's their community, it's where they make their friends, it's where they get entertained, it's where all this stuff that their mum and dad aren't watching is.'

For many young people it embodies their values – open, democratic and meritocratic. Good content rises to the top. They trust it because they feel like they are in charge. Unlike Facebook, which tends to reinforce connections between existing networks, YouTube is helping young people forge new communities with strangers, often from around the world. Despite the ever-present issue of trolling, the YouTubers I spoke to all felt they were part of something special, using video to create real empathy and connection across all normal boundaries.

Charlie McDonnell (charlieissocoollike) is one of the most popular UK video bloggers on YouTube. Describing himself as a 'professional internet human', he started videoblogging in 2007 and now has global reach, with over two million loyal subscribers. At the time of writing his most popular video is one where he spends four minutes trying and failing to speak in an American accent (9,598,711,162 views)[45] but the video he says he is proudest of is one called 'I'm Scared' (1,775, 666,390 views).[46] In 'I'm Scared' he talks about his writer's block, his fear of disappointing his audience, his anxiety about what people think of him, his need to be liked. It provoked a wave of video responses, with other YouTubers posting videos about their own fears. Charlie later posted on his blog about the experience: 'I think it was the video response that got to me the most. For me this experience has been a stark reminder of how powerful video blogging can be ... I think there is something incredibly important about the real connection you can make when you just talk directly into a camera and decide to share it with the world.'[47] He shared his favourite responses. There is one that really stands out: a young woman in the US (Neverbeenpinker) left a video saying she had been watching Charlie since 2009 but she was so shy she had never responded to anyone she follows before. She explains that she has been dealing with clinical depression and panic disorders her whole life and when things get too much all she can do is go to sleep or sit down and cry. But when she listens to him she no longer feels alone.[48] It's such a brave and powerful video to someone she has never met. 16,932 people watched it, 913 liked it, hundreds of strangers sent supportive comments.

It's impossible to watch this young woman so publicly face her fears and not to feel moved or believe how strongly she cares about Charlie, a complete stranger. These two young people who have never met and live across the world from each other are able to connect over a shared human experience.

Suli Breaks is a spoken-word artist whose video on education, 'I will not let an exam result decide my fate', went viral. He said when his message about education hit a nerve not just in the UK but globally it brought home to him the possibility of civic dialogues across national borders. He now sees the promise of the internet as enabling global communities and connection. He tells me, 'I think it's just [a community] that people are not used to, because usually we're used to physical communities, but for me personally the community has just opened up on a bigger scale.'

The process of creating an online dialogue has gradually altered his sense of his own identity, allowing him to see himself as a global citizen. A round-the-world tour he did where he met his fans embedded this. 'It was kind of like an outlook experience for me to look at myself and be like: I've only been looking at myself from one way, now I need to understand that it's so much bigger than I had perceived it.'

A global identity means he increasingly feels a responsibility to try to create social change on a bigger scale: 'I'm trying to form a kind of global conversation, so for that I need broad ideas. I need universal ideas, I need to project ideas which if you're in Hawaii, if you're in Istanbul or in Israel you can still connect, you know?'

While he is thinking globally, the methods he uses are similar to the young leaders creating local networks, empathy, respect for the individual and inspirational leadership.

'There's a simple framework – treat others as you'd like to be treated – that I try to live by. In everything I do, I try to inspire people. Once you inspire someone it's easier for them to give on information, rather than just regurgitate information. My number-one prerogative is to inspire ideas and if you give value to those ideas then I've done my job.'

Suli is religious but he doesn't want to be defined or pigeon-holed by his faith but focus on a common humanity.

'It's kind of idealistic but I think the best way to do that [engage individuals to build a community] is, to an extent, to get rid of the things that make us different. Not by losing our individualism but by focusing on the things that connect us and by getting rid of the barriers that divide us, like race, like religion, because what you find is on the internet, you connect so much because someone has a username but you don't know where they're from, you don't know who they are so automatically you're looking at them more neutrally. You take what they say before what they look like or where they're from. That's why the internet creates such large communities, because the barriers are not as apparent.'

YouTube is an ecosystem made up of functioning global communities. One of these is a land called Nerdfighteria, created by American brothers, bestselling author John Green and environmental blogger Hank Green (vlogbrothers).

They have created a genuine movement under the banner 'Raising nerdy to the power of awesome'. With eighteen channels, over four million subscribers and half a billion views, several fan sites and millions proudly calling themselves nerdfighters, they are a global force. Their largely teen followers, including many British young people, are united by the catchphrase DFTBA – Don't Forget To Be Awesome – a whole vocabulary of in-jokes and even a hand signal. Think *The Big Bang Theory* meets *Glee*.

The young person that just twenty years ago would have to go through school as an outsider, wondering why they weren't like everyone else, now has a whole community that feel exactly the same way. Popular themes include *Harry Potter*, social awkwardness, *Star Wars*, tech, gaming and politics. It all started in 2007 with an experiment called Brotherhood 2.0. The two brothers had been living in different cities for ten years and decided to experiment with how they kept in touch, committing to a year of back-and-forth public YouTube videos. Very quickly they built up a small but loyal band of followers, mainly fans of John's books, who quickly began to identify as nerdfighters. Their community rapidly expanded when one of Hank's videos, *Accio Deathly Hallows*,[49] chronicling his anxious wait for the last Harry Potter book, became a huge success. Lines like 'I need Harry Potter like a Grindelow needs water' launched the video to the front page of YouTube with over a million views and quickly gained their site over thirty thousand new followers. The community has kept growing ever since. It's also deepened, with nerdfighter gatherings now regular occurrences.

In a talk at Google John spoke about the power of the community in co-creating content. 'Our community is not us telling a bunch of people what to do or what's cool . . . It's not something they watch or consume, it's something that they become a part of, that they participate in, they're active creators of.'[50]

He tells the story of Canadian 'nerdfighter' Shawn Ahmed, who was inspired by a speech by Dr Jeffrey Sachs, in which he asked, 'You can see children dying before your eyes. What conceivable justification could there be for this?'[51] The next day Shawn decided to withdraw from graduate school, liquidate his savings and dedicate his life to trying to make a difference in Bangladesh, where both his parents were born. His vision is one where social media gives voice to people living in poverty and moves the dialogue from guilt and sympathy towards empathy based on genuine communication. Hank shared Shawn's story on their YouTube channel and other nerdfighters took up the call. Soon they'd raised thousands and Shawn is now a force in his own right.

YouTubers generally look bemused at the idea that community isn't possible online because they live it. They meet on YouTube but their friendships often spill into the offline world in the form of YouTube gatherings. For many it is the centrepiece of their existence, where they met their best friends and even their partners.

Seventeen-year-old Joe Dytrych found a similar sense of community within the world of open-source coding. He tells me that because computer science teaching has been rare in UK schools, most young coders are self-taught. 'That means you've learnt via this online global community who just write stuff and put it out there.' It creates strong bonds of reciprocity: 'When you owe that much to that community it's impossible not to be part of that.'

He believes opening up creates value for everyone. 'When you give back it starts a dialogue and it will make you better at what you do because people will give you feedback and people who you have amazing amounts of respect for and people who you've learnt huge amounts of stuff from, you almost idolise, will see your projects and say: I really like that; yeah, that's cool. Or they'll give you feedback on it or even build on some of your code.'

While Joe thinks relationships are possible online, he still thinks face-to-face connection is more powerful. Like other YouTubers, many of his relationships have developed into real-life friendships through global conferences, in his case through Mozilla. 'I may have met people online and developed relationships online but eventually I get to meet them face-to-face and that's nice.'

He thinks this is integral to the way the culture of the whole coding community works, in which you are required to be generous, open and give back. 'You could just read all this stuff and you could code [and not contribute yourself], but you won't actually gain any traction within the community even in terms of employment. Most employers, especially in places like Silicon Valley, will demand that you have a GitHub account full of open-source projects before they even look at you, so you are expected to give back.

'You're part of this community and you know if you put something out there people are going to feedback on it constructively and even contribute to it and you're motivated to do it because you know people are going to be interested in what you're doing and listen.'

He feels genuine ties of reciprocity to this virtual community. Joe is also a member of a canoeing club where there are no teachers and students but long-term members teach the newer arrivals. Joe has now been a member for seven years and explains his satisfaction at seeing people he taught begin to teach others. The point is Joe doesn't see any difference in the real obligation to the people he meets week in, week out at the canoe club and the strangers he meets coding. Both are real, functioning communities where knowledge is passed down and members feel part of something.

An online following or community can also form a protective blanket against internet trolls. The best online community becomes self-censoring. The community acts the exact same way you would if a complete stranger interrupted a group of friends in a pub screaming obscenities and abuse, by asking or rather telling them to leave. One young mental health campaigner told me about looking down at her phone after dinner with her family and seeing hundreds of notifications. Someone had left a critical tweet and her followers had swarmed in to defend her.

There are just as many stories of online bullying, of witch hunts and abuse. We all know those stories because they are the narratives we hear about young people and the internet, as I explore in Chapter 6. However, it is important to understand that real connection and reciprocity can exist online and work with young people to enable this kind of experience. We also hear a lot about the internet as a tool for exclusive identities, but it is also important to remember that the internet can enable a global citizenship based on a shared sense of humanity.

Sharing is caring

For some young people, the internet is allowing them to embed community values into how they consume. I remember as a cash-strapped pre-teen going to the Music and Video Exchange in Notting Hill and exchanging my old videos and tapes. I didn't realise it then but I was engaging in collaborative consumerism (no one had given it the hashtag #collcons). Apart from some second-hand books, that was where my engagement with the shared economy stopped. However, others of my generation were a bit more pioneering.

The sharing economy has exploded in the last four years. This can be sharing space, goods, skills, knowledge and even your household pet. The lawnmower lying unused in your garage, the sofa bed in your living room, your old course textbooks, the empty space in your car or the year you spent au pairing in Paris all become potential sources of revenue or exchange.

There is a scale from direct exchange through to sites based on altruism. The point is you are renting, swapping or buying directly from other individuals – and millennials are particularly involved in this.

Global research from Havas Worldwide shows that 49 per cent of sixteen- to thirty-four-year-olds agree that 'In the future, I expect to belong to a number of sharing services', compared with 27 per cent of those 55-plus. 51 per cent say they 'prefer to share things rather than own them', compared with 37 per cent of over fifty-fives, and 41 per cent said they had 'already contributed to a crowdfunding project or expect[ed] to do so within the next year', compared with 18 per cent of the over fifty-fives.[52]

The sharing economy is starting to have serious economic traction, especially in the US. In 2014 *Forbes* calculated that the revenue flowing through the sharing economy will be over $3.5 billion, with growth exceeding 25 per cent.[53] The UK is beginning to catch on. In the UK it was valued at £22.4 billion in 2013, which is 1.3 per cent of GDP and predicted to rise to 15 per cent within five years.[54]

Advocates say we're moving away from an ownership economy. At the UK-based ThePeopleWhoShare, a global campaign to support a sharing economy and the creators of 'Compare and Share', a comparison site for the sharing economy (named one of the top twenty start-ups of 2013 by Startups.co.uk), 'Owning was yesterday, in tomorrow's world everyone is a supplier of goods, services and experiences and can access the goods and services they need when they want them – on demand – at a price they can afford.'

This economy is reliant to a large degree on generalised trust and reciprocity. While there is a big gap between buying someone's old book on eBay and sharing a car to a festival, there is no doubt that much of this economy is both reliant on and actively building greater social trust between strangers. It is also opening up ideas about how we collectively use resources and carry out our shared responsibilities. Technology start-ups are creatively trying to bridge barriers to cooperation, for example distrust and fear of freeloading. Whether it is transparency around reputation, virtual points for contributing to a community or insuring risk, they are actively seeking to create a currency of trust.

However, this is by no means a universal movement. Often those who could benefit most lack the necessary trust themselves or the ability to inspire trust in others to engage. Research from the Joseph Rowntree Foundation found that while many graduates are offsetting the costs of privately renting by flat sharing, young people from disadvantaged backgrounds are reluctant to do so. While the sharing economy is most popular with millennials this is by no means a mainstream movement. Unsurprisingly given the divides highlighted earlier on in this chapter in terms of social trust, the sharing economy is currently powered by the young, urban and degree-educated middle class. Research from The People Who Share shows that 61 per cent of sharers (two or more activities) are from an ABC1 compared with 39 per cent from a C2DE background.[55] They are also more likely to come from London and the south. In some sense the producers are most likely to be the consumers and early adopters are most likely to be tech-savvy.

There is also no doubt that the sharing economy is competing against some strong cultural precedents in favour of ownership and it would be a mistake to think that young people have managed to escape this. They are avid consumer and their aspirations for home ownership are very similar to older generations.[56]

Those caveats aside, there are signs that this is a trend that young people are leading. There are also some major push factors. This is a generation with less money in their pocket, and that alone encourages alternative forms of consumption. Environmental concerns offer a moral cause that will continue to push innovation in this space and technology will continue to remove barriers to cooperation. There are no shortages of enterprising companies trying to find new ways to allow the collective pooling of knowledge, assets and resources.

Research by Cooperative UK shows that there is a potential for more sharing. 81 per cent of those in the UK say it makes us feel happy and 75 per cent say that we feel better about ourselves when we share our time and possessions. 53 per cent of us would love to find ways to share our time and resources within our local communities, and it is eighteen- to twenty-four-year-olds in the UK who are the age group most willing to share.[57] This is encouraging businesses to think more about their impact on the environment, through the so-called 'circular economy'.

This is a snapshot of the many ways that young people are embedding community values into their lives. What can government, religious organisations and community groups do to support them?

Rebuilding community

Community as an ideal has not been ignored by politicians. In fact, most political leaders are as enthusiastic as my gran is on the subject. Politicians at a national level have a role in trying to set out the values that can bind a diverse nation together and what our responsibilities are to each other. They can also help to create institutions that can provide a sense of national unity like the NHS and the BBC. They can invest in volunteering and ensure that citizens have the time and resources to engage in community life. Equally, politicians at a local level have a vital role to play and can help build that shared vision as they interact with the many diverse groups in their communities. They can create the public spaces, the services and the discussions that bring people together. The evidence shows that an individual's perception of the quality of local services, the fairness of their allocation and how much power they have in local decision-making matters in how far they believe they live in a cohesive society.

But neither local nor national politicians have the power or authority to engage in some debates about personal morality, and nor would most people want them to. Politicians can only go so far. Ultimately how people choose to relate to their neighbours is outside of the politicians' control, and this is where civil society comes in.

Religious organisations have traditionally been able to do what politicians can't and start a discourse about moral questions. When interviewing young people about taking part in community action I was surprised by how many were motivated by their religious faith. This wasn't information they necessarily volunteered, or if they did they did so reluctantly, seeing a distinction between the aims of their organisation and their own personal motivations, but it was clearly still a strong source of inspiration for many. Research supports this, showing that young people who practise a religion are more likely to volunteer compared with young people who don't have a faith.[58] This is unsurprising, as religious organisations by their very nature provide a challenge to individualism; they are a reminder of something bigger than oneself and act as a call to consider the needs of others. They offer one of the few opportunities to engage in shared rituals and build connections across different ages and walks of life.

This is not the space for a debate about the merits of religion in society, and there are of course many who would point to how this sense of community can become exclusive and divisive. It is, however, important to recognise that religious worship can and does play a positive role and to ask where the 39 per cent of young people who have no faith can go to discuss moral questions and to find meaning and solidarity.

Many religious institutions face exactly the same challenge as political ones, struggling to engage a younger generation.[59] There is a sizeable minority of young people have a faith but do not engage in any formal worship.[60] Religious organisations prepared to open up to young people will find an audience looking for meaning in their lives and ready and willing to engage in moral questions.

The content, style and organisation of traditional community groups, whether they are a place of worship, a neighbourhood association or a trade union, are rarely set up to engage young people. While most community groups are desperate for new members, they don't necessarily make the effort to go to young people and they're not always willing to make the necessary changes to keep them interested. If their model of engagement is 'wait till young people come to us and then try to mould them into a pre-existing structure' they'll get nowhere. The zealousness of the enthusiast is great but it can create structures that actively exclude all but the most committed. This is not inevitable, and in Chapter 8 I look at some examples of organisations that are thriving by handing over some of the reins to the next generation.

We can't abandon all traditional institutions for fluid, shifting networks of young people. It is only through working with long-term institutions that we build up the levels of trust, abandon our selfish gene and cooperate. However, this doesn't mean they can't take steps to give young people the empowerment they are looking for, as I show in Chapter 8. We need to adapt our community groups, whether they are a religious organisation or a neighbourhood association, to appeal to young people. We also have to give space for youth-led institutions to emerge and grow.

We have to change our mindsets about young people and recognise that community values make sense to them. It is as simple as acknowledging their fundamental humanity. They are not feral animals, or so lost in technology that they don't know how to connect. They have all the same impulses as anyone else in society and in the right conditions they will show reciprocity and altruism. If this isn't happening, society is not providing the right conditions.

The baby-boomer generation broke through many of the old social ties with gains for individual expression and personal choice, but in so doing created a society that leans too far towards the individual and forgets what we owe to one another. It is important that we rebuild those connections without crushing individual expression. We have a lot to learn from young people in getting the balance right, but they cannot do it alone.

Shifting the balance isn't easy; it requires good leadership, the space for different groups to come together and the time in busy lives to dedicate to our communities. We all need to become community revolutionaries like MC Angel, forging relationships not just with people like ourselves but across difference, and in Chapter 7 I show how empathetic relationships hold the key to re-creating a sense of community.

Rampant and unthinking individualism creates a society that is unequal, harsh and ultimately unsustainable. It abandons some young people to poverty and alienation. The consequence is declining social mobility, as we will see in the next chapter.

Chapter 5

Declining Social Mobility

I first met Naomi waiting in the locker queue on my first day at secondary school. Within minutes we'd established that our favourite book was *My Family and Other Animals* by Gerald Durrell and have been firm friends ever since.

At eleven we both fell hopelessly in love with the same sixth-former and so great was our shared obsession that on one occasion we followed him home and stood outside a freezing-cold station for two hours to ask for his autograph. It was Naomi who pretended she couldn't sing for the first few years of our friendship so I wouldn't feel bad about not being in the school choir. And it was Naomi who introduced me to my favourite books, took me to my first gig and tried to teach me to dance. She came to my house every morning before school so we could walk the last bit together and she came on holiday with us every year. She gradually became part of my family. My dad always said he wanted to walk her down the aisle when she got married.

We were and are very different. Later, when we shared a flat, my room was filled with back issues of *Hoops* (the official QPR programme), hers with *Vogue*. Her role model was *Sex and the City*'s Carrie Bradshaw, mine was Labour Party revisionist Anthony Crosland. She loves to cook, I would be happy eating toast three meals a day. She was always effortlessly cool. She looked a bit like a young Kate Moss and knew all the latest bands. I didn't. She would drag me round niche indie nights chasing long-haired DJs and I would drag her round Labour Party leafleting rounds.

We came from really different backgrounds. Naomi never knew her dad and grew up with her mum in a council estate in Camden. Yet all along Naomi bucked the trend for young people from her background in our local area.

She had an amazing family; her grandparents lived on the same estate as her and she credits them with her strong work ethic. 'They didn't have much money, but they worked really hard and there was a real pride in their work. I think they instilled that in me,' she says, and they did everything they could to support her.

And she had a mum, Rita, who fought her corner every step of the way, working to get her into the best local schools and fighting to ensure teachers had high expectations for her. When she didn't get onto the school's gifted and talented scheme despite good SAT results her mum marched into school and fought tooth and nail till the school admitted their mistake.

Naomi told me, 'I remember when I was little and we had no money, my mum would bring home copies of *Vogue* from her cleaning job and I loved recreating the outfits with my clothes, even if they were just my cousin's hand-me-downs. So for me fashion was this aspirational thing that I would see in magazines, but it wasn't unattainable if you had a little imagination. I guess it allowed me to dream.'

Things weren't easy. 'There was a lot of anxiety about money growing up.' She remembers hating having to queue with her lunch ticket, miss out on social events, and haggle to get on to school trips. She got a job when she was fourteen and really considered leaving school at sixteen, but through the extra bit of cash from her Educational Maintenance Allowance she managed to stay on and she got a loan to study fashion, styling and promotion at Middlesex University.

But fulfilling her dream turned out to be a lot harder than she'd imagined. When she finished university she struggled to get any job at all: 'It was the most demoralising horrible thing when I was signing onto the dole; honestly, nothing can prepare you for how awful it is.'

As a friend I watched her get more and more disheartened. She was in a cycle where she'd work for a few months in a shop or a bar, save up to do an unpaid internship and start all over again. 'I knew I could do it but I felt like I couldn't because money was holding me back. The only reason I can't go on to get a job is because I can't afford to stop working and really go for it.' Eventually she was getting up at 8 a.m. to do an internship and working at a bar till 3 a.m. to make ends meet. In the end she gave up the internship as she was competing against people who could afford to work for free indefinitely.

Looking back she says she was definitely depressed. 'It was awful. It was soul-destroying, you kind of get stuck in this mindset where you think it's never going to happen.' It helped that my mum worked in publishing and was able to introduce her to her networks. 'I spoke to you and your mum and the contacts you gave me, I was incredibly lucky to have that.' Finally, two years later, after three long-term unpaid internships she got a break with a job in fashion PR. Now she is an account director and doing brilliantly.

Naomi was an exception. It wasn't what happened to most of the kids growing up on her estate, she tells me. 'I find it sad when I go back to see my mum and I look at the lives of the kids I grew up with. There was never any hope for them. I saw the mum of a guy I used to play with when we were kids working at Sainsbury's a couple of years ago. It was when I was working at Liberty. She said, "Thank God you got out of the estate, thank God you're doing something; my son is on the dole." It's so sad because you always knew that's what he would be doing. He didn't have a chance.'

In the course of my research I got back in touch with some old school friends I had drifted apart from. When I started at secondary school, Sarah* used to come round to my house every week. We had decided to formally become second-best friends after a telephone negotiation discussing the matter with the seriousness that only twelve-year-old girls can comprehend.

But when I met Sarah this year, I hadn't seen her in ten years. All I knew about her life came from the occasional Facebook update. As we walked to get a coffee, I characteristically started dropping all my belongings and she laughed. 'You haven't changed, Georgia, you were always so clumsy.' She asked me about my parents. I had to tell her my dad had died and she burst into tears. I realised she is the first person I'd had to tell. She didn't know him as someone involved in politics but someone who was nice to her.

We got talking about our lives in the ten years since leaving school. She told me that she has never had a job. Her grades were poor and the course she did at sixteen didn't help her into work. She didn't get any of the jobs she applied for and she didn't know how to bounce back from that, so in the end she stopped trying. She suffered with depression and struggled to leave her house. She didn't know what she had to offer an employer. Having a child was a way out and she credits her little kid with providing a purpose to her life but she is still struggling with housing and debt.

She told me that she sees herself as the lowest of the low; she blames herself for where she is. She desperately wants better for her child. She's doing a services course and she's taking her child to nursery but in reality she is not sure how to change their story.

Unfortunately in Britain today it is Sarah's story rather than Naomi's that is the most common.

Looking back at my early school years it's easy to see where the

* Not her real name.

divides emerged. My primary school was nestled in the Hallfield Estate and, like any London primary, educated children from around the world. It was just next to a line of hotels and hostels where the council would house people who'd just come over to the UK. There were children who'd been through terrible things. One boy, who had seen his parents killed in front of him, would regularly have panic attacks in lessons. I'd go round to one friend's house, where there would be three bunk beds to a room, and realise that not everyone got their own bedroom. Another friend would come round to mine most mornings and I realised that not everyone got breakfast every day.

By sixteen a lot of the girls I'd been friends with up to the age of fourteen had dropped out. They transitioned to adulthood earlier, starting work and having children. Facebook highlights the split even more clearly between graduates who are still single, moving up a professional career ladder, and their classmates who are getting ready to send their children to secondary school. I think of my friendship group now and most of us went to university. Of course there were middle-class girls who struggled and there were girls from disadvantaged backgrounds who went to university or who left school at eighteen and went on to build successful careers, but these were the minority. Unfortunately most of the girls I went to school with ended up repeating the educational trajectory of their parents.

If you haven't been at a school and watched kids who are just as smart or smarter than you fall further behind it can be hard to explain. For me, it was a fact of life. I knew from my education that we live in a society where your life chances aren't determined by how intelligent you are but by your background. I knew it because I went to one of the best state schools in the country and saw so many girls fail to fulfil their potential. I knew it because there were girls far brighter than some of the people I'd met at Oxford who had ended up not even making it to A levels.

An angry young person on the street isn't born like that; they become angry through a thousand small injustices. But segregation is so ingrained in our education system that too many people just see the angry teenager. They've never met the scared little kid.

A mixed classroom is one of the most important things we can give young people. Integration matters for young people like Naomi because it helped to broaden her career aspirations and gave her access to networks she wouldn't otherwise have had. It also gave her confidence – it helped to know that the only difference between her and the people who make it is money. It matters for young people like me because it forces us to develop humility about the opportunities we have been given, and hopefully emerging from this comes an obligation to share those opportunities. It exposes us all to different worldviews and ways of thinking. Of all the many things my parents gave me, I'm most grateful that they sent me to a comprehensive school. If they hadn't I might still have gone to Oxford but I'm sure that I would never have become a local councillor, I would never have been so angry about how much potential we are wasting and I would never have written this book.

What happened to the British Dream?

Unfortunately the story of my classroom is the story of Britain. Today young people from the highest social classes are three times as likely to go on to university as those from the lowest and twice as likely as students in the middle.[1]

This is striking, particularly if you compare it with the dominant narrative we saw in Chapter 3, the belief amongst young people today that if you work hard you can make it. When I spoke to Sarah she told me, 'I have no one but myself to blame, look at you and look at me. I could have done what you've done and apply myself.'

The truth is that by the time many young people are old

enough to make a conscious choice they are already far behind their peers. For too many young people the British Dream is a not a reality. They have all the aspirations but none of the tools to reach them.

As twenty-six-year-old Sarbjit put it, 'Thatcher wanted to empower individuals, like the American Dream she sold this idea you work hard and can make it to the top, it's about you and you've got to get off your arse and work hard. But everyone is not on a level playing field. Where you get to is not necessarily a function of hard work. I feel it's a bit of a con. You've sold us the dream and you haven't given us the tools to get it.'

There are too many young people leaving school without the basic skills to engage in economic or social life. 40 per cent of young people leave school without good English and Maths GCSEs when employers view these as essential employability skills.[2] At fifteen, 18.4 per cent of young people in the UK in 2009 had reading scores below Level 2, the reading age required of a seven-year-old, in other words they are functionally illiterate.[3]

As we saw in the previous chapters, this has a knock-on effect on citizenship and community life. But it is also a drain on our greatest resource as a country – our human capital. We are failing to enable the potential of the next generation. A study by Leon Feinstein found that on average children with low early test scores from affluent homes overtake children with high early test scores from working-class homes by the age of five.[4] This is a tragedy for that child, but when it is repeated again and again it is a national tragedy. How many businesses haven't been built, how many scientific discoveries missed, because we are not nurturing the full potential of our young people?

Declining social mobility

A socially mobile society is one where patterns of disadvantage and advantage do not repeat themselves over generations.

Most people believe that a socially mobile society is a desirable one, either on the basis of fairness, whereby people should be rewarded for their effort, perseverance and talents, or on the basis of economic success, which unlocks the full talents of our society. There is also general agreement that Britain is not a socially mobile society.

However, this is where the agreement ends. How to measure social mobility and how to ensure social mobility are highly contested political questions.

Much of the difficulty comes from trying to make sense of complex intergenerational processes. Every child receives a legacy from their parents, whether that be ability, inherited wealth, values, social networks, education or the nurture they receive at home. The environment a child grows up in affects their health, outlook and development. It also impacts the degree to which they are protected from changes in the labour market and family circumstances. The neighbourhood they grow up in is another important factor to consider as it determines their worldview and the level of opportunities available to them. All these conditions ultimately impact the likelihood of them finding work and the kind of work this might be.

The findings change depending on the measure used to compare mobility over generations; you get slightly different results if you choose to focus on social class, income, education or wealth. They also change depending on whether you are comparing generations on average or what an individual family's experience looks like compared with others.

For example, in absolute terms successive generations are more educated than their parents, whilst in relative terms data shows that affluent young people are likely to be better educated than their peers from poorer backgrounds. Both are important but they tell you very different things.

The story of absolute mobility is about the type and quality of jobs available in an economy. Absolute mobility will go up if there are large numbers of good-quality, well-paid jobs. In other words, if there is more 'room at the top'. Relative class mobility looks at where you sit in relation to the rest of your year group. It is therefore a zero-sum game. As one individual moves up, another moves down – not everyone can be at the top. It tells you about the extent of, or rather the lack of, equality of opportunity in a society by the strength of the relationship between an individual's social class and that of their parents.

When it comes to social class the evidence clearly shows that between the 1950s and 1970s there was a big increase in absolute mobility. However, the picture is more contested when it comes to relative mobility. Some studies show a small degree of opening up of opportunities for men[5] whilst others show stagnation.[6] Either way, the results show that even in the era of greatest social mobility relative mobility did not markedly increase.

The accepted conclusion has therefore been that the vast majority of social mobility was secured through structural changes in the economy, with the increase in professional opportunities rather than a fundamental opening up of society.[7]

Since the 1970s absolute mobility has remained stagnant for men, although opportunities for women have continued to increase.[8] Relative class mobility for both, however, hasn't changed.[9] This isn't anything to celebrate as rates of relative mobility were already low and are today below the European average for men and are at the bottom of the pile for women.

The picture is even bleaker if economists' favoured measure of social mobility – relative incomes (how far your parents' income determines your income) – is used. One of the major issues with this indicator is you can only start to assess social mobility once a young person has reached career maturation at around thirty-five years of age, and even then it only offers a pinpoint of complex trends. These caveats aside, the last measure of relative incomes looked bad for social mobility. According to research by

Jo Blanden and Stephen Machin for the Sutton Trust, 45 per cent
of boys born in the 1970s to fathers in the top 25 per cent earnings bracket were themselves in the top 25 per cent of their
generation by the time they reached their mid-thirties. This was
an increase in 'stickiness' of 10 per cent from the 1958 cohort,
meaning that there was a stronger relationship between the earnings of father and son for the 1970s cohort than for the 1950s.

Things look worse still when we start comparing social mobility in Britain with the rest of the world. The evidence shows that
when it comes to generational earnings, elasticity (the percentage change you might expect in a child's earnings compared with
their father's) in Britain and the US has substantially higher rates
of immobility than in Canada, Australia, New Zealand, Germany
and the Nordic countries.[10]

The focus in recent years has turned to the transmission of
wealth across generations, and unfortunately the picture doesn't
get any rosier here. Research by Abigail McKnight and Eleni
Karagiannaki shows that the combination of wealthier parents
and personal financial assets in early adulthood is associated with
better job prospects, health, educational outcomes and well-
being.[11]

What is clear is that social mobility isn't increasing and is lower
in the UK than in many other developed countries. Whatever
the measure used, it is evident that young people from poorer
backgrounds lose out.

Why isn't there more mobility?

There is no easy answer to why this is – or more accurately isn't –
happening. It comes about from the interrelationship between
family, education, culture, the labour market and policy.

The social mobility of the 1950s and 1960s was fuelled by
changes in the labour market. Technological change saw a massive
expansion in white-collar jobs, opening up more opportunities

than the middle classes could fill. The professions grew by 68 per cent between 1951 and 1971.[12] Supported by an expanded welfare state and educational opportunities, working-class children entered the professions in unprecedented numbers.

This growing professional class began to include women in larger numbers. Professionals were more likely to marry each other, move to the same places and, as we saw in the last chapter, form large social networks with other graduates. They were more likely to live in London and the south-east and their children were in turn more likely to get degrees.

At the same time technological change saw the automation of many manufacturing jobs. The long-term decline of manufacturing that occurred throughout the century was associated with a reduction in traditionally unionised sectors. Ultimately this led to a reduction in the power of labour in wage bargaining. Throughout the second half of the last century we see a growing polarisation between the career progression and opportunities available through education on one hand and the low-paid service options for those without post-eighteen education on the other.

As we increasingly enter a knowledge economy education matters, and it matters more in the UK than in other countries. Part of the change in the labour market is the higher premium placed on education. In the UK, for example, a graduate can expect to earn 71 per cent more than a non-graduate over their lifetime. This is one of the highest rates in the developed world, compared with 45 per cent in Australia, for example.[13]

The labour market keeps moving the goalposts of what is expected of young people, demanding higher and higher qualifications for the same roles. A degree becomes a starting point, not a guarantee of success.

Parents respond to this change by focusing more on their children's education. Middle-class professional parents not only have personal experience of educational success, they also have the resources to invest in education. Their social networks provide children with role models, and as they get older these same role models act as a source of professional advice and help.

These same parents are driving the rise in private tuition[14] and education, and when they are not opting for a private education for their children, middle-class parents tend to cluster around good state schools. Even when they don't they are more successful at navigating admissions. They also provide implicit support – securing work experience through professional networks, paying their children's rent when they take up internships, buying books, investing in cultural experiences – and invisible support, through the kind of expectations and conversations they have around education.

The state has had to work harder to keep up with parents furiously investing in their children. In the 1980s, when it needed to do more to level the playing field as technology disrupted the labour market, it actually started to do less.

In 1979 12.6 per cent of children were living in poverty. After eighteen years of Conservative government this figure had risen to 32.9 per cent.[15] Whole communities were abandoned to unemployment, with little support given to re-educating those who found their skills dormant in the new economy. The number of low-skilled men out of work increased from 2.2 per cent in the mid-70s to 15.8 per cent at the turn of the millennium.[16] Many communities descended into mass unemployment, with all the family breakdown and alcoholism that accompanies lack of opportunities. These families had little hope or skills to pass on to their own children.

There is some hope that the efforts put in to reducing child poverty, early years support and educational investment in the 1990s have had a knock-on effect, increasing social mobility and stalling the rising inequality that Britain witnesses in the 1980s and early 1990s. But it appears that the Labour Party were more successful at halting the decline and less so at reversing it.[17] In absolute terms young people brought up in the 1990s are more qualified than preceding generations, but levelling the playing field has proved more difficult against deep-seated and entrenched inequality.

Today we are left with two separate but related problems:

1. The professions are increasingly dominated by upper-middle-class young people at the expense of young people from disadvantaged and average backgrounds. 'Unleashing Aspiration', the Panel on Fair Access to the Professions 2009 report, highlighted this shift, showing that younger professionals, born after 1970, typically had a family income of 27 per cent above the national average compared with 17 per cent for older professionals. To take one extreme example, journalists and broadcasters born in 1958 typically grew up in families with an income of around 5.5 per cent above that of the average family; but this rose to 42.4 per cent for the generation of journalists and broadcasters born after 1970.[18]

2. Those young people who don't end up in the professions increasingly face low-paid, insecure options or unemployment. In the past you could have a poor education and still gain a decent standard of living. This is no longer the case for the majority. Mid-skill-level jobs are hollowing out, with an increase in poorly paid unskilled jobs at one end and highly skilled jobs for graduates at the other. By 2020 high-skilled, white-collar occupations are projected to employ 46 per cent of the population, with two million additional managerial, professional and associate professional roles. At the same time low-skilled jobs will increase by over three hundred thousand and skilled trades will decrease.[19] As this happens, a vacuum opens up in between, and there is no longer a staircase to work your way up.

Why inequality matters

People of all political persuasions acknowledge that we have a problem. As an idea, 'equality of opportunity' shares, along with 'democracy', almost universal political support. And like debates about democratic practice, a cursory look reveals deep divisions. The issue comes when it begins to conflict with other strongly held values – for example, autonomy of individuals, families or the market. If some families are investing more resources in their children, do you stop them? Most would argue no because it would remove their autonomy. Should the state then invest the same amount in young people in poverty? Many would say no because that would require redistribution on a scale that might distort market incentives or compromise individual autonomy. Yet 'equality' in contrast to 'equality of opportunity' is one of the most contested ideas in modern politics.

In my view we can't have equality of opportunity unless we start to address some of the inequality. If inequality is too high the gap between the rich and poor is too big to cross. Globally this has been proven time and again. Where we have more equal societies, social mobility is higher.

We saw this in Britain. When we invested in the welfare state, social mobility increased. Looking at how we can more equally share resources has to be part of any debate around equality of opportunity. Dealing with inequality is not just about redistributing income or wealth, it is also about skills, social capital and power.

We know that during the 1980s the very wealthiest began to pull away from everyone else. The top 1 per cent doubled their share of total UK income from 7.1 per cent in 1970 to 14.3 per cent in 2005; in fact, most of this increase came from the top 0.1 per cent.[20] For the top earners this can be explained by a global market for talent, changes in pay norms and tax policy.[21] However, the gap also increased between those on low earnings and everyone else.

These trends weren't specific to the UK; inequality since the 1990s has been rising even in traditionally more equal societies like Germany, Denmark and Sweden.[22] A comprehensive study from the OECD found that the most powerful catalyst for this has been technological change.

Under New Labour the high levels of inequality by no means disappeared but the rapid increases stalled for all but the very top. The Institute for Financial Services has shown that without Labour's redistributive tax-and-spend policies inequality would have increased much faster.[23] It is taking more and more effort by states just to stay still as globalisation and the mobility of capital constrains their options.

Accepting high levels of inequality means accepting that some are deserving of vastly higher rewards than others. The kind of society we want is bound up with how we view the purpose of our education system. Is it to identify the brightest and the best and to sort the young people most deserving of exceptional reward? Or is the purpose of education to ensure everyone has the opportunity to develop their talents to the best of their ability?

These two approaches to education create very different systems. The first may lead you to design a system akin to the grammar schools. But in my view, this cannot work. The only way to achieve the former is to design a system around the latter.

Imagine we started from scratch in a society where every child had exactly the same education and upbringing and at eighteen they all did a test. The top quarter got the best jobs and rewards, but the further down the list you were the worse off in terms of jobs and rewards you would become. Aside from any cognitive ability that was passed down, unfairness would be built into the system for the next generation. High earners would be incentivised to invest more in their children's education and they'd have the resources to do so. In one generation we have inequality of opportunity.

Any system that helps a minority and dooms the rest ultimately fails to create a socially mobile society. The grammar school was one such system and meant that my dad, who failed the eleven-plus despite being the smartest person I've ever known, left school at sixteen with one O level.

Our vision of social mobility can't be restricted to siphoning off the 'brightest and the best' working-class children into the professions and abandoning the rest.

If you are not academically focussed but you are compassion-ate, conscientious and hardworking you should have the opportunity to work hard, gain a qualification and earn yourself a good life. On the basis of fairness but also on the basis of social mobility. If you then have a child who is exceptionally talented you have the resources to ensure they fulfil their potential.

Things have gone too far when one person who works hard in the same company can be struggling to meet their basic living costs whilst another is struggling to spend the wealth they are accumulating. When half of all inheritance between 1996 and 2005 went to just one in fifty adults, we have to accept that we have got it wrong.[24]

These proportions matter when it comes to social mobility. But they also matter because evidence shows that more equal societies are happier, more cohesive, healthier and safer.[25] Scandinavian countries such as Norway and Sweden are more equal and invest heavily in early years and they have both low levels of infant mor-tality and reduced heart, liver and lung disease in middle age.[26]

A society where over half of people in poverty are in working families makes a mockery of social mobility and it entrenches the wasted potential of the young.[27]

The poverty trap

Young people growing up in poverty have to navigate a whole stream of hurdles to get the same opportunities as young people from more privileged backgrounds. It isn't that this isn't possible – there are many young people who do go on to succeed – but there are many more with all the talent in the world whose progress is halted by factors outside their control. This is the real tragedy of wasted potential.

Not every young person growing up in poverty experiences every hurdle, but even one can be enough to halt their progress. Firstly, the difficulties poverty gives parents in providing a secure, stable environment to develop the resilience and social and emotional skills young people need. Poverty can provide its own trauma and when it interacts with other forms of deprivation, such as drug and alcohol abuse, this can significantly hold back a child's development. Education is meant to level the playing field, but if expectations of poor children are low, teaching variable or leadership poor it can widen gaps. This can leave young people without the self-esteem to imagine other options or the resources and networks to make it happen. Finally, elitist beliefs can hold back individual young people and prevent these issues being tackled.

The importance of early years and parenting

The most important period for a child's development is the part they have least control over: the first five years of their life. Research show that 80 per cent of brain cell development takes place by age three.[28] This is where poverty first starts to impinge on the life chances of some children. A study presented to the Sutton Trust conference on social mobility and education following children born in 2000–1 split households into five income bands and looked at development in each band across a hundred-point scale. For every measure the pattern forms a staircase. The vocabulary of five-year-olds in the poorest quintile was twenty-six places below the richest and poor children were sixteen to seventeen places higher on the scale of likelihood to have conduct problems and hyperactivity.[29] Vocabulary at age five is one of the best predictors of later social mobility.[30]

As we saw above, parents can pass on a number of material and non-material assets to their children. Research strongly shows that secure parental attachments are crucial for children's sense of security and their ability to form attachments in later life. It also helps to provide the competencies that make them effective learners. One study following 267 American children from early years into their thirties found that parental care at four years old was a better indication of whether a high school student would graduate than IQ or achievement.[31] The psychologist Angela Duckworth has also found that students' scores on self-discipline tests predict their GPAs (grade point averages) better than their IQ scores.[32]

Likewise a parent's involvement in their child's education is more important than any other factor in determining a young person's educational success. This plays out in school choice, attitudes to learning and vocabulary.[33]

It is easy to blame parents and many do – if only parents cared more, engaged more, took more responsibility or wanted more for their children.

However, these arguments ignore the fact that the vast majority of parents have very high aspirations for their children. 98 per cent of mothers from the Millennium Cohort Study, a multi-disciplinary research project following the lives of around nineteen thousand children born in the UK from a whole range of backgrounds in 2000–1, wanted their children to go to university.[34]

It isn't that parents don't want their children to succeed; many just have no idea how to make it happen.[35]

Most research shows that the majority of families living in poverty display huge resilience in the face of multiple challenges and many parents living in poverty make huge sacrifices for their children. One study of low-income families found that a fifth of parents had gone without food to feed their children.[36]

However, they are still finding it difficult to make the aspirations they have for their children a reality.

At the same time parents who have struggled to achieve at school don't always know how to support their children's education. It is hard to pass on a wide vocabulary if you have a limited one. It is difficult to check that your teenager is doing their homework if you are a single parent doing evening shift work. It is tough to find the language to encourage learning if your experience of education was negative and it is impossible to read to your child if your literacy is poor. Parents need more support, as I will show in Chapter 10, and some families need that support to be intensive.

Childhood trauma

With poverty comes a whole host of other issues – housing instability and overcrowding, debt, low educational achievement leading to low-paid work or unemployment. Poverty is also associated with higher rates of post-natal depression and depression more generally.[37] I think of some of the parents I meet at my surgery. The one trapped inside her flat every day with her two kids because there isn't a lift and she isn't able to carry them up the stairs; the one trying to keep their eviction from her son so it didn't disrupt his exams. So much of their energy and resources have to be put into just getting by.

Not all children growing up in poverty experience childhood trauma, and trauma is not exclusive to families living in poverty. However the stress associated with poverty can make consistent parenting more difficult. Poverty can also compound other problems families' experience, putting up even more barriers for children. Evidence from the Millennium Cohort Study found that 42 per cent of young people who had experienced poor parenting but not poverty had reached a good level of development by age five compared with 19 per cent who had grown up with poor parenting and persistent poverty.[38]

There are a section of parents that struggle to support their children, held back by untreated mental health concerns, alcoholism, drug abuse or their own experience of trauma and emotional neglect. Many young people are growing up in households where their parents are just not able to provide the basic nurture and care they need.

This is not a minority. In 2003 the Department of Health estimated that four million out of the eleven million children living in England 'were failing to meet their developmental goals due to stress in the family caused by mental illness, domestic violence or the presence of drug and alcohol abuse, or by social and material conditions causing stress and chaos'.[39]

So many of the young people I met throughout the course of researching this book and as part of my continued work with young people in Camden were struggling to come to terms with the legacy of their childhood. Human bodies and brains carry the stress of childhood trauma well into adulthood. One study found that 47 per cent of children assessed as having a mental disorder had parents who themselves scored poorly on a test to measure well-being.[40]

Childhood trauma can prevent young people developing non-cognitive skills, such as resilience and self-control, which not only allow them to be good learners but also enable them to form relationships, sustain jobs and navigate life's many challenges.

Paul Tough sums up the available evidence in his book *How Children Succeed*: 'The part of the brain most affected by early stress is the prefrontal cortex, which is critical in self-regulatory activities of all kinds, both emotional and cognitive. As a result, children who grow up in stressful environments generally find it harder to concentrate, harder to sit still, harder to rebound from disappointments and harder to follow directions. And that has a

direct effect on their performance in school. When you're over-
whelmed by uncontrollable impulses and distracted by negative
feelings, it's hard to learn the alphabet.'[41]

Anna* is one young woman struggling with a childhood
legacy of neglect and violence. She told me how she still finds it
difficult to form relationships, sustain a career or find peace of
mind. Her day-to-day life has for years been peppered with
uncontrollable anger, anxiety and panic attacks. 'Sometimes I felt
like I wanted to roar, hit my chest like a bear. Literally, get it out
because when I get that angry, something inside me just needs to
leave. The only way I knew to get rid of it: get in a fight and hit
something.'

As a student of psychology she has been able to trace this back
to a childhood spent in 'survival mode' and the lack of a secure
parental attachment. She describes the impact that it still has on
her life. 'I am quite anxious all the time. In a relationship I don't
believe anyone cares or loves me.'

What is missing for Anna, and young people like her, is the
healthy brain connections that maternal love and affection produce. 'That is why so many teenagers and adults seem to behave
like children,' she tells me. 'It is not because they just want to, it
is because connections are not there.'

When a child comes into the classroom carrying profound
trauma they need more than a good teacher to break through.
Rachel, a twenty-year-old from Edinburgh, was brought up by a
mother battling drug addiction and experienced all the poverty and
chaos that came with this. She described how a couple of teachers tried to reach her but she didn't know how to accept help. 'I
was so shut down I couldn't take that help. I just couldn't've. I was
scared so I pushed everyone away from me because I didn't want
them to see what was going on.' By fourteen she was on drugs herself. 'I couldn't cope with feelings that were coming up. And that's

---

* Not her real name.

why I used because it gave me that numbness so I didn't have to feel anything.' She hadn't learnt any other way to manage her feelings. 'I didn't know how to be. The only thing I knew was how to use; I didn't know how to live life. I really didn't know how to do anything.'

It is important not to be fatalistic or deterministic about this. These young people can be reached and there is strong evidence to show that attachments formed later on in life can start to combat some of the trauma in early years. Sometimes this might mean supporting parents to re-form attachments. At other times, where this isn't possible, another adult can provide the strong relationship. However, helping these children requires investment, patience and time.

Rachel is now clean and mentoring other young people, but it took the support of her coaches at Street Soccer, a social enterprise that uses football to build relationships with those experiencing homelessness and other types of disadvantage, backing her through relapses, to get there. She thinks young people need a bit more compassion. 'If you're not engaging with services it is like, "Right you are out." They need someone who won't give up on them. Lots of young people experience difficulties at home, no confidence, no self-esteem, very little belief in themselves; they feel excluded from normal society because of the issues that are happening in their lives. Just dismissing them is not the best way. You need to work with them, help them believe in themselves, give them a bit of hope.'

Or as Camila Batmanghelidjh puts it, these traumatised teenagers need an unconditional base. They need you to 'hang in there through thick and thin. Slam the door, call you a fat bitch, come back and apologise.'

In Chapter 7 I show how charities like Street Soccer and Kids Company are re-parenting traumatised children through strong empathetic relationships. But there is still massive unmet need and too many young people are falling through the cracks.

These children are the innocent victims of a society that has tolerated the poverty and alienation of far too many of our families. If these young people continue to be neglected society will pay the price. And when people question where the morality, empathy or kindness of these young people is, the response might be, Where was yours?

Education

In theory, school should help to narrow the gap, enabling young people to catch up. In fact, in the UK it does the opposite: the gap widens as young people go through the education system.[42]

In Britain we have a highly segregated education system where a higher proportion of our national income is spent on private eduction than almost all OECD nations. The grammar schools that remain are very much the preserve of middle-class young people; only 1.9 per cent of their intake are on free school meals.

However, even within the state sector there is substantial variance in the quality of education, and children with the same background will achieve very different results depending on where they end up.[43] Too many schools have tolerated long-term chronic low achievement. And too many children from disadvantaged backgrounds end up in the worst schools.

Even within the same school, the gap can be incredibly wide. There has been a culture within some schools where certain pupils are considered 'unreachable'. Too often behavioural and emotional problems are conflated with lack of ability. A poll of teachers conducted for the government's Social Mobility and Child Poverty Commission found that 1 in 4 secondary school teachers reported that some of their colleagues had lower expectations of poorer students.[44] Too often the worst teachers end up in the bottom sets. Schools were predominately judged by the number of pupils gaining five A* to C grades (including English and maths), which meant that students on an E/D borderline didn't get the same investment as higher-performing students. This culture is shifting, with Ofsted now focusing on the progress each student makes against their past performance, but it still has a long way to go to change the culture in some schools.

The quality of teaching, how engaging the lessons are, the level of personalised support and the focus on character development all matter more for disadvantaged children who aren't necessarily getting support with education at home.

Schools also do not leave young people equipped for the labour market they are set to enter. The CBI regularly pick out non-cognitive skills such as the ability to communicate well, resilience and empathy as important for employment opportunities, yet schools don't don't always focus on these areas.

As Simon Devonshire, Director of Wayra, Europe, Telefonica's accelerator programme to support tech start-ups, put it, 'I have a very strong belief that we don't have an unemployment crisis, we have an employability crisis. That fundamentally education is pouring out young people without the right skills for work and that work is transitioning unimaginably at an incredibly fast rate. The work landscape now is fundamentally different and yet we're educating people in pretty much the same way that we did in Victorian times.'

Disadvantaged students are most dependent on schools to give them access to the networks, experiences and skills that they don't necessarily get at home.

Sometimes sensible points about expanding the breadth of our education system get shouted out in a bid to knock down straw men. As Michael Barber, educationist and Chief Education Adviser to Pearson, put it, 'The road to hell in education is paved with false dichotomies'[45] and in this country we are addicted to them. A knowledge-based curriculum or a competency one? Vocational or academic studies? While the debate rages on, other countries are managing to combine the best of both worlds and our young people are getting left behind. This isn't the teachers' fault; too often the targets, accountability framework and exam system encourage this narrow focus.

Finally, careers advice has to be fit for purpose to help young people make the vital choices about their future, and this is more important for young people who don't have parents that can help them navigate this. A survey of 11,759 thirteen- to eighteen-year-olds found absolutely no correlation between young people's aspirations and projected labour market demand.[46] Young people can only imagine the professions they have heard of; many young people I met from disadvantaged homes wanted to be social workers or youth workers as these were the only adult professions they came into contact with.

Many schools and teachers have put huge effort, resources and energy into narrowing this gap. It isn't easy; it requires professionals willing to go the extra mile for young people and often for their families. However, there is still a long way to go. As I discuss in Chapter 10 it is not just about censure, it is about valuing teachers, supporting professional development, sharing best practice and challenging low expectations.

Bridging the divide between home and school for white working-class families

When I was at school the group in my class that were most likely to fall out of education early were those from white working-class backgrounds. Looking at the data when I was elected as a councillor, I saw this was a problem across Camden.

Camden is a London borough where most children are likely to attend a school rated as either Good or Outstanding, but in 2013 only 25 per cent of white British free-school-meal pupils gained five A* to C grades, including English and maths, at GCSE, under half the Camden average and well behind the next-lowest-performing group (Congolese students at 52 per cent). This reflects a national problem.

The Strand Report showed that while socio-economic factors affect young people across the board they disproportionately affect white British young people (see graph below).

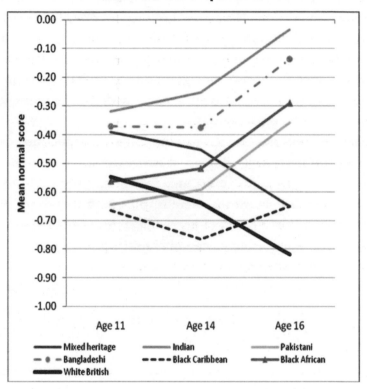

SES bottom quintile

Source: Steve Strand, 'Ethnicity, Gender, Social Class and Achievement Gaps at Age 16: Intersectionality and "Getting It" for the White Working Class', *Research Papers in Education*, 29:2 (2014)

One of the first things I did as a councillor was set up a committee to look into this, interviewing parents, teachers and other local authorities, and speaking to other communities who were having more success. The problem that we kept coming back to was the relationship between school and home.

I think this is not about race but about how many generations of a family have lived in the same area without experiencing social mobility.

In contrast, immigrating to a new country is an aspirational act and, despite the challenges of integration, language and cultural change, the generations that follow inherit the same sense of possibility in spite of the challenges they may face. Many immigrants come from highly educated backgrounds. They may not understand the school system but they understand how to support and understand the value of education. Every year I attend Camden's Somali Achievement Awards, where the community come together to celebrate and reward their children's achievements. There is a sense of momentum as each year the results and achievements improve, and they celebrate the first Somali graduate or the first Somali councillor, and so on.

This doesn't mean it is easy and it certainly didn't happen by chance. In 1999 only one Somali child in Camden got a GCSE and the community decided to come together with schools and the local authority to do something about it, investing in link workers, supplementary schools, homework clubs, mentoring and awards ceremonies, and results have improved year on year. Across London there was an acknowledgement from schools, local authorities and communities that language and cultural barriers could mean difficulty transitioning between school and home life for many young people, therefore many local authorities put resources into bridging these divides by working closely with communities to improve attainment.

Despite the substantial challenges many communities still face, including institutional racism, many feel like they are walking a path of progress. In contrast, many of their white working-class neighbours feel that they are on the opposite trajectory. This doesn't have to be the case, but it isn't going to change on its own. There has to be a catalyst to turn hopelessness into optimism.

Speaking to white working-class parents in Camden, it is clear that although they care about their children's education they are far less likely to engage with school life. Parents describe to me how it feels to walk in to their children's school. Suddenly they are back in the classroom where another teacher is telling them that they are failing, not as a student this time but as a parent. They are faced with jargon they can't understand and often what feels like a barrage of negativity about a child who is either misbehaving or not making good enough progress. They feel patronised. They hear it again on the phone every week or in letters. Eventually they stop picking up the phone or opening up the envelopes. Not everyone has the confidence to do what Naomi's mum did and fight for attention, so schools get the impression they don't care.

Many parents I spoke to put a premium on 'being there' and providing care themselves, but that care can only include the networks and knowledge they have.

They were wary of professionals, of services, of 'surveillance and control'.[47] They don't want interference in their lives and are especially wary of the police and social services. Afraid of an unequal power dynamic, they put up walls and keep away from the services that are designed to help. As one children's centre worker put it to me, 'White working-class parents pick up a leaflet and go.'

And they don't always have a positive sense of community to fall back on, at least one that promotes education. There aren't necessarily the resources within working-class communities to make sense of a changing labour market.

This is especially problematic for young men. They often have a very traditional view of their own role as breadwinners.[48] The boys I spoke to had an unrealistic sense of the opportunities available to them and little understanding of the changing nature of qualifications. Boys talked about academic achievement and reading as not being cool or 'for them'.

Within some white working-class communities there is also sometimes a defensiveness and anger towards other communities. In the interviews I did, I heard so often that all the support goes to this group or that group, whilst they were being left behind. This embeds their feeling of isolation and the sense that there aren't opportunities for them.

It is true that not enough resources have specifically targeted this group. It is obvious when there is a language barrier that a bridge between parents and school is needed, but when parents and teachers speak the same language it doesn't seem nearly as necessary. The truth is you don't have to speak another language to have trouble communicating.

While it is not the majority, too many teachers have told me that there is nothing that you can do with some children. If this is your worldview then when a parent doesn't turn up to parents' evening you think, Well, they must not care. When a child can't concentrate you think, Well, they aren't that bright anyway. It means you give up on them and lower your expectations rather than putting the extra time into building relationships.

Too many white working-class kids end up being what one parent described as 'invisible children', sitting silently at the back of classrooms, disengaged and disheartened. They are not troublesome enough to get special attention, not promising enough to be worth pushing. Children pay for the prejudices we hold as a society.

Too many schools are misinterpreting parental disengagement and too many parents are locked into negative stereotypes about education. We have a misalignment between schools and families and children end up being pulled between the two.

The working-class values Naomi's grandparents passed on to her – the powerful history of the British working class, the informal ties that make up white working-class communities and most importantly the aspirations parents have for their children – are all untapped resources for educators if only they took the time to understand and work with parents and communities.

It isn't easy to bridge this divide. It requires schools to reach out to parents on their terms and in settings they are comfortable with. It can happen because in the end both schools and parents have the same goal: wanting the best for the children. In Camden we have designed a pilot project taking a community approach to lifting white working-class achievement and we have found that, given the right support on their terms, parents are more than willing to engage.

Fixed mindsets

While parents may have high aspirations, their kids can struggle to believe in them. Stanford University psychologist Carol Dweck's research into educational achievement has shown that more important than a person's IQ is a 'young people's theory of themselves'. If you believe that intelligence is fixed and you are unintelligent, then effort becomes pointless. However, if you believe that intelligence is malleable and depends on hard work, then effort is an opportunity.[49]

Too often young people brought up in poverty have deeply embedded mindsets. There is widespread evidence of a 'stereotype threat', where the emotional baggage of being part of a stereotyped group can impede performance. One US study found that when a group of university students were asked to do a test, those from a lower socio-economic background did not perform as well when they were told it was an ability test to determine why low-income students underperformed relative to higher-income students. So deep are the stereotypes about class and attainment that the mere mention of the word intelligence managed to trigger anxiety and cause underperformance from working-class students.[50]

When your whole family is in the same position, it is hard to imagine a different future. A child brought up in a professional family has a map of how to reach their aspirations. If their parents can't help, often they know someone who can. A child brought up without this has the aspiration but not the map. Sometimes they respond by giving up, sometimes they hold on to these aspirations without any idea what steps they need to take to achieve them.

If the world seems to have low expectations of you, then you acclimatise to that. Instead of networks, connections or role models, these young people are labelled as 'NEETs', or stereotyped as 'thugs', 'chavs', 'delinquents' – and they absorb it. As one young woman at a pupil referral put it, 'You're not expected to get GCSEs, let alone go to college. You're told it every day in school, on the news.'

When whole communities share poverty, they share low self-esteem, bunkering down against a world that seems to reject them. It is terrifying to imagine an alternative life. In a community centre in Easterhouse, an estate in Glasgow, a group of young people tell me they think 80 per cent of Britain lives in poverty on around twelve thousand pounds a year. The number of people living in poverty today is around 20 per cent and average income is around £26,500. If you have such a distorted worldview, then it is difficult to imagine an alternative future.

The thick ties of family and friendship can be a source of strength and comfort but they can also hold people back out of fear of what high aspirations means in practice – the debt, moving out of local communities or losing touch with family.

I was reminded of this when speaking to a group in the Welsh valleys. They were all being paid the minimum wage for jobs in retail, hospitality, low-skilled factory work or farming. They were unanimous that these were stop-gaps as they worked towards what they actually wanted to do. One nineteen-year-old told me several times that he was only working in a factory to make a bit of money in the short term, but long term he wanted to go to university and become a social worker. However, as we talked it became clear that he didn't believe it would ever really happen for him. 'I always say to myself I want to move away but I know really deep down that I'll probably live here for the rest of my life. I know when the actual time comes to do it I couldn't leave.'

He is too afraid to leave the tight-knit community he grew up in. It gives him safety, security and a sense of belonging but it also puts a cap on his aspirations. 'People say go away for university, it's the best time of your life, but I know when I'm on my own I'd want to be back where I am. Here I've got my family, my friend only lives across the road. There you're in a situation where you don't know anyone at all. No one to turn to if it goes wrong; you're completely on your own. So I always know, even though I say I will, that I won't. I know even if I became a millionaire I wouldn't move, unless I could take everyone with me I'd just buy a massive house here.'

I hear this a lot – the conflict between young people's desire to branch out and their fear of losing what they have, even if it's not a lot. It is the tension between security and opportunity, family and career, housing and education costs. Failure is more daunting when there is no safety net. It's the difference between wanting something and believing it can happen.

Class prejudice and elitism

The low expectations projected onto poorer children don't happen in a vacuum. Our education system reflects the prejudices we hold as a society. As Owen Jones chronicled in *Chavs*, class prejudice is alive and well in the UK.

Many young people are left without anything positive to hang their identity on. They feel separated from a working-class identity, so when asked to define themselves they reflect back other negative perceptions.

Too often in popular culture 'working class' has become synonymous with 'fecklessness', while education and hard work have become monopolised as middle-class values. Naomi describes how as soon as she got a job, began visiting art galleries and started holidaying abroad, people told her she couldn't be working class. 'Everyone is convinced I'm middle class but they're wrong. I think it's so rude to assume because someone speaks nicely and they're dressed a certain way that they're posh. I think that kind of attitude really holds people back in society. I mean, I've worked really fucking hard to get where I am and I'm still working hard and I come from a background that taught me you have to work your arse off to get anywhere. I see myself as working class and I think I always will.'

Just as pervasive as class prejudice is the 'talent myth'. This is an issue linked to the individualism we saw in Chapter 3, where we over-ascribe success to individual talent, flair and brilliance. This in turn leads to a binary view of talent and intelligence – either you have it or you don't. In fact, much of the recent evidence from Malcolm Gladwell to Carol Dweck shows that effort is far more important in determining success than any innate talent. Despite this we continue to favour the 'heroic genius' or 'natural talent' explanations for success rather than highlighting teamwork and effort. Over-emphasising the individual can quickly reinforce elitist ideas.

In his book *Injustice*, Daniel Dorling, professor of human geography at Oxford University, highlights elitism as one of the five new evils in society alongside greed, despair, prejudice and exclusion. He writes about the rise of 'IQism', which he believes is being used to justify elitism. When the IQ test was designed in 1905 it was never meant to be a measure of intelligence but rather as a tool to identify where students needed more support at school. It has turned into something much more prescriptive and has become an easy way to label people or place them on a scale.[51]

This becomes dangerous when we mistake differences in opportunity for innate differences in intelligence. Humans are prone to over-exaggerating their own talents and many individuals who succeed find it easier to subscribe to the view that they have made it because of their own brilliance instead of accepting that things were set up in their favour. Families find it easier to ignore the extra resources they are pouring into their child when they celebrate their successes. It is much easier to believe that talent rises to the top when you have already made it.

There is mixed evidence on the importance of genetics in determining intelligence, but what is clear is that children are not handed down a set measure of intelligence, rather a range of possibilities, and where they end up is in large part dictated by their environment. This is borne out by studies of identical twins conducted in the US. When identical twins are separated at birth and brought up in affluent families, there is a great deal of correlation between their IQs, suggesting a role for genetics. However, when it comes to twins brought up in poverty one study shows that the correlation disappears.[52] We have no idea what the potential of many of our children is because they are never allowed to develop it.

Numerous studies show that investment in children's education can improve their IQ. The IQ of children in more equal societies is on average higher than in unequal ones and in fact IQ results in general are increasing because intelligence is not static but evolving. We need to change our mindset from 'what are our children's limits?' to 'how far can they go?'

So deeply embedded is the talent myth in British and American education that it's easy to forget that it is simply a cultural construct. We seem to have resigned ourselves to the current situation. There are other approaches: many South Pacific education systems, for example, do not have the same association between low expectations and poverty. In 'Oceans of Innovation: The Atlantic, the Pacific, Global Leadership and the future of education', Michael Barber et al. describe two central messages running through many South Pacific education systems and societies – 'birth is not destiny and effort is rewarded'. Or, as one famous Chinese saying puts it, 'Diligence can compensate for stupidity.'

Elitism is reinforced by segregation, as mentioned earlier in the chapter. If you only come into contact with people from a similar background then these beliefs never get challenged. I remember naively thinking that elitism was a bit of a myth before I went to Oxford. I'd seen the films, I'd read the books, but I thought that this was a Britain of the past. I was shocked by what I encountered. I remember standing behind a group of boys queuing for a club who were literally laughing at the idea of speaking to someone from a state school: 'I wouldn't even speak to someone who went to Harrow.' I remember being left speechless by a London-educated private school boy who told me that it was a scientific fact that black people were less intelligent. On another occasion a group of day-school-educated girls told me we had to have private schools because we needed somewhere for the intelligent people to go. 'Not the intelligent people, the rich people,' I started shouting, much to the embarrassment of the person who had invited me. I remember turning up to my first and last 'Bad Taste Party' to be greeted by the sickening sight of my fellow students dressed up as everything from pregnant 'chavs' to an aborted foetus. There is nothing more unedifying than a bunch of rich white people making fun of people in poverty.

Of course this isn't true of every private-school-educated person I met and they are by no means the majority. But the fact that these views exist at all is a disgrace. The fact that these people have all gone on to have top professional careers is frankly terrifying.

Young people from elite backgrounds aren't necessarily getting the most well-rounded education but what they are getting is the best education for the elite recruitment that determines too much of the access to professions. If they were getting a broader education we would probably have a more dynamic and creative workforce and if there was a broader approach to recruitment we definitely would.

I have focused on the fixed mindsets of young people growing up in poverty but Carol Dweck makes clear that this is just as likely to afflict children growing up in affluent families. There are young people who are told from a young age that they are intelligent, smart and talented. Far from encouraging effort, these labels can make young people less likely to embrace challenges for fear of losing this status. In one example two groups of young students do an easy test; one group are told on receiving high marks that they are intelligent, the other are told that they must have worked hard. When asked if they want to do a harder test the majority of those who had been told they were intelligent declined – there was too much to lose.[53] Paul Tough believes this helps explain why so many graduates from top universities choose the safe corporate route – it is the path of least risk. If we want innovative, resilient young people then we have to look at how we enable growth mindsets across the board.[54]

Furthermore, affluent young people can't afford to exist in narrow networks where they only meet people like themselves. I tell anyone who will listen that sending their middle-class child to a state school is the greatest gift you can give them. They might not end up with the same sense of innate confidence and entitlement but they will be less susceptible to hubris and elitism. They will be able to negotiate difference and they will be able to communicate with people outside of their direct social networks.

Breaking into the professions

Even when young people make it all the way through to university it can still be harder to convert aspirations into tangible opportunities. Graduates who went to private schools are also more likely to be in the highest-earning professions three years after graduation, A third of those who went to private schools had earnings over thirty thousand pounds, compared with 14 per cent of those from state schools.

The networks and cultural experience a parent exposes their child to also matter. There is the intangible way they broaden horizons and aspirations, and the unconscious way they teach young people how to interact in different worlds, the unwritten rules to follow, the confidence they provide. Mostly they matter because they are the most important tools for finding work. This is true whatever your network. The majority of jobs are never advertised and some estimate that half are passed through word of mouth. Finally, the assets a child inherits make a huge difference to their sense of well-being and their capacity to take risks.

Sarbjit is from a working-class background in the Midlands and described to me the intangible benefits that come with a privileged upbringing. 'You lift your head above the parapet and you go to Oxford and you're around all these privileged people and you don't understand it unless you've come from somewhere else, that people walk around with a different sense of what they can achieve when they've been around success, it's what's expected, it's innate. You don't get that where I'm from. You might think everyone leaving Oxford has this degree, that they are on a level playing field, but they're not. You still have some people who will get their foot through the door.'

Young people who do want to break into the professions face an uphill struggle. Even if they do get an opportunity there is a high chance it won't be a paid one.[55] In 2013 48 per cent of employers said that relevant work experience was the most important factor considered when recruiting graduates.[56] The Fair Access to the Professions report stated that the 'exponential growth in internships in the professions adds up to a profound change in the British labour market. Access to work experience is a new hurdle that would-be professionals now have to clear before they can even get onto the recruitment playing field.'[57]

In 2012 the Fair Access to the Professional Careers report found that 'over one-third of graduate vacancies will be filled by applicants who have already worked for the employer as an under-graduate'. Job competition is so fierce that more and more young people are willing to take on unpaid internships.

But being able to complete unpaid internships requires accommodation and access to at least some disposable income. It doesn't help that many of the opportunities are in London and the south-east – the places in the UK with the highest housing and living costs.[58] Current projections are that almost half of the growth in jobs in higher level-occupations will occur in London, south-east England and the east of England.[59]

This means a degree is only half the story. You have to be able to fund yourself through an unpaid – or if you're lucky poorly paid – internship.

Unpaid internships disadvantage those living outside of big cities, they disadvantage those from low-income backgrounds and they prevent a level playing field in access to the professions. They're also in many cases illegal.

A YouGov poll commissioned by the National Union of Students estimated that there are approximately one hundred thousand young people doing unpaid internships and 43 per cent of young people see unpaid internships as a major barrier into work.[60]

Unpaid internships can be highly competitive, so it's not easy for young people to demand their rights, even if they know what their rights are. One poll showed that only 10 per cent of young people knew they were entitled to be paid the minimum wage.[61]

Intern Aware's young co-director Ben Lyons tells me that while his organisation has raised the profile of the issue and won widespread political support, there is a long way to go. 'Most young people can't afford to work for free, and increasingly when we speak to employers they understand that paying interns isn't just the right thing to do, but also helps them attract the best people. But unfortunately there are also companies which have shifted their business model to rely on unpaid, often illegal work!'

Ending this wasted potential

Ensuring every child meets their potential and combating elitism isn't something schools can do alone. Schools have to do more, but the idea that great teaching can solve the broader dynamics of poverty is a cop-out. The education system can't be expected to act as our poverty programme, our cohesion programme, our employment policy and our skills programme.

To change outcomes for young people, everyone involved has to believe it is possible – young people, their families, their teachers but also policymakers.

We need to support them not only because it is the right thing to do but because if we do we will unlock latent resources of creativity, energy and productivity. If we don't act then we push young people to make the wrong choices rather than supporting them to make the right ones.

There are many exceptional young people who manage to navigate these challenges. But you shouldn't have to be exceptional to get on in life. Of course there is a balance between an individual's responsibility for their own choices and the circumstances they are born into. However, no one needs to tell these young people to take responsibility for themselves. They're already internalising these messages and blaming themselves for failures. They don't need any more criticism. What they need is support: support in early years, support to develop non-cognitive skills, emotional support, support to access new and different networks, support to broaden their horizons and support to gain work experience.

There is no more important issue for the future of our country than this chronic waste of potential. The task of dealing with declining social mobility becomes all the more urgent as inequalities follow young people online.

Chapter 6

The Revolution Will Be Digital

Power to the geeks – Kevin Chandler, 22, Derby

Kevin Chandler talks like someone who spends a lot of time on a computer – quickly, about everything at once and with a sense of awe about the possibilities open to him. When he was a toddler he was always taking toys apart to see how they worked, at eleven he went to school dressed up as Bill Gates and by fourteen he was hacking his PlayStation. He tells me, 'I'm definitely part of a generation who can challenge the status quo.'

He is frustrated at the pace of change in society's views about the digital revolution. From 'being that nerdy guy in the corner . . . I went through the whole being bullied at school kind of thing' to the way people's faces fall when they hear that he studies gaming – they think violence, timewasting and obesity. For Kevin this bears no relationship to the creative beauty of interactive entertainment, games that can educate, empower and connect. 'I learnt maths through games,' he tells me; people don't understand that play can revolutionise learning.

When I ask him about community, he answers passionately, but he's not talking about Derby where he lives now or Aylesbury where he grew up. For him community is everyone he has an email address for, it's a network of online contacts that spans many countries. 'I'm not attached to a location. Talking to you now I see you as someone that I've networked with and someone great to speak to again. You're now part of the circle of people I've met and that's cool. I can email you. I don't need to know where you live or knock on your door.'

Coding for him meant greater social mobility. He lived in an area that still had the eleven-plus. He failed and went to the local comprehensive, which he enjoyed, but he felt that it didn't equip him for the route he wanted to take. 'There was no one in school who said that there is this amount of entrepreneurialism in the UK or here is a place where you go to learn about it. If they did maybe I wouldn't have lost so much time.' When he was sixteen his mum encouraged him to apply to do computer science at the grammar school. He would travel down the road once a week for computer science lessons. Despite not fitting in with many of the students, he found a teacher that believed in him, nurtured his talent and made learning fun. Kevin tells me, 'I owe him my life.' Kevin didn't know much about university, he was the first person in his family ever to go and he says it was pure fluke that he ended up at one of the best computer science games courses in the country. On his first day his lecturer joked that at least they weren't doing computer science and pottery at a nearby univer-sity. It had been Kevin's second choice. 'Clearly I had no idea what I was looking for but it turns out I went to the one of the best universities in the UK for games programming.'

It was at university that Kevin finally found his place. He can barely find the words to bring to life the buzz he gets from the flow of ideas and creativity in his flat. 'I cannot emphasise more how being around creative and empowering and enabling people helps.' It was from this creative spirit that IndieSkies was born, a games collective made up of eleven students from his course. Instead of taking the tried and tested route of an internship at a big corporation they decided to branch out on their own. He said the overwhelming response was negative, with concern even from his parents.

For Kevin, IndieSkies turned out to be life-changing. 'It was the most humbling thing ever. To see people play the games, to know we created them ourselves and we didn't have any help.' He shows me one of the apps he created for Nokia and Microsoft, which as we spoke was displayed at the South by South West festival in Texas. In one year he says his whole life changed. 'My confidence was zero when I started, now I see it as a hundred per cent.'

He thinks a lot of young people are still waking up to the potential the internet brings. 'The freedoms that come with the internet for young people are brilliant. I just don't know if young people know the power of the internet yet.'

He doesn't want the same bargain as his parents' generation, where money constrained options and a job was to pay the bills. For Kevin, the internet is the liberator. 'It's not that people didn't want to do it back then, it is just they didn't have the opportunities. If Facebook and all that tech was around back then I think my parents would be up for it. They would be doing exactly the same thing I am doing right now.'

He wants to make enough money to look after his family. 'My dream is to pay for them to have a cruise around the world. To facilitate that for them would be my personal goal. Success for me is to better the life of my parents.'

Most importantly he wants to love his work. 'I must enjoy every waking minute of life . . . I will not settle for something I am doing that I don't like. My God, there is so much creativity in this world. I haven't seen hardly any of it yet, but what I have seen is phenomenal.'

Kevin is a true digital native who has the skills to make the most of the internet. As a result he is finding deep personal empowerment, shaping his career on his own terms. However, his story says a lot more about the potential of the internet than what is actually happening with the majority of young people.

Stuck in the middle of the internet debate

'With their reflexes tuned to speed and freedom, these empowered young people are beginning to transform every institution of modern life. From the workplace to the marketplace, from politics to education to the basic unit of any society, the family, they are replacing a culture of control with a culture of enablement.'

Don Tapscott, *Grown Up Digital*

'It's a connected world defined by millions of "smart" devices, by real-time lynch mobs, by tens of thousands of people broadcasting details of a stranger's sex life, by the bureaucratisation of friendship, by the group think of small brothers, by the elimination of loneliness and by the transformation of life itself into a voluntary *Truman Show*. Most of all it's a world in which many of us have forgotten to be human.'

A. J. Keen, *Digital Vertigo*

Young people are living the communications revolution more completely than any other generation. It is in the fabric of their social lives. They would recognise both the quotes above as offering some element of truth about their lives online, two sides of the same coin.

Those who don't like what the internet is doing to society can draw on young people's 'narcissism', their inability to understand friendship and short attention spans. They ask how technology is changing the way young people's brains work. Those that do support the internet there is young people's creativity, their collaborative impulses and empowered attitudes.

This debate often misses two crucial elements in a bid to present either a utopia or a dystopia: a huge divergence in how young people use technology and young people's own agency in shaping the tools they use.

Firstly divergence: the truth is only a small minority of young people embody either extreme of an empowered digital native or a vulnerable digital outcast. For the majority the internet is neither a tool of great empowerment nor one of oppression.

This doesn't mean the idea of a young digital native is a complete myth. Young people do tend to be more immersed in the internet than older generations. They are more frequently online (24.2 hours per week for sixteen- to twenty-four-year-olds versus 16.9 hours for all adults in 2012). Their time is more likely to be spent on social networks. 96 per cent of sixteen- to twenty-four-year-olds look at social networks at least quarterly, compared with 69 per cent of all adults. They are more likely to have an open view of ownership online: 53 per cent of sixteen- to twenty-four-year-olds say downloading music and films should be legal compared with 36 per cent of all adults.[1] For young people who have grown up with the internet, they can't imagine life without it. The graph opposite illustrates the difference: while older generations couldn't live without their television, for younger ones it is their smart phone.

It is not that they are online that matters; it is what they do when they are there. This is where the diversity kicks in. The majority are still making quite limited use of the internet for entertainment, casual browsing and connecting with friends. They consume rather than create. Kevin holds most closely to Don Tapscott's vision of an empowered young person transforming and disrupting the world around him. However, he is in truth in a distinct minority. This minority are using the internet as a tool to create, whether it is enterprises, art, or political movements. It is

Most-missed media – top five mentions among all adults: 2013

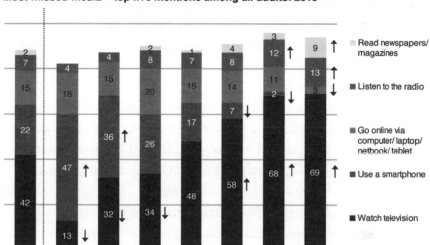

A2 – Which one of these would you miss doing the most? (Prompted responses, single coded) – NB Showing the five most popular responses in 2013 at an overall level
Base: All adults aged 16+ (1642 aged 16+, 224 aged 16-24, 260 aged 25-34, 270 aged 35-44,226 aged 45-54, 262 aged 55-64, 211 aged 65-74, 189 aged 75+). Significance testing shows any difference between any age group and all adults aged 16+

Source: Ofcom Adults' Media Use and Attitudes Report, 2014

an innovative, entrepreneurial, progressive mindset bent on shaping the tools, not led by them. As Joichi Ito, director of MIT Media Lab, put it, 'The internet isn't really a technology. It's a belief system.'[2]

It's affecting young people differently based on their digital literacy, their skillset, their education and their parental support. Some young people are digital outcasts. They are online but without much protection or support. They are getting the negatives – the vulnerability, the sharing without accessing any of the knowledge, growth or skills. The offline inequalities we saw in the last chapter follow young people online. Research from the Oxford Internet Surveys found that among all internet users, benefits such as saving money online, finding a job, finding health information and finding out about an event were more likely to accrue to those with a higher household income.[3] The link was even stronger around education: those with a university degree are more than twice as likely to be able to benefit from internet use compared with people with no education. For those young people who are already empowered it gives them new opportunities, audiences and global reach. Those who are vulnerable are put at even greater risk.

The vast majority of young people are predominately digital consumers. They are aware that they have access to a powerful tool but haven't unlocked how to channel it. They have a diluted version of Kevin's sense of possibility. They know it can make a difference but they are not quite sure how.

The task we have is to ensure that the great majority of young people stop being consumers and are given some of Kevin's creative awe.

While young people are predominately consuming rather than creating content, this does not mean they have no agency when it comes to shaping their experience online. We too often talk about the internet happening to young people – making them a certain way. However, this ignores the complex way young people are interacting with the communication tools at their disposal.

There is a constant dialectic, not between generations but across them. The pace of change is so fast that as soon as one set of behaviours becomes dominant, an opposing movement rises to meet it. Society always moved like this, but now this process is a dynamic, live one where trends are changing and transforming at breakneck speed. Pinpointing the direction of travel is very difficult. Young people are more comfortable than older generations with this dynamism and flux; it is all they know. They are less preoccupied with whether the internet is going to be a force for good or bad and much more focused on how to shape it.

Seventeen-year-old Yas demonstrates the ubiquitous nature of the internet. She was so worried about the effect of online pornography and the pressure on young girls to upload sexualised images on social media that she set up a campaign to better educate young people on some of the dangers of the internet. Her campaigning vehicle was, of course, the internet. Young people like Yas live the paradoxes of the internet every day. They are less concerned with a theoretical debate about whether it will be a force for progress and busy responding to the actual impact on their lives.

The tentacles of the internet creep into every aspect of young lives – how they date, work, learn and communicate. I focus on equality, empowerment, truth and connection as four areas where the internet is important for shaping not only young people's lives but also the future of our society. In each area I will address the divergence in how young people are using the internet and how far they are able to shape it.

Kevin may be an outlier in his sense of agency but the important thing about young people like Kevin is they show what is possible. Channelled correctly, these tools can allow a young person to find new connections, take up new opportunities, discover, learn and broaden horizons. Our shared task is to ensure that the promise of Kevin's story is not an exception but the lived experience of the majority of young people.

The promise of equality

In a TED Talk, Andrew McAfee, co-founder of the MIT Initiative on the Digital Economy, described the possibility of a technological age and the automation we saw in the last chapter.

'Now, when I talk about this with my friends in Cambridge and Silicon Valley, they say, "Fantastic. No more drudgery, no more toil. This gives us the chance to imagine an entirely different kind of society, a society where the creators and the discoverers and the performers and the innovators come together with their patrons and their financiers to talk about issues, entertain, enlighten, provoke each other." It's a society, really, that looks a lot like the TED Conference. And there's actually a huge amount of truth here. We are seeing an amazing flourishing taking place. In a world where it is just about as easy to generate an object as it is to print a document, we have amazing new possibilities. The people who used to be craftsmen and hobbyists are now makers, and they're responsible for massive amounts of innovation. And artists who were formerly constrained can now do things that were never, ever possible for them before. So this is a time of great flourishing.'[4]

This is the world Kevin already inhabits, a world of possibility and creativity. However, this is by no means the assured future or the lived experiences of many young people.

McAfee goes on to contrast this with the doomsday path of the world characterised by increasing inequality: 'My biggest worry is that we're creating a world where we're going to have glittering technologies embedded in a kind of a shabby society and supported by an economy that generates inequality instead of opportunity.'[5]

We are already seeing the unemployment caused by automation. As software becomes more powerful and integrated into our lives, it will reduce the demand for many traditional jobs. This won't just be in manufacturing: think of how much of the work done in the legal and accounting professions could be done by a computer.

What is crucial is that in the glittering new world that Andrew McAfee describes, young people from poor backgrounds aren't left behind and that in practice freedom from drudgery doesn't simply mean alienation and unemployment.

Task-biased technological change means many mid-level routine jobs have been automated. Technology is creating new jobs but they tend to be highly skilled. The Royal Academy of Engineering estimates that over eight hundred thousand jobs will be created for science, engineering and technology professionals by 2020.[6] Anecdotally, people working in the tech world tell me that most investors and entrepreneurs come from top universities. Matt Robinson is a twenty-seven-year-old Oxford graduate who left his job at McKinsey to found GoCardless with two of his colleagues. Set up in 2011, GoCardless is a direct debit provider for small businesses; regularly voted one of London's top start-ups and having been backed by $12 million of investment from major UK and US venture capital firms, it is a company that is growing fast (800 per cent last year). Matt described the profile of his company: 'Most are young graduates from red-brick universities. Generalists typically come via arts degrees and consultancy, and engineers via computer science degrees.' Other tech employers tell me that they target Oxbridge graduates.

The dislocation that will be caused by automation will only continue. This affects everyone and indeed creates new types of inequality that disproportionately affect the digitally illiterate and socially excluded of all ages. When I organised a careers fair for young people in my ward, half of those who turned up were people in their forties, fifties and sixties who had lost their jobs in the recession and had no idea how to even apply for jobs in a digital age.

The internet does provide new opportunities. The barriers to entrepreneurialism are lower than ever. There is access to so much of the world's knowledge online. A young person could feasibly get a degree, learn to code, speak a new language or start their own business all from their bedroom. It shouldn't matter whether that bedroom is in a tower block or a mansion.

Tech entrepreneurialism is highly competitive and the practicalities of housing and living costs are hard to deal with for young people with no safety net. An unpaid internship might last two months; a start-up could mean living with no pay for two years. For some young people it is just not possible, however good their idea.

There are very few winners.

Matt Robinson described to me the struggle to make it as an entrepreneur: 'I don't think people realise how hard this is. My biggest comparison would be that it is like a computer game. Every level you complete, all that happens is that you go up and have an even harder one. We got nowhere to somewhere, raised a bit of money; great, now you've got to actually use that money sensibly. Then you build something tangible and raise a few million, but next you have to make proper revenue. Then you make proper revenue and you raise a large sum, well now you're responsible for a lot of people's careers and customers' businesses and you have all the worries that come with that. Every time, all that happens is that the bosses get bigger and the levels get harder. It's exactly the same if you mess up: you die. Game over. You know there are no second goes.'

But those that do succeed gain huge rewards. A very small number of people are amassing a huge amount of money creating inequality on a new scale.

The internet is fulfilling its promise of equalling opportunities for a minority. The way it is used at the moment is in fact in danger of entrenching inequalities.

Empowerment online

The power to be heard does not necessarily come from an established position, it comes from a following, and this applies to national and local structures as well as to international ones. Power can be created and built from nowhere. Take nine-year-old Martha Payne, who blogged her dissatisfaction with her school lunch every day and the council leader and headteacher that tried to close her down.[7] The girl was technically powerless, but a media storm, three million hits and a global audience meant she was able to win her cause and lift the ban. Her blog has turned into a movement, with over ten million hits and children sending in pictures of their school meals from around the world.

She has raised over a hundred thousand pounds for Mary's Meals, a charity that helps provide school meals in some of the world's poorest countries, started campaigning nationally around healthy eating and published a book about her experiences – all before her eleventh birthday.

The internet can turn on its head traditional power dynamics where youth and inexperience are an advantage. Young people can offer a fresh perspective; they are in touch with the latest technology and less encumbered by how things have always been. PayPal founder Peter Thiel has been actively investing in the principle of unconditioned young minds with a programme that gives twenty-four entrepreneurial teenagers a hundred thousand dollars each on the condition they don't go to college. Institutions, he believes, saddle young people with debts and impart 'conservative, career-minded mindsets'.[8]

Jordan Hatch was seventeen when he decided to leave his school in Preston. He had already taught himself to code and he was more excited by what was happening in technology in London than by the prospect of going to university. He saw his friends graduating and finding it hard to get jobs and he just didn't see the point. Programming had always been a tool of empowerment for Jordan. Learning to code in his early teens, he was soon helping build his school's intranet and earning his own money as a freelancer. At fifteen he started to attend tech meet-ups in Preston and the networks he found there led him to Manchester and eventually to London and the first big hack event of Young Rewired State (a global community of pro-grammers under the age of eighteen). It was here that one of his presentations caught the eye of someone from the then nascent Government Digital Service, which was set up to try and help make government digital services simpler, clearer and more accessible. He was asked to do two weeks' work, which he completed in two days, finding himself the department's youngest employee. Three years later he is still there, helping the government channel technology to provide better public services. He talks with pride about the first page he built, which is now used by millions. For Jordan the great empowerment the internet offers is the power to create, to develop the ideas he has into tools that others can use.

Here again the promise of the internet seems extraordinary. It can give young people the tools to educate themselves and start their own careers. No longer wholly reliant on gatekeepers like television or record producers, they can create their own platforms. There are new models emerging like the crowdfunding site Patreon, which enable fans to become patrons of their favourite artists by encouraging small donations.

The internet has enabled an explosion in citizen journalism. The wave of youth media keeps on coming, from YouTube channels to online blogs. Susana Giner runs the Youth Media Agency and told me that she calls it the 'Jamal Edwards effect', where young people are increasingly creating their own platforms and building their own audiences. 'The power of a positive role model, the collateral that can have is massive. It's why we support youth media, especially young people creating their own media. It eases frustration and it gives young people a voice.' When we met there were around one hundred and fifty youth media companies in her network; she thinks in a year it could be a thousand. 'Ultimately,' she tells me, 'it is coming from "I want to have a voice". "I want to say something positive about young people." No youth media is negative about young people. It's trying to support people.'

Once again the reality is that these examples are still outliers. The majority of young people understand that the internet could be a tool for empowerment. 73 per cent of eighteen- to twenty-five-year-olds in the UK say social media is a force for change.[9] However, the majority are not actualising that potential in a creative, entrepreneurial or political sense.

In 2013, according to polling by Ofcom, only 16 per cent of

sixteen- to twenty-four-year-olds have set up their own website and 16 per cent their own blog.[10] In 2013 only 0.4 per cent of A levels taken in the UK were in Computing or Computer Studies.[11] Figures from the Department for Business Innovation and Skills show that we have actually been moving backwards on digital skills, with a 23.3 per cent drop in the number of under-graduates studying Computer Science.[12] From 2001 to 2011 the proportion of young (sixteen- to twenty-nine-year-old) IT pro-fessionals actually declined, from 32 per cent to 19 per cent.[13] While steps are being taken to address this, as I will show in Chapter 10, we have a long way to go to give young people the skills they need to take advantage of new opportunities in the digital economy and to become true digital creators like Kevin and Jordan.

The same is true of political empowerment. The internet allows people to bypass the media to contact MPs directly and start their own campaigns. However, as we saw in Chapter 3, despite a strong desire for new powers it is only a tiny proportion who had set up a petition online.

Part of this is that young people don't think that anything will change and don't feel there is much point in engaging in a system that doesn't give them real power.

The internet allows a level of participation and coordinated decision-making unprecedented in history. Just as the internet is replacing gatekeepers with the crowd in some of our industries, it is feasible that the same could be done to our democratic insti-tutions. This forces us to ask real questions about the kind of democratic institutions we want, and our commitment to rep-resentative democracy.

From Plato onwards there is a strong tradition in democratic thought that is afraid to hand over too much power directly to citizens. John Stuart Mill, whose ideas did so much to shape the institutions of representative democracy, believed that votes should not be equally distributed but weighted to the more educated and cultivated. Fear of the rabble – the heightened emotions of the crowd, the tyranny of a uniformed majority – has been a major factor in how our institutions have developed with relatively little say for citizens. The question is how to reform our institutions to give young people the power they want without threatening our rich tradition of individual rights.

For some, this has led them to reject the idea of representative democracy altogether and look to the internet to enable self-rule. On the right this represents a kind of extreme libertarianism and on the left anarchism, which I refer to here as techno-anarchism.

Myles Dyer is a twenty-six-year-old YouTube star who believes the internet will usher in a new political reality. For Myles, the most disruptive political force is centralised power. He tells me, 'People instantly say, If you have decentralised power who makes the rules? It's actually about creating a society where people know how you arrive at decisions rather than people having to tell you what to do.' Myles is embarking on a project to try to bring this about. It is essentially a crowd-sourced platform called the 'Universal Solutions Project', based on his view that humanity collectively holds the answers to the challenges we face and that oppositional party politics just stands in the way. He is optimistic about our potential to self-organise but not for our current power structures to let it happen. He sees such a chasm between the worldview he is articulating and our current political structures that he thinks they are incapable of reform. He tells me, 'I honestly think things will have to collapse before they get better.' For Myles it comes down to a clash between generations. He believes a generation used to hierarchy and control will not be able to watch their power structures crumble.

YouTube epitomises the crowd-sourced principles that form the heart of his worldview. He trusts it because the content that finds its way to the front page gets there because of popularity among users, not central direction. 'Of course it could always switch to centralised power; the moment it does it will lose all credibility and people will shift.'

Sitting in Regent's Park listening to Myles talk about the inevitable collapse of our current political structures I was reminded of the thesis of the former Conservative (and now UKIP) MP Douglas Carswell's book, *The End of Politics and the Birth of iDemocracy*.

Carswell describes how the internet is unlocking the power of collective intelligence without direction from above and compares the free and open internet to market forces. 'The web is, by its very anarchic, decentralised, unplanned and hyper-networked nature, a repudiation of the notion that things are best done by design. It embodies the idea of a spontaneous exchange and trans-action. It hands the decisive advantage to those who hold that human affairs should be best ordered by the invisible hand of mil-lions of individual transactions rather than by top-down design.'[14]

Like Myles he thinks we will be able to rely on our 'collective brain' or 'market-derived intelligence' to provide answers, removing the need for 'experts'.[15] Carswell says the internet puts gatekeepers, from politicians through to civil servants, and their grand designs out of a job, as it 'pulverises monopolies and smashes hierarchy – not just in the world of business and com-merce but public life too'.

Also like Myles he ultimately ends up with direct democracy: the internet 'will realign politics neither to the left nor the right but instead pull it down from elites to people'. In his view, state bureaucracies will give way to the istate, characterised by personal budgets, personal education and tailor-made retirement plans. The future according to Carswell is a smaller state that does less and an empowered population who together do more.

There is a need for greater empowerment, as I show in Chap-ter 8, and I agree with Myles that political institutions have to change, but Carswell's free-for-all represents an extreme individ-ualism which I think will ultimately let young people down. It links with the view propagated by some software experts of the internet as a free space that should not be subject to any regulation. Pushed too far this approach could mean that young people are encouraged to reject institutions and laws altogether. While techno-anarchism is currently at the edges of youth debate, there is a rise in political groups like the Pirate Party putting forward an internet agenda. If institutions continue to ignore young people's demands for more power, ideas like this have the potential to fill a void for young people with potentially adverse consequences.

Young people's willingness to engage in traditional political institutions is intimately connected to how they are finding and interpreting news online.

Search for the truth

Gone are the days where everyone sat round the radio for the daily news broadcast. News is constant and fragmented. Everyone accesses a personalised diet of information from their networks, friends and choice of news sites. Many are choosing to cross-reference different news channels or switch to alternative and entrepreneurial news sources. As Sarah, a seventeen-year-old from Birmingham, told me, 'Each newspaper has a very biased point of view. If I read only one I only get that one opinion. Type it into Google and I get a whole load of websites, you can develop yourself and your own opinion on things.' This causes issues for governments trying to set a national agenda and a set of shared norms, rights and responsibilities.

The digital communications revolution has helped contribute to a breakdown in deference and authority. Information is contested. The crowd offers an alternative to an individual expert. People have access to a whole range of opinions on every topic.

There is no need for young people to passively consume information; they can compare, cross-reference and decide what to believe. As Kevin said, 'You can no longer be easily bullshitted and I think that's great. It makes people think about things a lot more and a lot harder. It makes people work, which is good. People can no longer easily brainwash you into thinking something that they want you to think.'

Finding the 'truth' online or at least a reliable source of information can mean wading through a lot of ill-informed, poorly researched, half-truths. Knowledge is contested and young people have to increasingly decide what to believe.

Too often healthy scepticism crosses over into what I believe is unhealthy conspiracy.

Many young people overestimate their ability to decipher information online. Googling a topic, it can be a lottery whether what emerges as the top few entries is a trustworthy piece of journalism, a popular myth or a piece of propaganda. However, many young people may never know the difference, as 45 per cent of sixteen- to twenty-four-year-olds only look at the first few items in a search engine compared with 35 per cent of all adults.[16] The think tank Demos found that only one in four twelve- to fifteen-year-olds makes any checks when visiting a new website. Less than 10 per cent ask who made a website and why and a third believe that information generated by search engines must be true.[17] 86 per cent of young people claim to be confident in judging what they read on websites.[18]

This belief that they are finding the truth online mixed with a lack of critical analysis of what they are reading can be a toxic mix for some young people.

At a BBC Free Speech debate I was sitting next to an eighteen-year-old Londoner who when I told him I was a councillor proceeded to enthusiastically enlighten me about politics. 'It's just a distraction, to stop people working out the truth,' he said. 'I don't want to be labelled a conspiracy theorist but everything is just run by the elite. All this debate is meaningless; we're ignoring the big questions. Watch *Thrive*, then you'll know what's going on.' A couple of others agreed: 'They're trying to brain-wash us.'

Thrive is a two-hour YouTube film that has been viewed 8,479,853 times. It is a tour de force through the world of conspiracy theories: 9/11 might have been an inside job, free energy and cures for cancer are deliberately being kept from us and we're all being controlled by an invisible elite with a global-domination agenda.

It appears credible, with high production quality and a flashy website. It deals with issues a lot of young people believe are not addressed in mainstream political debate – for example inequality and environmental degradation. It blends some credible voices with long segments from David Icke, a man who has publicly claimed that a predatory race taking a reptilian form is enslaving humanity. Social activist John Robbins was interviewed for *Thrive* but penned an open letter condemning the conspiracy elements of the film: 'The *Thrive* movie and website are filled with dark and unsubstantiated assertions about secret and profoundly malevolent conspiracies that distract us from the real work at hand.'[19]

A 1995 *New Yorker* magazine article coined the phrase 'fusion paranoia' to describe the coming together of far left and far right narratives in the 'Us vs. Them' of conspiracy theories. The article states that 'it's only a matter of degree' that separates the critics who feel the media, politicians and lobbyists are not working in the public interest from those who see a deliberate and dangerous conspiracy. 'Where the realists see tacit collusion among members of the governing elite, the radicals see flagrant treasonous plots. But the root of the paranoia – the belief that government isn't working in the interests of the people – is the same, and it is on that common ground that populism and conspiracism, healthy mistrust and crackpotism, meet.'[20]

As we saw in the previous chapter, many young people already feel disengaged, disempowered, and sometimes like they are under direct attack from politicians and the media. They talk about politicians as an indistinguishable elite. They frame much of the debate as 'us' (their friends and family) and 'them' (those in power). Some feel that the world is set up against them. They go online and find films like *Thrive* that put voice to those feelings. Reviewing the evidence on belief in conspiracy theories, psychologists Viren Swami and Rebecca Coles point out the link between distrust in authority, political cynicism, powerlessness and low self-esteem. There is no shortage of material online to convert that disenfranchisement to a belief in real conspiracy.[21] It's not even a massive jump.

Communities that advocate these views have sprung up online and can lead to 'confirmation bias', where young people only come into contact with those that reinforce and embed their worldview.

A belief in conspiracy theories intensifies young people's alienation from democratic institutions. It encourages them to opt out and reject politics altogether. It discourages debate, campaigning or a critical analysis of our institutions. It kills passion and encourages isolation. It meant that the eighteen-year-old I started a conversation with was sitting with MPs and campaigners but felt it was pointless to engage with puppets of an oppressive system.

Research by Karen Douglas at Kent University supports this. She found that people exposed to conspiracy theories about climate change and the death of Princess Diana were more likely to withdraw from participation in politics and less likely to take action to reduce their carbon footprint.[22] So young people who are consuming this content are stuck in a vicious circle where their alienation feeds more alienation until the only thing they believe in is that no one can be trusted.

As one youth worker I spoke to in Brixton put it when talking about some of the disenfranchised young people he works with, 'They're very, very political. Not so much in to true politics, but into the conspiracy theories. They're all up on the new world order. This is the crux; why they don't want to work for anybody. Why they don't want to be in employment. It could be deemed one big trick, it's all about control. They're very aware of that. You talk to any person round here. It's quite heavy. To have your whole belief system smashed apart.'

This anecdotal evidence is supported by research by Demos that found that 48 per cent of teachers have argued with pupils about conspiracy theories;[23] one in twenty say this happens on a weekly basis.[24]

Of course not all young people who feel disenfranchised believe in conspiracy theories. However, their exposure to these ideas can lead to a kind of generalised scepticism.

Research from Ofcom supports this finding that young people are disengaging from mainstream news. In 2006 64 per cent of sixteen- to twenty-four-year-olds believed the news was not relevant to them, compared with 44 per cent in 2002.[25]

There is something wrong if young people feel so disengaged they are willing to believe there is an active conspiracy locking them out of power. Conspiracy theorists will always flourish where people feel powerless. Political institutions and mainstream news media need to take seriously the disenfranchisement that young people feel.

Faced with multiple news sources, young people are going to be demanding, sceptical and questioning. This should be encouraged. The real problems occur when they think they are uncovering truth but they are actually being misled.

This is where the importance of education comes in, equipping young people with the analytical tools to process the vast amount of information they are confronted with on a daily basis.

Connection

For all the sensationalism, most young people are using the internet to spend more time talking to people they already know. The most active social networkers are those that spend the most time with their friends. Ofcom's 2012 survey showed that 92 per cent of sixteen- to twenty-four-year-olds said they used their time on social networks to communicate with friends and family they see a lot.[26] The Pew internet report shows that rather than replacing phone conversations, text has enhanced them for some young people; the heaviest texters are also the heaviest talkers: the heaviest texters (those who exchange more than a hundred texts a day) are much more likely than lighter texters to say that they talk on their cell phone daily.[27]

When young people carefully curate their private lives online or snap pictures of themselves, they are not like Narcissus lost in his own reflection but deeply concerned about the perception of others. It is all about the audience. They are not obsessed with themselves as much as they are obsessed with other people's perceptions of them. Young people are constantly snapping pictures not because they want to record memories but because they want to share them. They are expressing a very human desire for approval, connection, validation and acceptance.

This has a flip side. The digital world can be isolating at the very point it should be connecting. 51 per cent of sixteen- to twenty-four-year-olds say they use their profile to look at other people's profiles without leaving a message. A Prince's Trust survey showed that 40 per cent of sixteen- to twenty-five-year-olds said they regularly compare themselves to peers online in terms of how successful they are. 34 per cent had felt depressed as a direct result of something they'd seen on a social network. 65 per cent of sixteen- to twenty-five-year-olds had been left feeling inadequate compared with their peers at some point by social media. However, they don't feel like this all the time. Only 11 per cent often felt like this, 23 per cent sometimes did and 28 per cent rarely did.[28]

As one twenty-two-year-old I spoke to in Glasgow put it, 'It's just nosiness. If people post photos you're obviously going to have a little look.' This can lead to a strange situation in which you watch the most intimate moments of people's lives – graduation, birthdays, engagement and marriage – without ever being in touch. There is a comfort in knowing you're connected but also complacency, a feeling we're more embedded in each other's lives than we are. It creates an uncomfortable voyeuristic quality to some relationships, where the connection is more curiosity than care. This isn't necessarily caused by social media. Social envy is part of the human condition, but it does make it much easier to compare lives when you can browse through the archive of anyone's life, from your primary-school classmate to your work colleague.

For some young people the dislocation is more serious. In a group in Glasgow the topic led on to social media. They started talking about a young teenager who had been filmed without her knowledge during a sex act; they'd all seen the video. One girl said, 'It's all about having a good reputation, the whole world knows her for that one act, no one is ever going to want to get to know her.'

There are small lapses in privacy and then there are privacy breaches that can destroy lives. The prevalence of smart phones means it is easier and easier to take and send explicit pictures. This can be freely done as part of a relationship or even flirtation, but can turn ugly quickly. Or it can be done without knowledge, like the trend of boys taking pictures of their sleeping sexual conquests.

If some of these pictures sitting in servers or on someone's phone surface later on, they become a problem. Once you've lost control of an image it can multiply out of all proportion.

Today you don't need to be in a national newspaper to feel the humiliation of exposure. The same effect can be created by posting something to Facebook or Twitter. The people most important to you – your mum, your cousin, your colleagues, your mates – are all in one place. This is brilliant if you want to share your new haircut, a side venture in jewellery design, or ask advice on what to do if your headphones get lodged in your iPhone. But it can be seriously exploited. With the click of a button your life can be destroyed by a malicious ex, or an internet troll vindictively trying to cause harm. We are so connected that bad news spreads as fast as good. We've seen the hopelessness the threat of blackmail can cause – people tricked into exposing more than they ought and then blackmailed into worse to try to cover it up.

It is a minority of young people that experience online bullying – according to a Prince's Trust survey, 14 per cent of sixteen- to twenty-five-year-olds (and 18 per cent of those aged sixteen to eighteen) – but the impact can be devastating. Social media brings it into their bedrooms, means they carry it with them in their pockets. It's hard to escape. One teenager told me of how her friend was driven to a mental breakdown after online bullies followed her from school to school.

For some very vulnerable young people who don't have strong friendships to fall back on, the internet can entrench their sense of loneliness and isolation. The lucky ones may find a community that recognises and celebrates their differences like the Nerdfighteria we saw in Chapter 3. However, not everyone finds a community. Some broadcast without a response. Others continue to post in abusive forums, an act some teenagers call online self-harm. And a small number are tricked, coerced or groomed into abusive relationships by adults pretending to offer care.

At one end of the spectrum very vulnerable young people are finding themselves alienated online, but at the other, as we saw in Chapter 4, a minority are managing to carve out new communities that form real connections and genuine empathy amongst strangers.

May Gabriel (@itsOkCampaign), set up a blog when she was sixteen to challenge some of the stigma surrounding young people suffering from depression, self-harm and suicidal thoughts. I interviewed May over a couple of meetings in a London café

where she took me through her battles with mental health, suicidal thoughts and how she ended up running her online
campaign.

She knows the natural reaction is to step back and keep it
private. To open up a vulnerable situation to a sometimes unforgiving world seems counterintuitive. She was worried about her
future, about university applications and applying for jobs.
'Nobody I've met would put their story up online. I think they're
afraid of it. Once it's online you have no control over it, you have
no idea what might happen to it. There's nothing you can do
once you've published.'

But despite all the risks May decided to share her story. In a
series of raw blog posts she shares her experiences of losing
friends, of depression, of her own battle with self-harm. They are
not easy to write and once she's finished she shares them as they
are: 'I never read back any of my blogs ever.'

For May a blog that was about sharing her personal experience
has enabled a global community based around shared experiences. She tells me, 'I get lots of people emailing me their stories,
almost just because it's someone they can share it with and it's still
a safe place for them to do it.' She is weaving a community out
of individual stories. 'I want people to know they're not alone,'
she says.

May, like Suli and Joe who we met in Chapter 4, remains an
outlier. It is possible to create communities online, as we have
seen, but we have to overcome significant barriers.

Firstly, it is difficult to form strong ties of reciprocity in essentially fluid, porous communities. This is particularly true where
there is anonymity. Newspaper comment pages can be some of
the nastiest spaces online, with high levels of anonymity, low
levels of accountability and controversial subject matters. One
twenty-eight-year-old in Birmingham told me he and his friends
play a game called '24 hours of rage' on dailymail online: they
leave the most balanced and human responses they can think of

and the winner gets the most dislikes. However as we saw in Chapter 4, there are also online tools that generate reciprocity through currencies, reviews and links to Facebook profiles.

Secondly, it can be hard to feel empathy or connection when you can't physically see someone. I know as a Labour Party activist that I am much more likely to get a positive response on the doorstep than on the phone – people are reluctant to slam the door in your face but the added barrier of the telephone allows them to be a little less civil. Text is one step removed from that. The cloak of anonymity or simply the barrier of a screen can detach some young people from the human nature of an exchange and the consequences of their actions. In a focus group in Glasgow of sixteen- to twenty-four-year-olds, the problems caused by the extra barrier of a keyboard were raised. One young man put it: 'Facebook causes a lot more fights. People think, I'm behind the keyboard so nothing bad can happen. I've had that a few times where people start to give you all kinds of abuse because they are behind the keyboard. If they were face to face they would just not say that stuff.' Myles Dyer, who met some of his best friends online and believes in the internet as a tool to break down barriers, described what happened when a video blogger hanged herself. A few people left comments like 'should have fucking done it sooner', which her family had to read. 'The problem is some people have no accountability,' Myles said. I asked him how that tallied with his belief that YouTube was creating real bonds. 'The reason it's hard to understand, they haven't had that connection yet, they don't realise the key strokes have an effect on the other side.' Education is an important tool in building up empathy and understanding about consequences online.

Finally, it can be difficult to be vulnerable online. May Gabriel's decision to share her battle with mental health is exceptional because it is out of the ordinary. People like May who expose their vulnerabilities are rare; most of us put our best selves online – the more together, attractive, fun, employable version, depending on who are audience is.

Despite the challenges we can't give up on online forums as a means of stimulating new connections and bridging social capital. We aren't going back to traditional neighbourhoods, so online tools have to be one way to create empathy, reciprocity and dialogue.

The most successful online communities are those that blend on- and offline contact to reinforce bonds. This was true of the YouTube gatherings and social coders we saw in Chapter 3. According to the Prince's Trust 63 per cent of sixteen- to twenty-five-year-olds said they'd prefer to discuss a problem face to face than over the internet. MaryLeigh Bliss from Ypulse, a New York-based youth marketing and millennial research firm, told me, 'I think that most millennials see online interaction as a means to create offline interactions and I think the idea that they are unable to speak to one another and only communicate through text messages is absolutely overblown.'

Harnessing the power of the internet

In the next section of the book I look at how we can ensure that the internet acts as a tool for equality, empowerment, truth and connection. This requires firstly that our education system is providing young people with the skills and support that they need to navigate a digital world, as I show in Chapter 10.

Secondly, our institutions have to respond to the world as it is, which includes a generation that are active users of the internet and who are demanding greater power, transparency and a more relational approach, as I show in Chapters 7 and 8.

Brie Rogers Lowery, UK Director at Change.org, tells me, 'I think that there is a lot of talk about how the public needs to adapt to how parliament works, but I want to hear a lot more about how parliament needs to adapt to how the public is operating. Parliament needs to get up to speed with digital campaigning and they need to look at how they can improve the two-way engagement.'

The answer is not pulling down our institutions but working with young people to reform them. The lived experience of young people is a resource that we can't afford to ignore. They can't be bystanders in a debate about the future because they understand most powerfully the risks and opportunities.

Path to the Future

Young people want to see authenticity and honesty from their leaders. They want good careers, secure housing and responsive services. It isn't a million miles away from what everyone else wants.

Real transformation is not going to come from a single policy decision or a speech in a party conference but from a change in society's mindset so that young people are viewed as partners. This would give them power and rebuild relationships with them.

It doesn't require one single change; it requires an infinite number of small ones. It is the slow, sometimes painful, incremental process of institutional change. It is every school, trade union, branch of a political party, residents' association and police unit asking how they can work better with young people. It is a shared agenda of reform to create institutions that are fit for the twenty-first century. It is media outlets showing responsibility in the way they report the next generation.

Involving young people is only half the battle. The other half is working with them to build a society that allows every young person to flourish. This means offering them more than just security but the opportunity to truly flourish. It is a job that gives them autonomy, purpose and mastery. It is the chance to lead and innovate in their work and in their communities. It is the opportunity to find their passion, the space and time to build real connection with others. It is an empowered citizenship that allows them to be active partners in shaping the world around them.

If you look at the opposite of these grievances, you will find a list that any sane person would be against – inauthentic and dishonest leadership, unfairness, disempowerment, alienation, loneliness, unemployment, boring and mindless work that lacks purpose. No one would actively choose to waste potential. Yet somehow this is what we are left with. Young people are calling for something that everyone wants. The question is how do we get there?

The next five chapters set out a path towards achieving this. This is not a blue print or an exhaustive list but some ideas that flow from the young people I have met.

I start in Chapter 7, not with big visions but with real relationships. The society we want will be created by each and every one of us making the effort to build strong relationships, firstly with our family and friends but secondly with those that are different from us. It is through such relationships that common narratives can be found between generations. It is these that will thread together new communities based on shared understanding. It is relationships that will engage young people that feel alienated and ignored.

However, relationships alone are not enough. Young people are also demanding power. In Chapter 8 I show how young people want empowerment at a very individual level – the power to determine their own future and to have a career they find meaningful and fulfilling. They also want power to shape their communities and their politics. If we want people to do more, we have to give them a reason to engage, which means handing down more power and listening to collective voices.

Part of an empowered citizenship is the ability to express civic values in how you work and what you buy as well as traditional acts of volunteering. In Chapter 9 I show that sustainable growth and human flourishing can only occur if business and public services are structured so that actions for the individual good coincide with the collective good. This means businesses with a social purpose and ensuring public services are living up to their core mission of serving the public.

Institutional reform is not going to solve all these issues. In Chapter 10 I show that a test of fairness will mean changing policies so that all young people have the opportunity to experience an empowered citizenship. There are real issues of intergenerational inequity around housing, debt and employment that have to be addressed. Government at local and national level has an important role in ensuring that there is a fair distribution of resources for current and future generations. Different groups are more likely to accept losses if they can see how they are helping to build a fairer society. We have to make a strong case for fairness so everyone understands that when young people lose out, ultimately so does everyone else.

It isn't going to be government alone that solves the problems I have set out in this book. In Chapter 11 I look at how all these elements can come together to provide a uniting purpose for the future. I took my gran to see the Ken Loach film *The Spirit of '45*. She spent the following week telling me everything they had got wrong but she said what was right was the sense of shared purpose it captured. A spirit that built the NHS and created the welfare state. A country that had just won a world war was ready to believe in the strength of their collective endeavour.

We can't go back to 1945, nor should we want to. The task is to find the spirit of 2015, a collective voice that might be more messy and certainly more diverse, but one that works for the modern world. There are big challenges to overcome: the aftermath of the financial crash, climate change, a generation set to have lower living standards than their parents. But we will not build a collective spirit on a foundation of fear and pessimism.

Cynicism pervades too much of our debate, clawing away at

initiative and hope. Young political activists tell me they feel locked into a divisive debate that more resembles an episode of *The Thick of It* than the good they want to do. There is a lot of fear about the way the country is changing, especially about immigration and globalisation. Too often our leaders hark back to how things were rather than how they should be. It is a strategy that makes it easier to win politically, to sell newspapers, but ultimately it leaves us with a society that nobody wants.

Young people deserve more, they deserve leadership that is optimistic and inspiring. They are looking for big, aspirational goals that match their personal aspirations. They are ready to create the spirit of 2015; they are waiting for their leaders to stand with them.

The changes young people are demanding don't have to start at the centre; in fact, we have spent too long waiting for someone at the centre to wave a magic wand. Cities, councils, parishes, businesses or citizens can claim a leadership role as so many young people have. To do this more power needs to be held locally. Location can offer a shared context to bind people together.

This means devolving power to the lowest possible level. It means giving more autonomy to those on the frontline and mechanisms for spreading innovation. It means opportunities for ideas to cascade up rather than down. It also means citizens having a stake in all the institutions that affect their lives, including global ones.

Finally it means leadership fit for the modern world. Leaders who are able to find big and uniting ideas, who live the principles they promote, who offer authenticity and a sense of purpose.

A future that makes sense to young people is one in which their individual effort is connected to others' in working towards a shared goal. This allows them to retain their individuality but still participate in a collective mission.

The changes we are experiencing are scary and we could easily turn against each other and try to close the doors on progress. The dog-eat-dog individualism could win out and the young people I have met will continue to feel alienated.

Or we can be a country where difference is celebrated, where the talent of every individual is nurtured, where communities come together around empathy, where active citizens help direct the services they use. We don't have to imagine this different future; we need to look for it. In every community there are young people and organisations bringing this to life. They show us what is possible.

Chapter 7

Building Relationships

Building a shared purpose in a diverse society ultimately relies on individuals negotiating their differences through relationships.

The young are no longer content with a blanket offer or a broadcast. They want to have a direct relationship where their preferences are considered and they feel valued. This is manifesting itself not just in relation to brands but in every area of their lives. Some of the key trends are:

- Desire for personalisation – individuals are increasingly used to a tailored experience and expect this in more and more spheres of life.
- Demand for authenticity in communication – brands with a personality and leaders who feel accessible.
- Social currency of stories – whether you are a brand, an individual or a political party, the story you have about yourself (or others create for you) is the most important force in shaping your success in a media age.
- Greater premium on face-to-face relationships in building a deeper level of connection.

These aren't always easy to marry together. If you are developing a modern GPs' practice do you increasingly automate, diagnose online and put the patients in charge (aided by software) or do you develop a system where an individual builds trust with a named GP who builds up their confidence in managing their own health?

In Chapter 8 I will look at how personalisation can give young people some of the empowerment they are looking for. However, we must remember that personal relationships are crucial in connecting with young people and helping them to navigate the noise, complexity and confusion of the modern world.

As we saw in the Chapter 6, the internet is putting a premium on face-to-face, human relationships. This will continue to be one of the most valued and important forms of interaction in the modern world and the key to transformative change.

Relationship building – what is happening already?

In Chapter 4 we saw how young people are leading the way in creating organisational structures built on personal relationships, whether it is spoken-word collectives, not for profits or loose networks.

Much of this work builds on the principles of person-to-person community organising. Neil Jameson from Citizens UK tells me that his organisation stands for an 'old form of politics', based on grassroots organisation. He points out, 'It is relatively new for there to be parties that represent working people. Prior to that the only option the poor had was to organise, which they did very well and very powerfully.'

This 'old politics' of local community organising has been hugely successful in engaging the young. Citizens UK's generally young community organisers have engaged young people in campaigns, debates and intergenerational conversations around crime, wages and housing. They have helped train thousands of young leaders. The youth-led CitySafe campaign has three hundred

CitySafe Havens where young people can seek refuge in a dangerous situation and sixty-two CitySafe Zones with a team committed to keeping the neighbourhood safe. Young people have also contributed to their Living Wage campaign, which has signed up nine hundred businesses as Living Wage employers.

The Obama campaign in the US managed to bring together all four of the components above – personalisation, authentic communication, a strong story and human relationships. By doing so they were able to mobilise large numbers of young people.

Marlon Marshall, who served as the Deputy National Field Director on Barack Obama's 2012 field campaign, tells me the community organising principles at the heart of Obama's campaign also represented the 'rebirth' of an old idea. But for the Obama campaign it was an idea that was re-imagined for an internet age.

The campaign was explicit about the importance of one-to-one relationships and personal stories in binding volunteers into their larger story. Everyone who volunteered had a 'one-to-one' session, not to teach them about Obama's policy objectives but to help them understand why they had walked through the door. These conversations deliberately pushed through to the deep sediment of each volunteer's values and worldview. As Marlon Marshall puts it, 'A lot of times you'll hear some powerful, powerful stuff on why people are engaged that they didn't even realise brought them to be involved in politics.'

The campaign helped volunteers weave their support of Obama into their narrative of self, which they would then be able to tell to others. Obama's own story was the centrepiece, connected to a multitude of individual stories, thus forming a movement.

As Marlon put it, 'You know a one-on-one is a chance to build, to connect the values of the campaign to the values of that individual because you are not saying "Hey I want you to come and volunteer", you are saying "Let me tell you why I signed up for the President's campaign, here is my personal story, tell me why you believe in the President". It is very powerful.'

The number of one-to-ones and follow-up conversations were metrics the campaign measured, helping to develop leaders and binding in support.

As one volunteer told me, 'You feel this integral part of this big thing and people are paying attention to you.'

The engine of the campaign, Marlon tells me, was personal relationships. They create their own momentum beyond the cause. As Lynda Tran, who served as National Press Secretary for Organising for America, put it to me, 'Obama may have been the catalyst that set it off, but after a couple of weeks of hanging out with your team you're not just doing it for the President, you are also doing it because you really like seeing these people every week.'

Relationship building may be time-consuming but the chain of one-to-one connections can form a powerful movement. This is not the transient power of the online crowd, which coalesces around an issue and then disperses, but a deep and durable power.

As Marlon put it, 'I think 2012 was a win for organising, even more than 2008, because there were so many more challenges in this election than there were in 2008. In many battleground states the numbers we organised were larger than the margin of victory.'

But how do you go from one-to-one relationships to scale? Not every volunteer can have a personal relationship with leaders, but they can have faith in a process where their ideas and contributions are shaping the campaign.

The Obama campaign bridged this through an online tool allowing individuals to report challenges and successes. Marlon thinks this helped volunteers feel part of the wider campaign: 'The fact that they were reporting and that they knew that people were reading their reports was a huge motivating tool and morale booster.' But equally leaders had a duty to listen and respond.

One young volunteer described to me a light–bulb moment. She had put in her daily report with a story that had moved her to tears, of the sacrifices a volunteer with MS had made to be part of the campaign. She got a reply from the Iowa state director. That one simple acknowledgement gave her the motivation to double her efforts.

At Citizens UK they use citizens' assemblies as forums to turn one-to-one relationships into powerful collective movements. Individual institutions decide their priorities and they are then negotiated in a locality, a region and then nationally. Ideas float up from the grassroots. Through this process a collective voice emerges and participants learn to navigate difference. In 2012 2500 people at the London Citizens' Mayoral Accountability Assembly were able to present the mayoral candidates with a shared 'Citizen Agenda' based on a nine-month dialogue with more than ten thousand individuals.[1]

Citizens UK aren't beholden to any one political agenda so they are able be more organic, a process that appeals to young people.

For Citizens UK, the face-to-face contact is the lifeblood of effective relationship building. 'The idea of people not meeting is terrifying,' Neil tells me. 'We have to meet face to face as that immediately neutralises the extremist.'

He sees their work as a direct contrast to the 'uninformed consent' of an online petition. It is the process of negotiating your views within a collective. This is not the simple choice of an online survey but a chance through dialogue to build empathy and slowly change perspectives.

Digital tools certainly have a role in relationship building; online strategies that use video and personal testimony are more powerful and effective in creating empathy and engagement. Online tools can help enable scale, but the story of Citizens UK shows that it is not a flashy web strategy that creates really powerful change but depth and relevance.

Marlon Marshall sees an important role for digital tools in gathering information, targeting messages and reaching out to new supporters. However, he tells me that for the Obama campaign digital tools were always just that: tools, never the strategy. 'For us the digital tools are a tactic for our strategy of organising young people in teams, and our door-to-door tools were a tactic to getting people mobilised to go out.' The online tools were there to seamlessly blend with offline ones and encourage action in the physical world. The end point was the face-to-face connection, building 'the family infrastructure'. This is where the magic happens.

Relationships as a tool for transformation

Developing relationships becomes more important than ever when supporting young people living in poverty. As we saw in Chapter 5, poverty can be a barrier for young people in forming the secure parental attachments that allow them to develop healthy relationships in later life.

On the other hand strong relationships even later on in life can help overcome some of these barriers. When I asked young people who were exceptional in overcoming barriers of childhood trauma and poverty what had been the turning point for them, the answer was almost always the same: someone believed in me. Sometimes it is their mum, their dad, their grandparent or sibling, but often it is a teacher, a mentor, a youth worker, a social worker or an employer. The role was unimportant; what mattered was that this was a person who invested in them, who cared, who gave them second chances and fundamentally reflected back to them a better version of themselves.

In the US Geoffrey Canada was running a charity in Harlem and feeling frustrated with interventions that were more about keeping young people alive than changing their lives. He was tired of the chronic poverty that blighted children's lives and the fact that it was only ever a tiny minority that beat the odds and went on to university. He started to ask, What would it take to transform not just one life but the whole neighbourhood? In his book *Whatever It Takes*, Paul Tough charts the story of Geoffrey Canada's organisation, the Harlem Children's Zone – an ambitious vision to give the children in twenty-four blocks of Harlem the best of everything.

The principal aim was to take families on a journey from 'cradle' through to college by providing them with intensive and coordinated support around health, nutrition, parenting, advice, community organisation, mental health, technology and employment. This starts with 'Baby College', which are workshops and home visits helping parents understand the tools for early development through to college preparatory classes. At the heart of this was building relationships with families and staying with them on their journey till their children had reached adulthood. The aim was that every child in that locality made it to college. The zone now has 95 per cent college acceptance rates across their programmes.[2]

Paul Tough told me when we spoke that part of the power came from thinking small. The zone was about deep and intensive interventions in a small neighbourhood.

Paul Perkins runs a youth centre in Camden called The Winch. He had a similar sense of frustration. He felt that too often his organisation was putting a sticking plaster over the issues young people were facing rather than dealing with the root causes. I remember him telling me that there can be an intrinsic belief in youth work as a good thing without considering how it is actually changing lives. He'd heard about the Harlem Children's Zone and decided to take a group of young people over to America to find out more about it. The experience of the Children's Zone and other projects focusing on the power of relationships began a three-year process of learning and organisational change. He coined the phrase 'from cradle to career' and went about building his organisation and in fact the whole community around the child.

When I first met Paul Perkins it was just a vision. Two years later when I visit The Winch again, it has come alive. In the office, which is now a huge open-plan space, 'promise workers' – who do the day-to-day work of relationship building – are meeting with some of the young people they mentor. Young people are busy on computers in 'The Company', a support hub for young social entrepreneurs. Downstairs the play project is in full swing and across the road mother and baby groups are meeting in the local library, which they now run. Later that evening The Winch will open its doors to the community for their weekly family dinner. These interventions don't happen in isolation but are part of a holistic support programme to help overcome the barriers of poverty.

Creating a neighbourhood approach requires leadership. It can come from the state, from business or from the voluntary sector. Paul Perkins told me they mapped where the families using their services lived, established a 'promise zone' and approached everyone within it asking what they could contribute. He has managed to bring in philanthropists, volunteers, local services and families themselves around a shared vision.

In developing this approach, it is key to nurture two relationships: the relationship with the child or family and the relationship between service providers (health, social work, schools, employability services, and so on). Paul tells me, 'Relationships are a universal human currency and adopting a relational approach is as important between services as it is in relation to young people.' Strong relationships between service providers mean it is the professionals that have to manage a complicated matrix of services rather than a struggling family. It allows services to provide a holistic support structure that takes account of the individual needs of each young person. Rather than having to meet a whole range of professionals who half understand their story, the young person builds a rapport with one person who knows them and can help them navigate everything else. Whatever ambitions we have for young people – education, employment and entrepreneurship – relationships are the starting point. As Paul Perkins tells me, 'It is only those who have built enduring, genuine relationships with young people that they may feel have earned the right to support and journey alongside them.'

It is these kinds of intense mentoring relationships that Kids Company, a charity started by Camila Batmanghelidjh in 1996 to support vulnerable inner-city children in London and Bristol, specialises in. Visiting the London office it feels like a nerve centre for combatting childhood disadvantage. Maps line the walls, outlining all the areas Kids Company operate. Staff are on hand to answer questions from key workers who directly work with young people on the ground about benefits, housing, services and changing legislation. They put the relationship first, so the young person doesn't have to manage lots of expert advice – the key worker does this for them.

One key worker may have only five to fifteen cases, as they feel adolescents need so much intensive support. Staff tell me their approach is to do what is necessary. The child comes first and everything is judged on whether it is in their best interests. They are not just available nine to five, they are available when the child needs them.

It's an organisation run on commitment and a kind of unconditional love; nobody is here for the money, someone jokes. According to a staff survey carried out by the London School of Economics, there is a 96 per cent satisfaction rate among their six hundred staff members. 97 per cent of their staff and eleven thousand volunteers feel proud of what they're achieving.[3]

Staff talk in terms of providing the family that some young people don't have. I visit a brightly coloured room named 'positive experiences'. In this department they play the role of an aunt or uncle – a source of advice, connections and crucially second

chances. If you drop out, mess up or find you don't enjoy something, the Kids Company is there to help you pick yourself up
and try again.

Around the country I found different youth organisations with
the same theory of change.

In Camden when we looked to redesign our youth mental
health services the feedback from young people was clear – they
didn't want staff wearing a badge reflecting their expertise:
'mental health', 'sexual health', 'substance abuse', 'careers'. They
wanted someone who would view the whole person not just deal
with their section.

Relationship building isn't always easy. It can be painstakingly
slow. Charlie Howard, a young psychologist, believed passionately
that young people involved in gangs and youth violence were
plagued by unmet mental health needs. The problem was she had
no idea how to get them to engage with therapy. So she decided
to go to them. She found the fish and chip shop that boys in her
area went to and she went there too. She didn't approach them,
she didn't hand them leaflets, she just sat there. And she did this
again and again for six months until one day one of the boys
asked her whether she was a policewoman. It was the start of a
conversation that went on for many more months. By then she
had proved consistency, she had shown she cared, there was a
thread of trust that she could build on. Charlie went on to found
MAC-UK – a hugely successful organisation that takes mental
health to the streets through street therapy. It involves wrapping
holistic mental health support around young people's interests,
such as music.

Jennifer Bradley, co-author of *The Metropolitan Revolution* and
fellow at the Brookings Metropolitan Policy Program, described
to me the process of city-led economic regeneration: 'It is only
by engaging in that conversation, which is slow and painstaking,
and there are no fireworks and there are no ribbon cuttings, but
this is how you learn to be responsive. It really is a constant,

exhaustive, painstaking conversation; there is no rubber-stamp, cookie-cutter, one-size-fits-all approach.'

She sees the role of the state as facilitating connections. 'Just go out and ask, meet with people you haven't met before, it sounds so crazily simplistic but the number of times I have been told by people, "Well, it really started when we just had a meeting." I wrote a book about meetings, basically . . . it just sounds so simple but it matters so much.'

The principles for successful relationship building

As an idealistic eighteen-year-old working as an organiser for Siobhain McDonagh, an intensely hard-working local MP for Mitcham and Morden CLP, I saw first-hand the principles of building good relationships and where it can lead to. Reading this I know that she would roll her eyes, tell me to stop banging on and go out and knock on some doors. This is what she started doing as a candidate in 1987, knocking on doors. She has continued to do so ever since – week in and week out, in the snow, rain and sun, good times and bad, asking people what their concerns are and then acting on them. Fuel poverty was a problem, so she got every company together to offer their best rates to her constituents. Her local hospital, St Helier, was set to close so she created so much noise that ten years later the closure still hasn't happened. Young people were facing unemployment so she created a local work experience scheme. Over the years she has turned a six thousand-strong Conservative majority into a thirteen thousand Labour one. Knock on any door in her constituency and young or old they will be able to tell you something she has done for them, more than likely they will have her calendar up on their wall. Turn up to one of the local branch meetings and you will find yourself swept up into a community that is more a broad extended family than a local Labour party and where no one is ever turned away.

Building relationships with young people requires effort but, as Siobhain would tell you, it isn't complicated. There are five principles at the heart of successful relationship building:

1. Go to them – knock on their doors, turn up to their youth clubs and schools, sit in their favourite cafés, hang about on their streets, find them on social media. Use intermediaries that they trust. Keep going if they don't engage.
2. Be authentic – be clear about your story and how it connects to theirs. Be transparent about your values, clear in your purpose and how it connects to them. Make an effort to be interesting, inspiring, funny, engaging, authentic or at the very least relevant.
3. Listen – ask them what they think and really listen to what they have to say. Give them the resources and information to make an informed intervention.
4. Feed back – It is not enough merely to listen, they have to understand the process by which their views and ideas feed into a decision-making process. This doesn't mean that they can always get what they want, but there has to be an open process of negotiation, conversation and dialogue. They have to be taken seriously. If your starting point is to 'teach them something' or 'make them feel involved' or if there is no flexibility in your strategy then you might as well not bother to engage, as young people will eventually see through it.
5. Be consistent – this applies if you are building a social media strategy or a new service. Young people, especially more vulnerable young people, are used to being let down. Consistency of individuals is ideal because trust is the biggest premium in any relationship, but also important are consistency of

provision, message and communication. If you can
only be involved in a time-limited way with a young
person ensure that the transition to independence or a
new service is well managed. There will be a time
young people have to move on, but put extra resources
into helping them manage that change.

As Heather Smith, Chairwoman of Rock the Vote – arguably
the most successful youth mobilisation organisation in the US –
put it when I asked her the advice she would give to an organisation trying to reach young people: 'Be authentic and true to
who you are, and just go talk to them.'

Properly applied this is the start of people-centred politics and
services. These are strategies political parties need to use if they
want to engage people and garner support. However, equally
important is how they are used by civil society.

There is a crucial role for the institutions of civil society in
rebuilding a social contract – community organisers, pressure
groups, trade unions and campaigning groups. They have an
easier job in reaching out to young people because of their independence. They can more easily put the power into young
people's hands and let them set the agenda.

For young people the purpose, funding and powers of the
person reaching out are important. The trust barrier for a young
person to engage with a politician or a member of staff at a job
centre with the power to sanction them is going to be much
higher than with an independent community organiser. As Neil
Jameson from Citizens UK puts it, 'They always want to know
who is paying you ... that's why civil society raising its own
money, booking its own halls, building its own agenda is a
responsible thing to do.' The messenger matters.

We saw in Chapter 2 the depth of young people's distrust and
cynicism about formal politics. Civil society can provide a bridge
for young people, building trust and teaching them how to take

power into their own hands. As Neil put it, 'For many young people there is one main alternative to organising, that is dropping out (not voting or participating). For a tiny angry minority it may also be rioting.'

An informed and organised youth population creates an eco-system where political parties and corporations are held to account. It will ultimately build a better political system.

For this to work the starting point has to be relationships. We all have to become community organisers. This does not mean a collective or global agenda is impossible but it has to be built on the blocks of local relationships. The future is coalitions and net-works, the threading together of local agendas into a national and global narrative.

When I interviewed Robert Skinner from the UN Foundation, he told me that the most successful campaigns were built on the bedrock of strong local groups like the environmental campaigners in Austin, Texas, who became involved with the UN Foundation through a local traffic scheme. He told me, 'It is the old cliché of think globally act locally. If you're worried about education you'll think about starting education in your own community.'

In the same way that secure family attachments are the start-ing blocks for developing friendships, local engagement can be the starting point for a national or global political voice.

Neil described to me how starting local with Citizens UK cre-ates the conditions for wider political involvement. Young people are given the opportunity to lead locally and celebrate it and then they start to ask, 'What else can we do?'

Take an overworked geography teacher in Lewisham who used the principles of Citizens UK to help his students start a project around litter, then build a local youth club, and eventually run a campaign for safer streets. They grew from a small group to a ten-thousand-strong movement led by sixteen-year-old Camilla Yahaya. She went from being afraid to speak in class to meeting the President of the US. Camilla told me, 'When we first started it was small numbers, we didn't feel like we were achieving any-thing. Over time we noticed it build up. The more we got things changed in the local community, the more people wanted to listen to us, the more people wanted us to do something, the more people wanted to help. It is about safety but before we can save lives, before it can do that, it's all about community build-ing and relationships.'

Some of the most powerful relationships are ones with those from different backgrounds or perspectives, which cause you to challenge or change an assumption. These kinds of relationships take on a democratic quality as they help us to negotiate differ-ence. They are the bridging bonds I focus on in Chapter 4 – bridges across socio-economic class, ethnicity and religion and ages.

Camilla Yahaya was brought up in France and her heritage is French-Ghanaian yet her inspiration for the 10,000 Hands campaign was the murder of Jimmy Mizen, a white Catholic. Through her work on their son's behalf she has formed strong relationships with Jimmy's parents. More than anything she wants the loss of young lives like Jimmy's to spur on a transfor-mation of their community: 'It is like there are so many young people who die each year, it feels like their deaths are in vain, nothing is coming out, it should shock and change and drive people, that is what has given us strength. We are not really doing it for ourselves; we're doing it for other people and in the memory of someone. Personally I do it in the memory of Jimmy.'

Marc Stears, Oxford academic and Ed Miliband's adviser, writes in *Every Day Democracy*, 'What makes a relationship specifically democratic is when it takes place between people who might otherwise be in tension with each other who through that relationship learn to respect each other in ways that they oth-erwise would not.'[4]

These are the relationships that underpin a healthy political process, that allow unified action and common cause. However, building better relationships won't unlock the full capacity of citizens alone; it has to go hand in hand with handing over power. As political theorist Danielle Allen puts it, 'Nascent interpersonal trust will never mature into full-blown political friendships until it is given serious work to do.'[5]

Chapter 8

Sharing Power

As a society we face major challenges with fewer resources to meet them. Without citizens doing more than passively receiving services we will never be able to deliver our collective ambitions. The good news is young people are ready and willing, in fact demanding, to take a more active role in political and community life. To be successful this has to be on their terms, not directed from above but negotiated in our communities. It will require huge change at every level, but the effort is worth it because if we are successful at giving young people the empowered citizenship they are looking for we will unlock a new wave of civic entrepreneurialism and energy.

I was recently sitting next to a Conservative baby boomer at a dinner at Oxford University who looked bemused as I enthusiastically espoused the importance of empowering young people. The problem, he told me, was the misconception that anyone has power and that rather than persuading young people that they have autonomy over their lives, it would be better to make it clear to them that everyone is powerless.

There is some truth in this. As we saw in Chapter 3, the power of elected representatives is severely constrained. Despite the fact that I am a cabinet member in a governing local administration I feel in my own work the gap between everything I want to achieve and the formal powers available to me. The greatest resource I have is the opportunity to build a coalition and bring people together.

My dinner companion may have been right in the sense that the power of an individual is limited in the modern world, but the power of a collective is limitless. A key part of any conversation about how to empower young people has to break down the 'hero myth' – the idea that there will be a knight riding over the horizon and that power is vested in an individual – and establish the rationale that power as a collective force is stronger. The more young people see themselves as part of a movement that is exercising power the more engaged they will be.

The problem, of course, is that in a youth culture that celebrates the individual young people struggle to find stories they can turn to for inspiration. As Lewisham's former Youth Mayor Jacob Sakil puts it, 'No one can actually give us an example of when people worked together for a long-term result.' Their parents and grandparents may well tell them tales of trade union strikes, anti-apartheid campaigning, CND and women's liberation; but they are from a different era, which can be difficult to relate to. The good news is that young people are starting to create their own movements, but these stories need to be shared and celebrated not derided as slacktivism, as we saw in Chapter 2. The question for our political institutions is how we provide young people with both the tools and the inspiration to exercise collective power.

What is happening?

A model of citizenship restricted to voting at an election every five years or the occasional charitable act is not going to work for many young people. They are calling for a much deeper engagement with the future of our society, which in turn calls on us to re-imagine what it means to be a citizen in the modern world.

However, this does not mean tearing down representative structures and rushing head-on to a system of direct democracy.

Oscar Wilde famously said, 'The trouble with Socialism is that it takes up too many evenings.' I may be happy rushing between two meetings every evening but I have never forgotten the first thing legendary campaigner Alan Barnard told me on my first day working for the Labour Party when I was eighteen: 'Never fall into the trap of thinking we are normal.'

Young people don't want to run every service or make every decision; however, they do want mechanisms for their ideas to be heard and opportunities to shape the direction of the policies that directly affect them.

They want to be authors of their own destiny and make choices about their own lives. Meeting this demand will need us to be much more ambitious in our understanding of citizenship. This will mean new responsibilities for citizens in exchange for more power.

British political theorist David Held offers an approach for thinking about modern democratic theory that connects to young people's desire for empowerment with the idea of Democratic Autonomy. For Held, autonomy is 'the capacity of human beings to reason self-consciously, to be self-reflective and to be self-determining'.[1]

To realise this vision he proposes a process of double democratisation, 'the interdependent transformation of both state and society'.[2] He feels that whilst both need to change this must be done with respect for their independence and integrity as separate but parallel spheres of action. His vision includes new broader political, economic and social rights accompanied by new obligation for citizens. I agree that the promoting of a new empowered citizenship requires nothing less than a parallel process of democratic renewal.

In the first section of this chapter I look at the role of the state in allowing empowered citizenship. In the second half, I give some practical examples of how the institutions of civil society can empower young people at a grassroots level to find their collective power. Institutions that are local, not for profit and serve the public interest can be a bridge between citizens and the state.

The purpose of this democratic renewal is to create the conditions of an empowered citizenship where every young person has the following:

First, the opportunity to negotiate difference and find common cause through relationships with those who are different from them, as we saw in the last chapter. Secondly, an understanding about how their actions contribute to a broader purpose for society, which I discuss in the next chapter. Thirdly, the opportunity for creative self-expression. Fourthly, the opportunity to be part of the conversations that govern them – the power to initiate political change, the power to engage in 'enlightened debate' and the power to co-create the policies that affect them. Finally, dynamic representation through open political parties. It is these last three that this chapter focuses on.

The starting point for young people is that they have autonomy in their own lives.

1. Opportunities for self-expression and creativity

For young people, collective empowerment is intrinsically linked to personal empowerment. We saw in the first half of the book that young people want to be creators and entrepreneurs in record numbers.

Matthew Taylor made a speech in July 2014 setting out a new vision for the Royal Society for the encouragement of Arts, Manufacturing and Commerce (RSA) entitled 'The Power to Create'. He asserted that all citizens can and should live creative lives. Their vision combines 'an idealistic view of human flourishing with democratic inclusiveness'.[3]

The truly radical idea in the RSA's vision is that the power to create is not the purview of the elite, but belongs to everyone.

When Aristotle wrote about the good life it was not a million miles away from this. But it was one enjoyed by a male elite and underpinned by slavery. The advancements in technology mean that much of the world's repetitive labour will eventually be done by robots and that humans will be free to be creators, crafters and carers. As we saw in Chapter 6, there is no guarantee that this will be where technological change takes us and it could just as easily create larger inequalities between those living creative lives and those stuck in dependency. In Chapter 10, I show the importance of social and economic rights to give young people the security to find this kind of personal empowerment.

When it comes to work, it is about moving away from the take-what-you-can-get approach to one that looks to support young people into the career they want, if not help them create it.

Rajeeb Dey, who founded Enternships, quotes Confucius as his inspiration: 'Find what you love and you'll never have to work a day in your life.' A budding entrepreneur put it another way: 'Work out what you love doing and find a way to get paid doing it.'

This doesn't mean every young person has to become an entrepreneur, but as Rajeeb says, 'Everyone has the ability to be entrepreneurial in whatever they choose to do ... I think it is important to create the space to be creative and innovate, to take some risks.'

Unlocking young people's entrepreneurialism and creativity means taking a much more personalised approach to developing young people's aptitudes and interests. Author and philosopher Charles Handy talks about the idea of 'a golden seed', where everyone has some sort of skill or aptitude that, if it is identified and nurtured, builds a feeling of self-confidence and feeds into other areas of life.

The idea that every child has something valuable to contribute, and thus taking the time to find and develop their passion, is a model of true personal empowerment that would mean a big change in our education system. Later on in this chapter I look at practical ideas for how schools can deliver this, but it also needs national accountability and resourcing.

With the right tools, empowered young citizens can use their creativity and entrepreneurialism in their communities.

2. Providing citizens with the power to initiate and lead

The definition of a good democratic life is one where we have some kind of rule over ourselves.

To achieve this, the state will need to become more responsive to the demands of informed and active citizens. In South Korea, the Seoul Innovation Bureau is a cross-departmental unit that is putting substantial resources into trying to forge real partnerships with citizens, creating a number of avenues for citizens to get their voices heard. They can submit an idea online or vote on someone else's idea knowing that City Hall will look into the most popular every three months. They can visit one of the many temporary town halls set up across the city. They can go to City Hall and express themselves at the open speakers' corner and see their views shared online. They can attend workshops on a broad range of policy areas – to date, six hundred thousand people have attended six thousand workshops. Some 250 citizens have even participated in budget decisions to allocate £16.3 million of the city's £607.4 million budget.[4]

Citizens can be partners in improving their cities and towns, as the Boston Mayor's Office of Urban Mechanics has shown. They have developed 'Citizens Connect', a mobile app for residents to upload and track problems they see in their daily lives, and 'Street Bump', an app that monitors the road surface as residents drive around the city, helping planners to spot problems.

They can provide real-time feedback and accountability to public services through social media.[5]

Finland has taken an active approach to involving young people in decision-making. The 2006 Local Government Act ensures that 'the opportunity to participate in the handling of issues relating to local and regional youth work and policy must be provided for young people. Additionally, young people must be heard during the handling of issues concerning them.'[6] This is assessed by an annual youth survey through telephone interviews with two thousand fifteen- to twenty-nine-year-olds. As many as 40 per cent of young people have also directly submitted initiatives under this Act.[7]

Secondly the state will need to move away from simply delivering services and start providing citizens with the tools to help one another. As well as giving citizens new opportunities, the Seoul Innovation Bureau is supporting them as they take a more active role in their community through facilitating neighbourhood schemes like 'The Sharing Bookshelves', which promotes neighbourliness by setting up libraries in blocks of flats, and 'The Generation Sharing Household' scheme, which helps match elderly people in need of day-to-day help with students in need of cheap housing. These types of sharing schemes are looking to utilise technology to enable citizens to help each other. Nor are they exclusive to Seoul. 'Tyze' is an app used by Camden Council that uses cloud computing to bring together all the different people involved in an elderly person's care – families, friends, neighbours, care professionals – and allows them to share updates safely and securely, and to schedule care responsibilities.

The Conservative–Liberal Democrat Coalition has an ambitious agenda for opening up public data through freely publishing government data. Visitors to youdata.gov.uk can browse hundreds of apps created using government data, from 'Commutable careers' that lets you map job opportunities easily accessible by public transport, through to an A-level students' computing project of an app comparing schools based on their A-level results. There is still much more that could be done to use digital tools to open up policymaking.

Government also has to support the kind of deep, informed deliberation that leads to enlightened debate. There is evidence to show that consultations that skate on the surface of issues intensify dissatisfaction whereas those that go deeper, exploring trade-offs and negotiating options, lead to higher satisfaction rates. But it can be hard to convince residents to take the time and energy to negotiate complex decisions. At the local level this can be done with those who are deeply invested in a community service, such as members of a youth club. One way to get over this challenge at a national level is through deliberative processes. This is a kind of civic jury duty where a representative group of the population are asked to learn about an issue and then debate and discuss it. It has a minimum obligation on the citizen but ensures that the basis of participation is inclusive. The Greater Geraldton City Region of Australia's 2029 initiative involved two thousand people in a debate about the future of the region. Forty volunteer community champions led deliberative events across the region, and an online platform, CivicEvolution, was commented on by four thousand residents. This led to real policy implementation, such as the planting of a million trees as a one-day deliberative event agreed that the City Region should become carbon neutral. A three-day deliberative event involved hundreds of residents in creating a City Regional Plan. The region now has a vision for their future set out in a community charter, co-owned by citizens.[8]

If we want people to do more, the state should help provide the infrastructure and support for a service nation. In the US, Bill Clinton described a visit to City Year, where eighteen- to twenty-five-year-olds give a year of service mentoring younger children in inner-city schools, as a light bulb moment. It inspired him to create AmeriCorps, which pays young people a stipend to deliver a year of service, unlocking substantial mutual benefit for corps and the communities they serve.

Sophie Livingstone, Chief Executive of City Year in the UK and co-chair of Generation Change, an organisation creating a shared agenda across youth social action, tells me that creating a similar programme to AmeriCorps in the UK could unlock a new wave of voluntary youth service going beyond education into health, social care and the environment. 'You need the establishment to endorse this saying – we will recognise it, we will take it seriously, it will get you a job, it will get you into university because this is what you do as a citizen of this country. And that bit is missing.'

The support needed to actively engage will vary. In my ward middle-class, middle-aged residents are knocking down my door to take on more power and responsibility. When the new neighbourhood planning legislation came through they were ahead of the council in the way they organised themselves. Their commitment, effort and confidence were immense. No one needs to tell them where the access points are. They will turn up at my surgery, email officers directly, sign up to planning bulletins and organise resident committees. They bring deep expertise as architects and lawyers, and they play an important and valuable role. They are, however, only one section of the community; they cannot speak for everyone. Younger voters may have a different attitude about the night-time economy; different groups may feel more or less protective of the local pound shop and so on. Many of the white working-class mums I work with lack the confidence to engage with professionals at all – the idea of entering a school fills them with fear, let alone the possibility of taking on a leadership role. If we just devolve power down and let it fall where it will, we may end up entrenching inequalities. There has to be a dual process that simultaneously hands over power while supporting and building relationships with those that never turn up to meetings and have no idea how to engage.

Innovation units around the world are using technology to create new solutions. At the heart of the majority of these schemes is a belief that, through methods of co-creation, listening to citizens can drive innovation. However, local and national governments have to embrace this mindset as the new norm. There are plenty of examples that show what can happen if they do not. The Finnish Brickstarter project, designed as a kind of Kickstarter for communities where individuals could donate to community-based projects, say they ultimately floundered because of a lack of local government interest.[9] Many of the apps on Civic Exchange (an online portal for civic engagement tools) have failed to find local authority take-up.[10] Often new practices are slow to take root. Bureaucracies are not nimble. Change will not happen overnight. But what is clear is that institutions' default position makes many well-meaning and innovative projects impractical.

This also requires a change in our attitude to failure, both for our institutions and for our citizens. We need to be more forgiving of those that try to innovate, whether they are young would-be entrepreneurs, politicians experimenting with YouTube or organisations trying a new engagement tool. Change will always incur risks, especially if it is in the direction of openness and autonomy. As a society we need to value and embrace failure as a step on the path to innovation.

This vision for the future means that the agencies of the state will need to change and they will have to be more responsive and connected to users both in their design and accountability. However, the state will need to retain its responsibility for ensuring equity and standards: standards that offer targets and accountability but also space to innovate.

3. Open parties

As well as engaging directly with government agencies, citizens also need avenues to influence political policymaking.

Party politics is theoretically the avenue through which citizens can exercise their collective power and influence. However, far from seeing them as their route into decision-making, most young people bristle when party politics is mentioned. Political parties are seen as self-serving and disruptive to co-operation and coalition-building.

The majority of youth-led organisations I met told me with pride that they aren't 'party political'.

Political parties have to sell themselves better. They have to convince young people that it is powerful to be part of a movement that stands up for something; that there are values that unite us; and that at the heart of political parties is a purpose and a cause. They have to inspire. They have to mean something. They have to show young people that there is room for mavericks, independents and dissenters. And that they are willing to have an open and frank dialogue with all of them.

The truth is that the idea of party politics rejected by young people is not the party politics I know. Behind closed doors, some of the most impassioned debates are taking place about our values and our future, debates that could engage the most unpolitical of citizens. The party members I work with are almost all trustees, school governors, community activists and volunteers. They are some of the most deeply committed people I have ever met, but too often their community and party roles are separated.

Parties should take on more forms of direct participation and issue-based campaigns but they, in my view, still have an important role in coordinating political demands and in shaping democratic choices into something that makes sense for people living busy lives.

But they have a long way to go. We need to reclaim the idea of party politics as a deep expression of principle. We need to out ourselves as party members, talk about our principles and explain to young people what and who we are. Go to them with a story that they can relate to. We need to be seeking out the kind of young leaders I've written about and giving them every bit of support to take up leadership positions as councillors, party officers and eventually MPs. Their leadership will be the strongest sign to young people that party politics is for them.

It has to be far easier for them to join in without joining up. This means opening primaries so that the selection of party candidates is open to the wider public, not just party members. It also means allowing young people to register as supporters and campaigning directly on issues that relate to young people. Parties need to be embedding themselves in the lives of local communities, campaigning on the things people care about, and online tools need to be far more localised and linked in with community life. We need to open up our debates, processes and thinking.

The young people I spoke to had a vision of a much more co-operative politics based on dialogue, compromise and consensus. Name-calling and pointless debates just turn them off. We have to show that where it is in the public interest and there is clear agreement, parties can work together.

There has been some movement in the right direction. In 2009 the Conservatives held their first open primary to select the parliamentary candidate for Totnes, and there have subsequently been at least fifteen open primaries. To select their 2014 European candidate the Green Party ran a Europe-wide open, online primary. In the Labour Party, Ed Miliband has introduced the concept of registered supporters, who can affiliate and vote in Labour leadership elections without becoming paid-up members, and introduced Labour's first open primary for the selection of the London Mayoral candidate. In 2010 David Miliband founded Movement for Change to reignite the tradition of community organising within the Labour Party. Based on the principles of one-to-one relationship-building we saw in the last chapter, it employs professional community organisers to help build the capacity of communities to campaign on the issues important to them. Take the young Labour councillor and

Movement for Change activist Mitchell Theaker, who found that the biggest issue facing a group of young Swansea mums was the actions of payday lenders.[11] He worked with them to build a campaign, and one of the highlights of the 2013 Labour Party conference was two of the mums, who'd never before engaged in politics, getting up and demanding action on payday lenders from a future Labour government.[12] It's an important step in the right direction. These are examples of party politics at its best, as its values are lived out in the community.

Over the last half-century parties have become increasingly professional and centralised. This was driven by a mass media and the need to speak to the public more than to party activists. However, the world has moved on and parties need to do the same.

Opening up isn't easy. The impulse to control messages under the media's unforgiving glare is strong. We are all guilty of becoming comfortable with our traditions, processes and familiar faces. Change is time-consuming, difficult and challenging.

In *The Revolution Will Not Be Televised*, Joe Trippi describes how he threw out the rulebook while running Howard Dean's campaign for the Democratic nomination for US President. They crowd-sourced funds by publishing targets, they blogged their strategy and they created tools that allowed volunteers to take action on their own. Their methods were the genesis of the Obama campaign.

It wasn't easy. Trippi likened the act of handing over power as jumping without a net off a fifteen-storey building.[13] The hope, of course, is that hands will catch you, but there are no guarantees.

Opening up and letting go is daunting, but it is the only way to give young people the power they are looking for.

What happens when institutions share power with young people?

Institutions, whether political or civil, have to take steps to engage young people by devolving more power. This isn't easy.

As with political parties, many of the traditional institutions of civil society, such as religious organisations and community associations, have seen declining memberships, and those who are involved in them are often older generations deeply committed to the status quo. They can be reluctant to share power with a generation whose engagement is likely to be more transient, casual and open.

Modernisation is often painful. It will almost always come with tough trade-offs. Take the Church of England, grappling with its position on homosexuality and female leadership, or trade unions looking to represent both their often older, often public-sector core constituency while at the same time trying to recruit young members who sometimes have conflicting priorities.

Institutions can either open themselves up to young people or face steady decline. They have to be bold and recognise that huge positives will accompany this change – fresh thinking, creative solutions, renewed energy and a fruitful dialogue between generations. They will also have to come to terms with some loss of control, an abandonment of some traditions and new ways of doing things.

I found one of the most powerful examples of empowered youth leadership in a Sikh gurdwara in Glasgow that acts both as a place of worship and as a community hub.

Glasgow's new and first purpose-built gurdwara is an oasis of calm in a bustling city and a source of huge pride for Glasgow's large Sikh population. When I arrive a community member is busy pruning the already pristine flowerbeds. The gold dome shines in the midday heat. The kitchen is already full of volunteers, chatting and laughing as they prepare tea and snacks for visitors, a custom called *langar*, where meals are prepared and available for anyone who requires them. One older volunteer is carefully cleaning paintings from the old gurdwara, explaining to me as he does so, 'This is how we remember what we have been through, these paintings are our history.'

At the heart of all this is Charandeep Singh, a twenty-three-year-old Scottish Sikh. He takes me to remove my shoes and fasten a headscarf, then begins to show me around. 'I do this tour almost every day,' he tells me, 'but I never get bored because everyone's reaction is different.' He proudly explains how they raised the millions needed for the building. He shows me the vast dining room where anyone can come and eat for free – all they ask is that guests share their meal sitting on the floor together, a symbol of equality. He shows me the crèche, the homework club, the teenagers' meeting room, and he introduces me to some of the young volunteers.

It wasn't always like this. Charandeep became involved in the community well before building works began. One Monday evening he popped in to the West End Gurdwara on the other side of the city and what he found surprised him. There was a group of young people waiting for a class to start but no teachers had turned up. This experience spurred him to get involved and eventually he began leading the class. The students were not much younger than him, so he changed the whole structure. 'We were able to create an atmosphere of dialogue, rather than a classroom, lecture-style environment. Because it was youth-led, it became more exciting.'

In four years the class went from twenty members to over one hundred and in the process became a self-sustaining community. Charandeep then turned his attention to the Southside Gurdwara. He knew plans were in place for this new building and he wanted to see young people leading the process from the start.

To his dismay what he found was that young people in the Southside were even less engaged than in the West End of Glasgow. 'There was nothing happening.' There were lessons for primary-school children but teenagers were not provided for. 'They felt a need to be there, affiliation and connection with the institution itself, with their family, with their friends, but they weren't getting anything from this experience.' Again he felt he had to act. 'I don't like young people standing in a corner thinking, Why are we not going home yet?'

He established a Saturday class in which he wanted to replicate some of the experiences from the West End Gurdwara. At first it was just a few family friends he begged to come. It began with an intensive three-month course on values. 'We can't really do anything unless we know what our community believes in or practises, otherwise we are not doing things that are relevant to the membership of the organisation.'

He found he'd unlocked huge, latent reserves of energy within the young people. He said sometimes he was afraid to walk into the room because they were so energetic. Formal session would finish at 5.30 p.m., but he wouldn't go home until 8 p.m., sometimes later, as they were so eager to carry on the discussions.

Eventually they decided to establish the Young Sikh Leaders Network, a formal group which was committed to the gurdwara and to the community. He said it was hard at first to get young people to see themselves as leaders. They thought, Yes I am Sikh, yes I am young, but am I a leader? Slowly they became more confident and they decided to put forward a plan for the opening ceremony of the new gurdwara, a landmark event for the community. Charandeep took the plans to the executive committee, who not only liked them but decided to give young people the responsibility to run the entire event.

Suddenly the leadership dynamic began to change. It was the young people updating the elders. He tells me because of the young people's leadership the nature of the event changed. It was bolder, brighter and more energetic. In the past he said you might have had a few speeches and a ribbon cutting, but the young people wanted something to rival the Olympics. They also wanted something which was open and inclusive. It was the young people's idea to involve other faith leaders – personally delivering letters to other community groups to invite them to be part of raising the Nishan Sahib (the Sikh flag), which was the most symbolic part of the event. It was their idea to have a procession through Glasgow to show that the new space belonged to the community.

The opening of the gurdwara was covered by seven national papers, BBC Scotland and international Sikh media. The Young Sikh Leaders truly found a global platform. When I visit a few months after the ceremony it is clear young people are deeply embedded in the organisation. Young Sikh leader hoodies are draped over the door of the main office and posters for the entirely youth-organised summer school cover the noticeboard.

Importantly, the young people work hard to ensure that the building is open and inclusive, acting as guides to visitors. They know what it is like to walk into a building and feel like outsiders, so they put everything into making sure their gurdwara is welcoming. 'We are grateful to have over fifty thousand visitors to the gurdwara. If one person gets an experience that doesn't match our foundation values of humanity,' Charandeep says, 'we can't really be wearing that hoodie any more that says Young Sikh leader.'

He thinks there is some unease towards the more inclusive and open approach among some of the older members and he understands it. 'Obviously for a few older members of the community when they see non-Sikhs it worries them, they think, This is our space, our sanctuary, and we want to protect it.' But he says the young understand the power of an open approach: 'If a tile breaks we can fix it, if a child marks a wall we can paint over it, if two people walk in and we don't welcome them straight away we can never fix that.'

These Young Sikh Leaders have not stopped at the borders of the gurdwara. They are now looking outwards to the broader community. Charandeep says they see the gurdwara not as a building but as a living and breathing institution. When a local hospital needed funds, they came together and raised ten thousand pounds.

Also many are increasingly turning their attention to politics. He described what happened when one of the young people came into a session distressed after hearing their mother talk about a Sikh man in Panjab, India facing the death penalty. The group started to do some research and realised no one was talking about it.

They decided the answer was a debate in the Scottish Parliament and armed with the optimism that comes from success, they set out to make this happen. 'We created a role for ourselves. We might not know everything about politics, we might not know everything about community engagement, we might not know everything about dialogue and discussion and funding, but we can learn it. And we can take action. Who likes to learn and who has enough energy and excitement? The young people do.'

Two weeks later they were on a coach to Edinburgh to lead a protest. Charandeep tells me there was a team of young people coordinating things from the back of the coach. 'I had my phone, someone had an iPad, someone had a laptop, we had people on social media duty, one person doing a press release, another in touch with the Scottish Parliament.' Three hundred people turned up and the story made headlines. Six weeks later the Scottish Parliament debated the issue.

I could go on about many more of their successes but the point I am making is clear: these young people don't feel alienated, they feel deeply empowered. Every victory gives them more confidence and they now look at the world and ask how they can shape it.

The older leaders of the gurdwara could have closed the door on change, ignored the young people's ideas and refused to engage. Instead, they allowed young people to take on more powers. In return they gained a more dynamic, optimistic and outward-looking organisation.

*

In 2012 the London Olympics celebrated a vision of Britain that was forward-looking, positive and diverse.

Greg Nugent, who served as Director of Brand, Marketing and Culture for the London Olympics and Paralympics, is certain this came from the values of young Britons. He told me that fundamentally they saw themselves as reporting to young people; along the way 'very senior execs would sit down and literally be panicking about what this meant for young people'. For his team 'they were our litmus test and our target audience, the strategy came from them'.

The Olympic organisers took the message of 'Inspire a Generation' literally and tested every decision against a central goal: to equip the next generation. It set the culture for staff, volunteers and athletes.

'We said to the athletes: "Look you've got one thing to do, which is to win, but please tell your stories about sacrifice, and struggle, and hard work and late nights and no pay, and ... tell your stories because we believe that that will transform the way that people think about the essential concepts."'

I asked him how they managed to empower so many young people. The answer was simple: 'We trusted them.' They started off by creating full-time positions for school leavers. Then as volunteers they invested in their training and they drilled into them that they were the public face of the games, the success or not rested in their hands. 'We were very demanding of them. We said, "If you get it wrong we are fucked! You can't get it wrong! We're not doing this because it looks good for us to be able to say corporately we've got loads of young people." What we said was, "You're the best people. You're gonna do the best job. Getting this wrong is not an option." So in that sense, we took them extraordinarily seriously.'

We sit on deep resources of energy, creativity and talent that can either be harnessed and channelled for the good of society or be wasted.

Putting it into practice

There is a powerful case for sharing power, but the next question is, how do we make it happen?

Re-engaging young people in our institutions requires that we value their contribution, provide them with the skills to partic-ipate and create space in our institutions to hear them.

1. Valuing and recognising the contribution of young people

Taking young voices seriously

The dominant narrative that portrays all youth as a problem means that too many organisations, youth strategy is based on the notion that they need to be 'improved' rather than learnt from. We have to change our default setting about young people and start recognising how much they have to contribute.

The mindset of an organisation's leadership is more important than its structures. An organisation with a leader who believes that young voices are worth listening to is more effective than one that has a youth structure in place, but is isolated from real power.

As Marc Kidson, Chair of the British Youth Council's board of trustees, put it when talking about local government, 'Where we see it working is when they do really believe that involving young people will improve the effect that their policies have, rather than give it a badge of legitimacy.'

The pressure to give young people a voice means that they are often consulted, but they are not yet listened to. When some research suggests that only 40 per cent of government consultations have a clear link to outcomes it is easy to see how a meaningless consultation exercise can do more harm than good.[14] The starting point has to be that an institution believes that embedding young people in the decision-making process will add value. The metric of successful engagement can't just be the number of young people spoken to; success needs to be measured by the extent to which young people's involvement has led to improvement in strategy, product or culture. Crucially, the difference that their input made has to be fed back to them so they know their intervention has been effective.

Trusting them

When an organisation believes in young people, invests in them and then hands over power to them the results always exceed expectations. There aren't short cuts, you actually have to trust them. Too often people and organisations involved in youth engagement will miss out this step, then wonder why they have failed. They ask young people to put in a lot of work but then don't let them take the lead. They ask young people a question without trusting them with the information to make an informed response. They try to fit young people into a predetermined structure without considering what might work best for them. They wait for young people to prove themselves trustworthy. These may be well-meaning interventions but they do more harm than good.

Sophie Livingstone, chief executive of City Year UK, tells me, 'You expect excellence and people will rise to that challenge. I have seen that through the years with different roles with young people. If you have high expectations of them they tend to meet them.'

The young people Sophie works with are sent into schools that have children facing a challenging set of circumstances and there is an expectation that they will partner with the school to help them deliver. What's more, they become role models for the children they support. Sophie says that they grow in confidence as they see themselves through these other kids' eyes.

Trust and empowerment are the basis of their culture: 'There is a philosophy here that you can do great things, we believe in you and you can do it and we will be here to support you, but you also have to challenge yourself and it will be hard but it will be rewarding.'

Part of trusting young people means giving them the knowledge they need to make an effective contribution.

2. Increase the capacity of young people to contribute

Citizenship and political education

Political and civic institutions have to believe young people can make a valuable contribution but young people also have to believe that they will be listened to. If they have a fixed mindset about political change then they could be offered all the opportunities in the world but would simply fail to engage.

Unfortunately, at the moment this is a generation with a fixed mindset about their own agency in relation to politics and community. Just as Carol Dweck discovered that state of mind was more important than intelligence in determining outcomes in education, a young person's belief about the futility of their effort in all walks of life is hugely important.

Research shows that for teenagers the most important determinant of their civic engagement is whether they believed their intervention would make a difference.[15] In one study, 63 per cent of young people who had completed a GCSE in citizenship said their political knowledge had increased by not very much or not at all.[16] In 2013, according to the Hansard Society's audit of political engagement, 47 per cent of the population wish they had learned more about politics and how democracy works at school.[17] The most important political education is not about the structures of politics but about how to exert influence.

Schools and youth services have a lot to contribute. Political education is not just about learning your rights but learning that your interventions can produce change. This is best learnt by action.

In Germany this is enshrined in federal law. It is incumbent on all federal states to ensure that schools not only teach democratic values but also empower students 'to critical action, political participation, citizenship and active participation'.[18] Students in Berlin, Bavaria and Schleswig-Holstein are represented on school councils alongside teachers and parents.[19] Students can learn a lot about their own agency, or lack of it, from the opportunities available to them to take the initiative and contribute to the decision-making of the school.

As the German model suggests, it means starting early. Some schools go out of their way to engage young people in their local community and politics. I was recently at a mock election at Eleanor Palmer Primary School in my ward, complete with replica polling stations and polling agents. On election day, seven-year-olds were dragging their mums out to vote.

Many schools could do much more to open their buildings up to the community, to bring citizenship alive through engagement with local groups and to support community campaigns.

Another resource, too often underused by schools, is local politicians. They could be providing youth surgeries, allocating funds and brokering local connections. In one Glasgow focus group that was generally damning about politicians, one girl said that her local SNP councillor had regularly visited her school asking their views – he even attended the Christmas play – and as a result she was the only one in the focus group willing to stand up for politicians.

The National Citizen Service (NCS) was set up by the coalition government to promote active citizenship and is now an independent social enterprise. I was initially sceptical, feeling it was another programme to teach young people how to be good citizens rather than recognising how much they have to offer. But

I was proved completely wrong. I first saw them in action in Bradford. I had spent the morning conducting a series of tough interviews characterised by division and community conflict. It was therefore all the more noticeable when I walked into a room to see a diverse group chatting and laughing together. They called themselves a Youth Action Committee and were busy planning a food bank for young people facing homelessness in Bradford. It turned out they were NCS graduates, who a year later were still working together.[20]

The NCS's Chief Executive Michael Lynas tells me that he sees the dual purpose of the organisation as empowering young people and transforming communities: 'We want to give them the tools and opportunities to lead change in their community. The idea is to hand over the controls and let them drive the car but support them along the way. My vision is to be a movement that belongs to young people.'

The NCS programme is a three-week full-time leadership course, two weeks of which are spent on an intensive residential retreat, which takes a diverse group of sixteen-year-olds from the same area and teaches them the principles of community organisation. It then supports them as they take their skills back into their community, with another thirty hours given back in community service over a month.

Six weeks at sixteen can never be a panacea but it is an important tool, which, built into a wider service strategy, takes young people from primary school to adulthood. It is something to work up to and something to be built upon. This type of service-learning activity has to be embedded in our national character. It should start in schools; then be supplemented by organisations like the Scouts, Guides and the NCS; followed by opportunities at university and then finally the option of taking a year out for service before starting work. Generation Change and Step up to Serve, a campaign to double youth social action by 2020, are seeking to create this framework of quality youth social action for young people and they need cross-party support at the local and national level.

Finally we have to show young people the link between personal and collective empowerment. The good news is they are starting to create their own movements, but these stories need to be shared and celebrated. I remember talking to a group of teenagers about Camilla Yahaya, who at sixteen engaged ten thousand young people in Lewisham to demand safer streets. Suddenly their belief in what was possible shifted.

Helping young people to find a voice

As well as motivation, young people have to have the confidence and the communication skills to make themselves heard.

Otherwise, as one young Community Radio host in Bradford put it to me, 'What's the point of giving people a voice if they don't know what to say?' He says he sees too many young people like him from working-class backgrounds dry up when someone puts a microphone in front of them. He thinks that we have to teach young people rules of rhetoric, critical thinking and the ability to argue a point.

On a visit to Eton it became clear that all these practices were already very much embedded in that school's culture. The students told me that they are treated as leaders from a young age; students are encouraged to run their own clubs and societies. They are responsible for managing their own schedules and setting their own goals. By the time they leave school they have a strong sense of their own agency. Speaking to three young people from inner city London schools who had gone to Eton for sixth-form on scholarships, I learnt how empowered they felt by the opportunities to follow their interests and set their own agenda.

These young men recognised that managing children with a variety of different needs and on smaller budgets placed more constraints on comprehensive schools. However, despite the challenges, there are state schools embedding similar practices. The Wren Academy in London is one such example. It is an outstanding school, taking a more holistic approach to education. Teachers support children to be their own coaches with the aim that eventually every pupil can oversee their own learning. Rather than only having a traditional school council they have 'curriculum lead advisers' responsible for helping to shape the teaching their peers receive. One lead adviser told me she helps design lesson plans, find resources and canvass students' views on what is being taught. A conversation with a fifteen-year-old curriculum lead almost felt like a conversation with a senior leader. She described how new teachers sometimes don't get the school's ethos, 'But that's OK,' she said without irony, 'we soon teach them.' She feels a deep sense of commitment to the school's culture and perceives herself as having an integral role in preserving it.

Peter Hyman set up School 21, a state-funded school in Stratford, east London, on many of the principles we see here. The school partners with Cambridge University to create a curriculum focused on oracy, so young people, often from disadvantaged backgrounds, can express themselves in a way that gets them heard. They focus on many of the ideas we have seen throughout this book – developing growth mindsets, grit and Daniel Pink's three drivers of motivation: mastery, autonomy and purpose. The twin aims for the school – 'to create beautiful work and to make a difference to the world' – are the foundation stone of an empowered citizenship. The school also helps young people to see how they can realise that citizenship in the wider world. Peter Hyman told me, 'The fashion at the moment is for schools that are boot camps, silent children – seen but not heard. Our school is the opposite – children allowed to express themselves, become eloquent, care about the world around them, ask difficult questions. If we have schools that stifle creativity, do not allow students to combine academic and emotional, personal skills, they will not become active citizens. What needs to happen in our schools is a massive recalibration where young people are treated seriously and the dialogue is interactive, personalised and empowering.'

As we saw in Chapter 5, the greatest tool for empowerment is access to knowledge. Learning and empowerment aren't mutually exclusive; in fact, they actively support each other. Work by the Education Endowment Foundation and Sutton Trust assessed evidence of educational interventions to help the achievement of disadvantaged pupils and showed that the strategies with the greatest impact on young people's learning are those that give them more responsibility over setting and managing their own learning goals.[21]

It is incumbent on schools to promote this kind of learning and on local authorities to coordinate it, but Ofsted and national education policymakers also have to regard it as something of value. In the RSA's 'Schools with Soul' paper, Angie Kotler of the Schools Linking Network summed up the difficulty of focusing on spiritual, moral, social and cultural education: 'We are working in a system that mainly reflects and transmits the overt values of capitalism and individuality, with a nod to the niceties of being "good citizens". While we are playing this game, I believe it is incredibly difficult to be truly effective in improving SMSC. Or at least we will have to be satisfied with sowing a few seeds and hoping they might reap fruit at some point, once the real business of getting exams passed, getting further or higher education and then work, is done with.'[22]

Increase interaction between groups of children from different backgrounds

DebateMate, founded by former barrister Margaret McCabe, works to ensure that access to debating skills is not just the purview of an elite group of young people. Not only does it give young people from working-class backgrounds debating skills, it also promotes integration.

I came across them watching a debating competition at Eton where young people from inner-city state schools were competing against students from Eton and other public schools. One of the teachers from a comprehensive told me that when they first arrived, his students were staring and pointing at the Eton pupils in their tails 'like they were from another planet'. However, as the competition progressed their confidence grew. Eventually, it was won by fifteen-year-old Ife from Hackney. He told me, 'If you asked me in Year Seven what I thought of Eton, I would have said that is where princes go to, not Hackney schoolboys.' He has now developed real friendships among the people he has met at debating competitions: 'I don't feel like they are higher than me and they don't treat me like I am lower than them ... we all treat each other as good debaters.'

Most of all, it has given him a confidence, which is breaking down doubts about what he is capable of in all aspects of his life. 'The thing that I would like to stress with schools like Eton ... from the time that they are in primary school they tell them they are going to be leaders, they have a mentality that "we are the best". When you get into the more underprivileged areas you don't get given that mentality ... you get the mentality of "despite" – I hate that word, "despite". *Despite* the fact that you are from Hackney you are doing so well ... So sometimes it is about changing the mentality among people ... Just because you're from an underprivileged area doesn't mean you can't do well.'

He sees himself as having a responsibility to share this mind-set with his classmates. Using his skills as an orator, Ife became Youth MP for Hackney. The deep sense of injustice he feels and the confidence to speak out is powerful combination which he is now channelling for the good of his community.

City Year UK seeks to give this kind of community spirit and confident mindset to the young people they work with. Sophie Livingstone says, 'We train them to speak in public. They will look you in the eye, they will turn up on time, they will be smartly dressed. We have what we call leader behaviours and we expect them to not swear, not to smoke in uniform, not drink in uniform, not chew gum, to stand up for people on the Tube, all of those sort of things. So they are role models in the school but also in the community.'

She feels the interaction between young people from different backgrounds is where the most powerful change comes from. 'I've had pushback from funders: who want to fund the most needy. But I want the really privileged kid in this corps with the kid who hasn't had many opportunities presented to them, because they will learn so much from each other.'

What National Citizen Service, DebateMate, City Year and many other organisations offer young people is mutually bene ficial democratic relationships, knowledge about how to create change and most importantly, confidence in their ability to shape the world around them.

Young people can have all the skills they need but if institutions don't let them in, they won't get heard.

1. Make space for young people to make a contribution in our institutions

Opening the door

Opening the door and letting young people in means being open and transparent about how and where they can influence decision-making. We saw this above with political parties but it equally applies to other institutions. This means making information accessible. But publishing a document and putting it on a website won't suffice. Information must be presented in a way that is simple, clear and relatable.

As Jude Kelly, Artistic Director of the Southbank Centre, put it, 'What I think public institutions are really lacking is some transparency in their methods of public engagement and being clear on the nature and consistency of involvement. It's often too random – where is the metaphorical "front door"? And who's invited through it and how often?'

The power of the Southbank's appeal for young people is that it is a space they can make their own. They don't have to pay anything or produce a membership card, they can just walk in. An open door can help unlock young people's creativity. Take the young dancers who started rehearsing in the downstairs corridors; no one stopped them so they kept coming back. Instead of turning them away, the Southbank encouraged them and when I visit the dancers from the corridor are due to have their own showcase at an upcoming urban weekend. Jess, Participation Producer, tells me, 'Our vision is that we create a community of young people that use this space spontaneously and experimentally and that begins in time to influence how we programme new work.'

It is important to be transparent about access points. It is also important to give young people the right support to take advantage of that access. It needs to be made clear to them that they are valued. It is not enough just to open the door, the next step is to show young people that it is there, which means reaching out to them on their terms and handing over real power.

Handing over real power

When a youth position exists in an organisation there are a number of questions that need to be asked. Does the post hold real power? Is the position paid? Are they being trained and invested in? Are they around the table with decision-makers? Is there a budget attached to their role? Do they have genuine responsibilities? If the answer to all of these is no, then young people will quickly see through it.

Jessica Santer, Participation Producer at the Southbank Centre, described how they give young people the opportunity to create part of their annual festival. They are trained for each project, whether it is photography or customer service, and are then given real responsibility. She tells me, 'It has to be a real experience. It can't be you in a room completely separate from the festival creating a brochure, but then actually we are not using that brochure, that is just a pretend activity. It has to be real otherwise it loses its meaning.'

Another of their projects is to invite primary school children to take over front-of-house jobs such as those of the ice-cream sellers and cloakroom attendants, wearing T-shirts emblazoned with 'Ask me. I am in charge'. She recalls speaking to a ten-year-old who told her that it was the best day of his life. He had been running a cloakroom. It wasn't the activity but the power, 'feeling like they are being trusted with a real job and feeling like they are in charge'.

There need to be young people in positions of power throughout our institutions as leaders, employees and advocates. Young people like Jacob Sakil in Lewisham will rise to the challenge: 'I knew once I became Youth Mayor there were a lot of things that I couldn't do. I knew smoking and drinking wouldn't be a positive example to set for other young people. It is a responsibility I took on because people look up to me.'

Institutional change works best when it is not focused on creating a separate youth strategy but when young people's desire for more power is used as a catalyst for broader reform. If we want to restore faith in our democratic institutions, empowering young people needs to be a national mission. But it doesn't have to start in Whitehall. It can start with a management committee of a Sikh gurdwara handing over the organisation of a festival. Every small step shows what young people are capable of and helps another group of young people to believe in their capacity to create the changes they want to see. Once young people have the belief, there is no stopping them. All it will take is enough organisations willing to make young people a priority and we will unlock a force of energy and innovation that will be impossible for our national institutions to ignore.

Chapter 9

Helping Me, Helping You

In Chapter 3 we met Edwin Broni-Mensah, who saw doing well for both himself and society not as separate aims but a shared framework to guide his business and personal choices. In doing so Edwin is expressing a principle of mutuality where personal success is only meaningful when it also helps others. Research from Demos found that 70 per cent of fourteen- to seventeen-year-olds aspire to a career that changes the world for the better.[1]

Young people's search for purpose in their work is often seen as further evidence of the over-entitlement of an already over-entitled generation. But imagine what the world would look like if every young person had the opportunity to work for the community, regardless of whether they step each day into a bank or a charity.

Enabling young people to find success through working for the collective good requires nothing less than a restructuring of business and public services around the principle of mutuality. Businesses will have to deliver for the community, not in terms of a Corporate Social Responsibility strategy but within their core purpose. At the same time, public services will have to fulfil their promise and create mutual agendas alongside citizens.

Mutuality in businesses: moving from shareholder value to shared value

As one sixteen-year-old in London put it to me, 'The fact that local businesses don't have a stake in society, other than taking money from these communities, is an issue. I think that's a problem of the society that we live in.'

The clear trend among millennials is that work should be more than just a means to make money; it should also be a place to find fulfilment, enjoyment and give a sense of meaning to their lives. Deloitte found that when considering a potential employer, 32 per cent of the millennial graduates they surveyed worldwide picked 'corporate responsibility and volunteerism' as a key consideration compared with 13 per cent of baby boomers. 63 per cent chose sustainability compared with 35 per cent of baby boomers, and while 55 per cent of millennial graduates chose creating a fun work environment, only 19 per cent of baby boomers felt this was a priority.[2] In a separate survey, Deloitte found that 94 per cent of their UK millennial employees rejected the notion of profit as the only measure of business success.[3] Research conducted by Demos found that 77 per cent of teenagers felt that being happy with the ethical record of their employer was essential.[4]

For many young people, doing what they love and feeling inspired by their work is synonymous with adding value. Rajeeb Dey, of Eternships, says to attract and retain the best talent businesses have to ask, 'What difference is this business making to society?' He says it can't just be about the occasional Corporate Social Responsibility project; it must be integrated into everything they do.

To achieve the kind of meaningful career options young people want, industry and business can't be an afterthought and they can't be the enemy. The public sector will have to work alongside the private sector to redefine a mutual purpose that is aligned with young people.

This is a matter of necessity: levels of public spending are likely to remain low in the near future and the state simply can't afford to deliver our collective aims alone. Even if this wasn't the case the power of global corporations is substantial and the choices they make will be as important as governments'. Young people are well aware of this; they regularly identify big business as a more powerful influence than governments. 42 per cent of young people in the UK 'believe that the things I consume have more power to change things than the people I vote for'.[5]

The power of mutuality is that it is built on a growing and enduring consumer demand to which it is in industry's interest to respond. In it lies the key of long-term, sustainable growth. Any strategy that relies on depleting human or environmental resources can't last for ever and ultimately lets down future generations. A motivated workforce that believes in what they are doing will deliver far more than one that is underpaid, undertrained and underwhelmed. Working with local schools and colleges will help create a workforce for the future. Society needs businesses but businesses also need society.

We already see the green shoots of this with the way young people are pioneering a sharing economy and increasing social entrepreneurship. But we also see the barren waste of the current situation with the numbers of young people who feel disengaged, let down and frustrated by the work options available to them.

Commentators spend a lot of time bemoaning the fact that the young aren't fit for work, but just as problematic is that work is not fit for young people. According to research by Gallup in 2013, only 17 per cent of British workers are engaged with their work while 57 per cent are disengaged and 26 per cent actively disengaged. This leaves us with the highest actively disengaged workforce in Western Europe, joint with France.[6] One hundred billion pounds is lost each year through health-related work absences[7] (often stress-related).[8] This is something that affects

everyone, but young people, sitting at the bottom of the remu-
neration scale, are more affected by it and less willing to put up
with it. It is another instance where the changes they are looking for will improve things for all.

Increasingly, voices from within capitalism are questioning the
short-termism of a strategy that only focuses on shareholder
value, and turning to think about value to society.

In his book *Grow*, Jim Stengel makes the case that the world's
fifty highest-performing companies are those that hold a purpose
beyond profit. 'A brand ideal is a business's essential reason for
being, the higher order benefit it brings to the world. A brand
ideal for improving people's lives is the only sustainable way to
recruit, unite, and inspire all the people a business touches, from
employees to customers. It is the only thing that enduringly connects the core beliefs of the people inside a business with the
fundamental human values of the people the business serves.
Without that connection, without a brand ideal, no business can
truly excel.'[9]

This new thinking is attracting many new labels – conscious
capitalism, impact investing, good business. It draws on the idea
of stakeholder capitalism. They are all pointing towards a vision
of capitalism that values people and the environment and
acknowledges our dependence on each other.

One of the most popular expressions of this is the idea of
shared value expressed by Michael Porter, the Bishop William
Lawrence University Professor at Harvard Business School's
Institute for Strategy and Competitiveness. Here social purpose
is not an offshoot or a periphery concern, but integrated into
every area of a company's work. It goes beyond Corporate Social
Responsibility (CSR) departments and sustainability initiatives
and expresses the powerful case that companies need to make
addressing social need their core business: 'Businesses acting as
businesses, not as charitable donors, are the most powerful force
for addressing the pressing issues we face.'[10]

When young people are starting businesses it is not in the image of those that came before; they are more likely than older generations to have a social purpose. 27 per cent of the young entrepreneurs want to set up social enterprises, 10 per cent want to set up charities and many more want to set up businesses with social value.[11]

Matt Robinson, the twenty-seven-year-old founder of GoCardless, who we met in Chapter 6, told me how his approach to entrepreneurship has changed from seeing money as a metric of success to focusing on his broader purpose. 'Over time, I have gained a richer view of what success is. It is not just building a big company it's actually building something that helps a lot of people for the better. And then on the flip side it's building a place that people can go and do great work.'

He believes that he and his young co-founders are breaking this culture with a focus on ethics. 'If a decision comes up for me, my compass is what do I think is right? We have turned away big clients because we don't think we're the right fit for them, or told customers about mistakes which they would never have spotted because it's the right thing to do. If we have to make a hard decision we will, because we believe there is more to success than the bottom line.'

One powerful way companies can provide shared value is through providing opportunities to young people and by doing so answering the challenge put forward by Natalie Robinson: 'What happens when older people retire? There will be no one to replace them because younger people have no experience; they haven't been given the chance. Businesses need to get behind young people.'

The unemployment, underemployment and poor employment options we saw in Chapter 1 waste a vital resource not just for young people but also for business.

As Sam Conniff, director of youth marketing agency Livity,

puts it, 'We are systematically wasting one of the most powerful, one of the most important, one of the most precious natural resources at our disposal, because every single day, we systemise the failure and deny the opportunity that we have within all of our young people. And instead of being distracted by the debate around deficits and cuts, which on their own will not get us out of this mess, I think we need to invest our time and energies into empowering the opportunity for creative, social and economic power that we have within our young people.'

Sam is angry because every day he sees young people who have been written off flourishing and contributing with the support Livity offers. One of those young people described Livity as 'a transformation engine' and Sam's challenge echoes Natalie's: What if every business was a transformation engine for the young?

Livity is housed in an open-plan office close to Brixton but it is unlike any office I have ever been to. As one visitor observed, it is more like a youth club than a marketing agency. Young people are everywhere, eating in the open-plan dining area, busy at computers, chatting in groups. The young people I speak to are passionate about the work they are doing as journalists for *Live*, Livity's youth magazine, or on Livity's various campaigns.

In one room a group of young men are being trained in digital marketing. It turns out they are all ex-offenders, part of a pilot project with Google to try to turn their social media skills into something they can sell in the marketplace through a digital marketing agency. Later I learnt that none of those young people had re-offended.

Their unique model is an open-door policy where young people can literally walk in and be given real work, mentoring, support and advice.

It is a business that looks like a charity and feels like a charity because its founding vision is a deep social purpose. But Livity isn't a charity. From the start Sam and his co-founder wanted to prove that they could be commercially successful working with young people. Their approach is paying off. They won 'Best Agency' at the 2013 Marketing Agencies Association awards. Their list of clients includes NSPCC, Big Lottery, Penguin, Barclays, Channel 4 and Google.

Their staff don't have to have a separate CSR strategy because they streamline their community support into everything they do; all staff members are also mentors. From May to December 2012, Livity employees spent 586 hours mentoring young people – excluding those in a full-time mentoring role. As a result their staff are highly motivated and 95 per cent say they are proud to work there.[12]

The formula isn't rocket science – an open door, tailored support and rewarding work – but for the young people Livity work with the effect is life-changing. Sam has so many stories of young people who walked in as one person and left as another. Shanize came in at fourteen having been expelled from every school she went to. She sat in silence for weeks. Through Livity's support she went on to be an Olympic torch-bearer, become Lambeth's Deputy Mayor and develop into the young person every client wanted in their meetings. When Sam asked her what the turning point was, her answer was simple: 'Someone believed in me.' I met many young people who had been mentored by Livity and they all talk about it as a transformative period that unlocked confidence they never knew they had.

When companies open their doors to young people from diverse backgrounds they find they gain as much if not more than the young people do. Creative Access is a scheme whose aim is to challenge the majority–white nature of the creative industries. The 2013 Employment Census published by Skillset showed that ethnic minority representation made up just 5.4 per cent of the workforce,[13] in spite of the fact that the majority are based in London, a city where 40 per cent of the population are non-white. They set up year-long paid internships at some of Britain's foremost creative industries, including my own publisher Little, Brown.

Nicola Howson at Freud Communication told me that initially they took part in the programme to do some good but she found that the Creative Access interns brought totally different perspectives, new ideas and references that led to more creative campaigns. One of the interns described the light-bulb moment for her: a room of executives at her publishing house were discussing their web strategy and someone asked what Instagram was; suddenly she realised she knew more than them.

Turning mutuality into a mainstream agenda

Achieving this kind of shared value requires businesses to recognise that this is an important agenda, and this is already happening. The evidence of Jim Stengel and others is making explicit the link between social purpose and long-term success. Richard Branson and Jochen Zeitz have founded Plan B, which brings together a group of business leaders across different sectors to make the case that Plan A – where companies focus on profits alone – has failed. They are calling for 'Plan B', where the purpose of businesses is to be 'a driving force for social, environmental and economic benefit'.

Secondly, it requires concrete reforms for companies to create and measure a shared value strategy. Plan B are promoting 'True Accounting', where the full costs of business, including social, environmental, human and financial costs, are accounted for. They are looking at new structures to promote transparency, remove perverse incentives, share profits and reward sustainable practice. PepsiCo's 'Performance with Purpose' ethos mean staff are given Key Performance Indicators relating to the purpose agenda.

Finally, it requires investors and shareholders to view this as important. Here again measurement and evidence are key. Puma have created an 'environmental P & L', which adds notional costs from their environmental impact.[14] In their report 'Measuring Shared Value', social-impact consulting firm FSG estimate that despite increasing rhetoric about the importance of social impact only 10 per cent of global investments are selected on the basis of environmental, social and governance performance.[15] They argue that shared value measurements that integrate social and business value take measurement out of CSR units and into business ones, with the opportunity to start a new dialogue with investors.

While there are promising signs, creating value for society is too often still used as a differentiator for brands. It will only be transformative when it becomes the norm, and there is a long way to go.

Business can be and is part of the solution, but it is naïve to think that this reform from within is the whole answer. Some companies are less public-facing than others; the demands of shareholders can still outweigh stakeholders.

This is something that we have to build together, through citizens, civil society and the state.

A mutual agenda across businesses and government

Government at a local, national and global level has a responsibility to set a framework that encourages companies to contribute to society and rewards those that do. They have a crucial role in identifying need, brokering partnerships and setting agendas around social purpose. They can also celebrate and promote best practice.

Nationally, they can demand transparency around issues such as pay differentials and taxation. A 2013 report of the House of Lords Select Committee on Economic Affairs suggested that transparency can help combat tax avoidance by multinational corporations by requiring companies with large operations in the UK to publish a proforma summary of their corporation tax returns.[16] Measures to promote transparency reward companies that do the right thing on issues such as corporation tax and expose those that don't.

They can also use their regulatory power to push businesses to address social and environmental concerns. Michael Porter, a professor at Harvard Business School, suggests that a regulatory framework should be based on clear and measurable social outcomes that stimulate innovation rather than prescribing a blanket method. In short, a focus on ends not means. In the future government can work with businesses to design a measurement and tax regime that favours businesses that incorporate social and environmental costs.

Local and national government can use their commissioning powers to choose organisations that pay the living wage, employ apprentices and give staff a stake in their ownership. European public procurement budgets 'make up 17 per cent of GDP' so this budget has substantial weight in pushing change.[17] Businesses can also use their procurement process and supply chain to create shared value.

Local councils can also do a lot through their planning system. Camden Council's relationship with the Francis Crick Institute, the largest medical research centre in Europe, started with a challenging Section 106 agreement (a legal agreement that puts certain obligations on a developer as a condition to approving their planning permission). Francis Crick are now building on this with science buskers at public events, a teaching laboratory for local schools and a satellite laboratory in a nearby secondary school, lectures for teachers, taster sessions for students, work experience, mentoring, forty construction apprentices and further apprentices on completion, a living centre to promote healthy lifestyles and community grants. Through strong planning policies this development is not just a building young people pass but something that is part of their lives.

Local government can set a shared agenda that identifies opportunities for businesses to help solve social problems. For example they can help in the development of research clusters linked to universities.

They can also help facilitate the relationship between employers and young people. The 2014 CBI survey found that 52 per cent of businesses are not satisfied with school leavers' communication skills, 50 per cent with their problem solving skills and 38 per cent their basic numeracy. Careers advice is seen as not fit for purpose by the majority.[18]

While 80 per cent of businesses surveyed had some links to schools, this can be time-consuming and sporadic. Local government can help facilitate strategic relationships that reduce the burden for individual schools and businesses.

A shared agenda could include:

- Educating young people about work – facilitating businesses being part of discussions about curriculum, contributing to careers advice, setting challenges, speed networking, encouraging employers to be mentors, publishing advice, linking with colleges around vacancies, mentoring start-ups or even developing an accelerator to incubate new start-up companies as Telefonica has done. The best projects are those that offer young people opportunities to contribute their ideas and engage with real business challenges. I would like to see reverse mentoring schemes where young people impart their knowledge of social media trends in return for careers advice.
- Offering young people opportunities – quality work experience placements when they are at school,

paid internships after school, training and
apprenticeship schemes for young people to gain
experience and, of course, good-quality jobs that pay
the living wage.

- Recruitment based on mutuality – job hunting is often
  a highly depressing experience for young people of all
  backgrounds. According to the Prince's Trust 36 per
  cent of young people have never heard back from a job
  application despite often sending hundreds, their
  confidence draining away the longer they wait. No one
  should have to wait for answers that never come,
  wondering what is wrong with them. An automatic
  response with a sense of the scale of applicants and
  some links to help them continue to search is better
  than nothing. Better still would be to change
  recruitment so it adds mutual value for job hunters and
  potential employers. Rajeeb Dey at Enternships is
  developing a learning-based approach to recruitment
  that incorporates learning and the development of
  candidates as part of the selection process. Everyone is
  better off, the unsuccessful candidates have gained new
  skills and the business wins new advocates. It also helps
  with diversity because there is less focus on CVs and
  more on how applicants can respond to challenges.

Local government can bring together a network of businesses
that can lead a transformative community agenda helping young
people but also building up a future workforce.

In Camden, a partnership between the council and Camden
Town Unlimited (Camden's Business Improvement District) won
Best Programme of Support for Small Businesses at the
Federation of Small Business and London Councils Small
Business Friendly Awards. The programme transformed derelict
commercial space into free desk space for creative start-ups and

provided a fellowship programme to support young people into work. As a result more than 120 creative businesses have been helped, creating over fifty jobs and supporting young people into self-employment. Walking down the street from my flat, I now pass four Camden Collective shops where vacant shops are used as pop-up spaces for creative start-ups, which have created twenty new jobs and over a hundred work experience placements for young people.

These very local solutions can unlock a huge amount of shared value. However, action can't just be taken at a local or state level. Corporations are global and so are the challenges, so governments have to work together to provide regulation and avoid a race to the bottom across national boundaries, where countries compete over investment through lower pay and fewer regulations. The UN Global Compact works with over twelve thousand corporations from over 145 countries who have voluntarily come together to try to find universal principles on issues of human rights, labour, corruption and the environment.

It can't be done by simply painting business as the enemy. It has to be by celebrating and working with responsible businesses and supporting their efforts through the mechanisms of the state and our power as consumers. At the same time we must all come together to demand change from those that do not meet these standards.

What can civil society do to encourage business to embrace mutuality?

NGOs and community groups can make an active contribution to a mutual agenda by brokering or facilitating relationships with business. They also have a role in celebrating good practice; badges from UK Citizens such as 'City Safe' or 'Living wage' employers create incentives for businesses too.

At the same time they have an important role to play in putting pressure on organisations that do not meet ethical standards. They can proactively mobilise young people to press home demands over pay, environment and employment globally and locally. London's living wage campaign is one successful example, as is the unpaid internship campaign. DoSomething.org actively supporting young people to take campaigning action and connects them with a global network of over two million young people committed to social change.

There are opportunities to empower consumer activism through online campaigns. Apps like 'Boycott' allow you to scan a product and find out not just where it was made but the kind of political campaigns the producer supports. Young people in the UK see the potential of their collective power as citizens; the majority think the young empowered by social media can be more powerful than politics and business.[19] Brie, UK Director at Change.org, tells me that companies are often ahead of politicians in seeing the digital space as a huge platform on which to engage with consumers. Her experience has been that they are very responsive to campaigns on Change.org and those who aren't 'are left looking very much on the back foot and having to reclaim their branding as a result'.

It is important to be cautious here. Stated ambitions for ethical consumerism don't always translate into action. This is a generation struggling with debt, unemployment and high housing costs, so price is also a huge driver.

It is still a small group of young people who are actively engaging in consumer activism such as organising boycotts, setting up and signing petitions, and changing the way they consume can have a disproportionate impact. But a small group, even an individual leading a campaign, can start to change the conversation and impact on a brand's image. Take McKenna Pope, whose Change.org petition asking Hasbro to produce a gender-neutral Easy-Bake Oven for her little brother garnered forty-five thousand signatures, worldwide attention and a new line of silver and black Easy-Bake Ovens.[20]

Issues that are the lived experience of the young can and will engage them if put across in the right way. These campaigns help businesses to link to communities and to recognise what is important to them.

The role of trade unions

Trade unionism, as we saw in Chapter 1, is an increasingly marginal force in young people's lives. In 2013 just 3 per cent of sixteen- to nineteen-year-olds and 9.5 per cent of twenty- to twenty-four-year-olds were members of trade unions.[21] However, if we are looking to create a mutual agenda across employees and employers then there is an important role for representing and coordinating the demands of young workers.

A mutual agenda for unions could see them work with employers to provide opportunities for training, networking, representation and empowerment, creating a more skilled and motivated workforce. It would also help them to re-engage with a generation who prefer a collaborative approach to an oppositional one.

I remember standing outside St Pancras station for a rally a couple of years ago and listening to leaders give loud impassioned speeches rich with the language of history and class identity. The audience was a tiny group of cold and beleaguered older Labour activists, but I could close my eyes and imagine myself in a thousand-strong crowd in 1900, and maybe that appeals to my sense of history and nostalgia. But this is never going to appeal to the majority of young people, and it lets them down because they desperately need representation. The truth is many young people are put off by appeals to traditional collective identities and class warfare. As a research report from Unions 21, a think tank focused on unionism, acknowledged when reflecting on focus groups into lack of youth member-ship, 'Unions being seen as militant, old fashioned, bureaucratic and aggressive, turns young people off.'[22] Many young people weren't able to articulate how union membership could bene-fit them.

Usdaw is one union that has been rethinking its approach to young people. A successful negotiation with Tesco over youth rates helped them kick-start a youth membership drive, led by young people. They have also looked at how they can facilitate and cham-pion life-long learning, establishing fifty-three on-site learning centres in partnership with employers, training 800 union reps to promote educational opportunities, signing provider partnerships with colleges and setting up joint company and union funds to give people the necessary financial support to continue learning.[23] This kind of thinking embeds the principle of mutuality, it serves those taking up the opportunities, it helps create more motivated and skilled employees and it drives up trade union membership.

I think there is space for unions to change the way they work, but also for new unions to come up that champion young people's needs.

They can do more to represent the unemployed and link them in to training opportunities, and by doing so support the indi-vidual through an insecure labour market. Growing numbers of young self-employed workers, entrepreneurs and young people moving in and out of work mean that there is a role for unions to provide support services for those seeking to build their own careers, as well as access to life-long learning.

Public services need to live up to the promise of mutuality

The entire purpose of public services is social benefit, so the expression of mutuality should be explicit and powerful. The providers of a service and the recipients should feel they are working together for a social good whether that is health, employment, education or cleaner streets.

However, this is not always the case. Young people using services such as the job centre can feel like their needs or opinions aren't taken into account. They can end up as passive recipients rather than partners. It can fuel the sense of dependency that we saw in Chapter 3. This is problematic for all users but it is particularly problematic for a generation who value autonomy and empowerment as much as this one.

Likewise staff in the public sector can end up feeling disengaged from the core public service ethos, and overburdened with bureaucracy and targets that reduce their capacity for innovation. The private sector doesn't have the monopoly on disengaged workers. A PwC report showed that only 30 per cent of public service workers were engaged, the lowest of all employees engaged.[24] Public services can become their own vested interest and removed from the needs of users.

Service provision should not be a paternalistic state taking care of passive citizens but a partnership between empowered citizens and responsive services. At a very human level this can come down to a relationship between two people, be it doctor and patient or job centre adviser and job seeker. The relationship will have to include challenge, but based on a real understanding of that person, their motivations and the support they need. Young people's engagement in particular relies on their being treated as active partners, and we must avoid a two-tier system where adults are given autonomy and the young are simply directed. Cooperative structures can be a powerful tool to unlock mutuality for service users and staff.[25] It is hard to ignore the demands of anyone who is a partner in running a service.

Cooperative councils are a growing movement seeking to embed a cooperative approach into local services. Lambeth Council was a pioneer of this, and a practical example is the creation of the 'Young Lambeth Cooperative', owned by young people and the community. Rather than budgets set by the council, the available money for young people has been pooled, with each area being offered professional support to analyse their needs and choose the interventions they want from youth clubs through to extra employment support, whether it is youth activities, employment activities or peer mentoring schemes. With a potential budget of nine million pounds over three years, this is real power handed down to young people and communities.[26]

Mutuality doesn't necessarily require new structures, it just needs a culture focused on sharing power and putting people first. In Chapter 11 I look at how this can help guide devolution so that it means more power in the hands of citizens rather than just government.

A mutual agenda for the future

The potential of this new world is a diverse set of structures all operating collaboratively around a shared agenda and purpose; social enterprises, shared-value businesses, public service mutuals and state-run services.

This is a change of approach because it removes the thinking about private sector as bad and state as good. It might be simple and clear but it isn't going to transform the world. We can no longer afford to devolve responsibility for solving society's problems to government or charities. The only way we can achieve the kind of society we want today is with businesses committed to a broader purpose. They can and have to be transformative agents of change.

Mutuality can help bind together diverse individual interests around issues of shared concern. We can start to see the potential of mutuality as a means to re-form a multi-faceted social contract between individuals, state institutions, public services and industry.

The important question to ask of each part is not what their structure is but whether they are delivering positive outcomes for society. Fairness can be a guiding principle in defining these outcomes and a check to ensure that nobody is left behind.

Chapter 10

What's Fair?

A belief in fairness is inherent to the human condition. Scientific experiments show that people will forgo individual reward in the pursuit of fair outcomes.[1] Fairness can be conceived in different ways by different ideological traditions, but the view of fairness that has most mainstream support is one based on reciprocal exchange. It was the basis of the post-war welfare state where those who worked hard would be insured against bad luck.

Today this relationship has broken down, and as we have seen throughout this book, our society fails the test of fairness for young people.

First, the circumstances of your birth and early years have a disproportionate impact on your life chances. This is deeply unfair as no infant can be held responsible for the nurture they receive.

Secondly, employment opportunities are a lottery of where you were brought up and can afford to live. Too many young people who want to work are finding it difficult to get into the workforce and make a contribution through paid work. Many more are working but struggling to make ends meet.

Thirdly, housing assets are increasingly held by older generations and young people are struggling to get on the housing ladder. Too often the access to home ownership and security increasingly depends on how far parents are able to support their children.

The unfairness many young people are facing is an issue for everyone because a generation that has not been treated fairly will not have the same sense of obligation to those who came before or after. Young people today will be asked over their lifetimes to fund the care of an ageing population and generous pensions the likes of which they will never see.

Addressing this unfairness requires investment, but we are living in a time of constrained public spending. It will mean we have to find the resources to pay for it. This must come from asking the private sector to do more, as we will see with proposals around rent regulation and wages. The second avenue is to end ring-fencing of universal elderly people's services. Finally we can look at more redistributive taxes, especially around inheritance tax.

It is not just that we need to invest in young people, we need to invest more in the young people who are being left behind. This case needs to be made not just to older generations but to young people themselves. As we saw in Chapter 2, some young people have given up on the welfare state's ability to deliver and taken refuge in a put-yourself-first form of individualism.

While there are young activists campaigning for a different distribution of economic power, at the moment they tend to be at the margins rather than in the mainstream. Many young people facing poverty end up feeling that there is something wrong with them, that their failure to get on is an individual one. The majority don't have access to democratic forums where they can explore these questions and find collective solutions, so the idea that success or failure is down to the individual rather than the structure of our society dominates.

However, this doesn't tell the whole story. As we saw in Chapter 3, the majority of young people don't support redistribution by the state, but they are concerned about levels of inequality. They may not invest pride in the idea of a welfare state, which they associate with a 'benefits culture', but there is strong support for universal services like the NHS.

When you dig down into young people's deeper views and
personal stories, there is much more compassion and empathy
than the hard numbers might suggest. As I showed in Chapter 3,
what they are against is the idea that some people are free-riding
off others' hard work, that some people make a choice to be idle
rather than take on a job. This is felt most deeply by those stuck
in jobs they hate with low pay and poor progression routes.
Through that lens the idea of paying taxes to support someone
else's leisure provokes enormous anger. The only way to build a
coalition for more redistributive policies is through winning the
argument on fairness in the welfare state. It has to feel like a welfare state that is set up to support young people's aspirations, and
to do this it must include an element of reciprocity and it must
provide young people with autonomy.

First reciprocity: when we look to design a modern vision of
a welfare state that young people will buy into, it has to be one
that recognises and rewards contribution. There are many ways we
could do this. Demos propose a two-tier system for job seekers in
which those with a strong contribution record would be entitled
to more during periods of unemployment.[2] Volunteering and
social contribution could be recognised in housing allocations or
discounts for services. Young people who have been helped into
work or by a service should be expected to volunteer to help
others. Time-banking schemes and local currencies can reward the
efforts of volunteers. In Chapter 8 I proposed a stipend for a year
of service for young adults across different areas of care, schools
and the environment.

At the other end of the society it is important to be clear that
young people don't support wealth accumulation at all costs.
They are receptive to the idea of entrepreneurs who have worked
hard and created tangible value keeping the fruits of their labour.
They are less sanguine about vast inherited wealth. When looking to design redistributive taxes we can start to target those that
are unproductive, rent-seeking and unearnt.

The second is that this welfare state supports individual autonomy. Young people will support state spending where it rewards
those who are trying to get on, such as the education maintenance allowance for young people to stay on at school. They
want the state to get behind individuals, whether it is around
employment, housing or education. They want concrete help in
meeting their aspirations and a sense that making the right
choices will be rewarded.

What has and hasn't been done?

Political parties have a mixed record in addressing the unfairness
faced by young people. In the lifetime of the people I focus on
in this book, the Labour government of 1997 came in with a
commitment to address social exclusion, to lift families out of
poverty and to improve public services.

They had a great deal of success. Sure Start centres were a
landmark policy to provide early-years support to families living
in poverty, and 2200 were created across Britain. Women were
helped into work through free childcare places for three- and
four-year-olds. Child benefit went up by 26 per cent. A new
minimum wage and the introduction of working tax credits protected low earners from stagnating wages, encouraged work and
were highly redistributive. The New Deal for the unemployed
put resources and support into job creation, helping 1.8 million
into work. Huge investment went into the NHS, creating new
hospitals, reducing waiting times, increasing staff numbers and
producing the highest-ever satisfaction rates. Social housing stock
was improved through a £40 billion investment programme. Six
hundred thousand children were lifted out of poverty. When
Labour came to power in 1997, education spending was at a historic low; it rose by 78 per cent from 1997 to 2010. By 2009/10,
80 per cent of primary-school-age pupils were achieving Level 4
in English and in maths, compared with 63 per cent in English

and 62 per cent in maths in 1996/7; and 76 per cent of sixteen-year-olds were achieving five A★ to C grades at GCSE, compared with 45 per cent in 1997.[3] University enrolment went up and crime down.

We hear a narrative of Labour overspending and waste, but without that money the problems I am describing in this book would have been far deeper. The social problems they inherited were immense. House building had stalled, public services were chronically underfunded, concentrated poverty and unemployment had created entrenched social problems across large parts of the UK. They had to do more just to stall rising levels of inequality.

There were failures under the last Labour government too. Too much power stayed in the centre, not enough focus went into house building, they didn't do enough to reform the welfare system to meet the needs of a modern economy and they didn't do enough to tackle market failures. Youth unemployment was steadily growing in the latter years of the Labour government and not enough was done to tackle this.

The coalition government came to power at a different time and with fewer resources. However, they also have less of a drive to focus on some of these areas, with some notable exceptions. In education, pupil premium (additional funding provided to publicly funded English schools to raise the attainment of disadvantaged pupils) ensures that money is pointed towards the least advantaged and a focus on the progress of all pupils by tracking their performance against previous results reminds schools not to ignore children at the bottom. They have introduced a new legal duty on local authorities to provide fifteen hours of early education for disadvantaged two-year-olds. Raising the participation age to eighteen for education, training or work and making schools accountable through Ofsted for progressions gives a greater incentive to support young people on their next step. The National Citizen Service introduced by the coalition puts money towards young people's service in the community, as explored in Chapter 8. Where they have been successful the Labour Party should offer support and continuity.

However, the general direction of spending is eating away at the support available for children and young people. The drastic cuts passed on to local authorities (The National Audit Office estimate that by 2016 they will have received a real-terms cut of 36 per cent compared with 2010), particularly the end to ring-fenced early-years support, mean around the country youth centres and children's centres are closing. At the same time progressive polices like the education maintenance allowance have been cut. As I showed in Chapter 2, young people, especially disadvantaged young people, have lost out in budgeting cuts. Since 2012 more than forty-one thousand youth service places have been cut, thirty-five thousand hours of outreach work by youth workers has been removed and 350 youth centres have been closed. Since 2010 spending on youth services has gone down by £259 million.[4] These are discretionary services to non-voters and so they end up being the first to go.

At the same time many families are seeing a triple blow – loss to their personal income through benefits squeezes, loss of support services from local authorities and a reduction in the voluntary sector traditionally funded by local authorities.

The deep injustice is that young people are paying the price for something they did nothing to cause. A failure of the market has somehow been turned into a failure of the state. A squeeze on state spending has disproportionately hit the non-voting young. There is nothing fair or just in this.

If government failed it was to properly regulate the financial markets and rebalance the economy, not to spend money on disadvantaged children. A debate about the economy has been skilfully turned into a debate about 'scroungers', a group that take up a tiny proportion of wealth in this country. And this proportion pales into insignificance when compared with the money that was spent bailing out banks that had lost their sense of accountability while making enormous profits for themselves.

This doesn't mean signing a blank cheque. We have to be radical in how we reform our services, manage waste and assess the impact of spending so the money we spend shows real outcomes. We have to utilise every partnership and squeeze every efficiency out of the support we give families. We have to make it clear we stand with businesses that create shared value as we saw in Chapter 8. We have to stand with banks willing to invest in growth, incentivise responsible behaviour and manage risk.

However, the test of fairness can't just be applied to the poor, it has to be applied to the wealthy. We need to be tough on banks that refuse to de-leverage, businesses that create social and environmental harm, wealth that is unproductive and unearnt. We have to demand pay ratios that are proportionate and linked to productivity.

As we saw in Chapter 9, young people want to see businesses do more. They believe they have responsibilities on pay, employment and the environment. The idea of pre-distribution coined by Yale professor Jacob Hacker, which looks to prevent market failures happening in the first place rather than through the tax system, has the potential to connect to this generation.[5]

Young people are not going to rally behind the idea of a free market if a proposal for regulation has tangible benefits for people like them. If these views seem contradictory in traditional ideological terms it is because they are not operating from an ideological stance, or making conscious choices about what is left or right. They are asking what seems fair; what helps us?

The test of fairness can be applied to any policy area, but here I focus on the four areas that make up the basis of a new social contract with young people – children, education, employment and housing.

We saw in Chapters 8 and 9 that in order to deliver on our collective aspirations citizens will have to take on more responsibilities as partners of an enabling state. This will require new rights, especially if we want every young person to have the opportunity to actively engage in democratic life. First, the right to self-determination through investment in early years and childhood development. Secondly, the right to an education that gives them not just a qualification but nurtures their curiosity and creativity, develops their sense of purpose and treats every child as capable of living an entrepreneurial life. Thirdly, access to a means of making a living through work, whether that is service, enterprise or paid work, and life-long support for learning that allows them to respond to a changing world. Finally, access to secure and adequate housing.

A fair children's policy

The greatest unfairness in this country is how far the wealth of your parents determines your life chances. To challenge this we need to direct more of our country's resources to young people growing up in poverty.

If we don't we will pick up the costs for allowing young people to experience all the insecurity and chaos that often accompany poverty later on. We will feel it in our welfare system, our unemployment figures and most tragically of all our criminal justice system.[6]

We need comprehensive investment in early years with particular focus on the first three years of a child's life. In areas of poverty we need to take a cradle-to-career approach that supports families from the very beginning.

As I show in Chapter 7, effort needs to be put into building relationships with parents to help them build up their own resilience and agency in supporting their children. It requires services at a local level to work together to support parents from pregnancy onwards.[7] This has to be done without stigma and by people that parents trust. It is important that parents have information about health, nutrition, attachment and early learning, but professionals must earn the right to be heard, which requires investment in relationships. Once a successful relationship is established it is possible to build a support plan based on a family's need, whether it is mental health support or housing advice.

There needs to be robust tracking of families and young children to ensure they are getting the early intervention they need. If they aren't followed up with support, the good investment in early years can be lost by the age of thirteen. There need to be protocols for sharing data across educational institutions and linked up local services, as we saw in Chapter 7.

Early intervention not only promotes fairness, it also makes good economic sense. Evidence from controlled trials in the US shows that quality early-years interventions save money in the long term, with 'rates of return ranging from $1.26 to $17.92 for every $1 invested'.[8] In the UK, social investment studies show a rate of return of £1.37 and £9.20 for every pound invested. The Early Intervention Foundation provides a list of different interventions and their cost-effectiveness for the taxpayer.[9]

Investment in early years is the best investment we can make as a society because it will be felt not just in savings for the taxpayer but stronger families, communities and economy.

A fair education policy

Young people deserve an education that pays attention to how they flourish as human beings. The mission for our education system has to be not just turning out good employees but turning out purposeful citizens with a love of learning and the confidence to lead full, creative lives. The character development of young people can't be an afterthought when the important work of qualifications and employability is finished, but the driving purpose of our education system. This isn't about replacing academic learning but passing on to young people a curiosity for knowledge and the confidence to take responsibility for their own development that will stay with them for life.

It is the right thing to do, and it also equips young people for a world where they will increasingly need to create their own opportunities.[10] As Reid Hoffman and Ben Casnocha argue in *The Start-up of You*, 'What's required now is an entrepreneurial mindset. Whether you work for a ten-person company, a giant multinational corporation, a not-for-profit, a government agency, or any type of organisation in between – if you want to seize the new opportunities and meet the challenges of today's fractured career landscapes, you need to think and act like you're running a start-up: your career.'[11]

To develop entrepreneurial, purposeful, creative young citizens schools need to embody the values they are trying to pass on. Teachers that love learning, who are entrepreneurial in how they teach and who go out of their way to empower and support students and work collaboratively together. At its most successful, a school will be a hub for the collective ambitions of teachers, parents and young people themselves.

To achieve this vision for every child the following has to happen:

- High expectations – as we saw in Chapter 5, the starting point is schools with high expectations of all their pupils. This requires careful tracking of the progress of all pupils and interventions where they aren't achieving. These are expectations for achievement and also their social and emotional development. Leadership is critical in setting a culture of high expectations. As a school governor for the past six years the big lesson I have learnt is that the most important decision in any school is putting in place motivated, values-driven leaders who are able to inspire and motivate staff, pupils and parents.

- Commitment to pupil voice, personal empowerment and character development – Finland has one of the most successful education systems in the world and explicitly prioritises this: 'The objective is to increase pupils' curiosity and motivation to learn and to promote their activeness, self-direction and creativity by offering interesting challenges and problems. The learning environment must guide pupils in setting their own objectives and evaluating their own actions. The pupils must be given the chance to participate in the creation and development of their own learning environment.'[12] Singapore, another highly successful education system, has just introduced a new curriculum for 'character and citizenship education'. As I show in Chapter 8, this starts in the classroom with students supported to set their own learning goals and develop mastery over individualised tasks. It goes out to the community with schools partnering with the youth sector to encourage service learning. Young people should be supported to become vocal, active citizens working within their communities.

- Focus on professional development and quality teaching – we must value teaching as a profession by insisting that those who teach in our schools are qualified to do so.[13] The world's best education systems invest heavily in the professional development of teachers.[14] Good classroom teaching is the most important determinant of young people's learning and the more teachers are supported with access to the best evidence, safe forums to experiment, peer-to-peer feedback and development opportunities, the better the experience for pupils.

- Collaborative networks – schools should not be in competition with each other but existing within supportive networks.[15] In Camden we think of our schools as a 'family of schools', where each individual part is committed to the success of the whole. This is tangibly felt in professional development across schools, with head teachers giving up their time to give feedback to peers. Collaboration is most important within the transitions between primary and secondary school, when the gaps widen for many young people from disadvantaged homes. More schools that combine primary and secondary will help, but so will strong links where data is shared, and secondary teachers visiting primary schools to teach shared lessons. Underpinning local collaboration has to be fair admissions. We saw in Chapter 5 that some schools have intakes of middle-class children disproportionate to their location. Schools should be given autonomy in how they develop their school curriculum and management, but this should be underpinned by an admissions policy that guarantees fairness. The temptation would be too great for schools setting their own admissions to choose pupils that are easier to teach. The basis of a comprehensive education system is integration and equality, and local authorities are the best place to safeguard this. Finally collaboration has to include private schools delivering on their charitable status by opening up their facilities and their places to children from poor backgrounds.

- Community and parental links – parental engagement is key to young people's success at school. Schools need to make efforts to reach out to parents where they are. I met one deputy head who regularly spoke at the local mosque to try to reassure parents about school trips and university opportunities. They also have to make sure schools are welcoming environments; a school I visited had worked to turn parents' evenings into socials with separate one-to-one meetings to discuss pupil progress. A pilot project I set up in Camden takes a community approach to lifting the white working-class achievement gap we saw in Chapter 5. Dedicated workers build relationships with parents in communities and give them the knowledge and support they need to confidently engage with schools. Parents are now leading a fortnightly book club, turning up to forums previously dominated by middle-class parents and changing school policies.

- Making digital skills a priority – as we saw in Chapter 6, many young people lack the skills to find empowerment online. Much is being done; the old ICT GCSE has been replaced by a new Computing qualification with a strong programming element, and this has been included as a science in its own right on the E-Bacc, equivalent to Physics or Chemistry. There are resources going into promoting coding as a hobby from after-school Code Clubs through to Young Rewired State hack days. However, fully embedding this in our education system requires a major cultural shift. There is still a dearth of qualified teachers. All adults working with young people need to see computing skills as core skills alongside numeracy and literacy. Finally schools need dynamic policies to keep up with how young people are interacting online.

- Links to business – schools need to give young people the advice, skills, experience and networks to prepare for work. This means nurturing links with business, as we saw in the last chapter. It also requires meaningful work experience opportunities – I met one young woman desperate to be a vet who ended up making tea in a beauty salon. It also requires a focus on enterprise education and opportunities to engage in the kind of active learning that young people want. Further education colleges should be hubs of quality vocational provision, linked to business needs and providing courses respected by industry.

- Strong accountability – we need to end the obsession with school structures. All schools should have the autonomy to develop solutions to the specific challenges facing their pupils, but this has to be in the context of strong accountability measures. Every school can't be directly accountable to the Department for Education – it is unsustainable – so there needs to be a strong middle tier of accountability. In the first instance, this should be local authorities, or failing that a school's commissioner.

The London challenge, which helped to drastically drive up standards through a combination of many of these shows the power of a collaborative approach.[16]

A fair employment policy

I have shown throughout this book that young people want to work yet hundreds of thousands still face unemployment. This is a long-term structural issue that needs addressing. In 1993, young people were twice as likely to be unemployed as adults, a differential that rose to over four times as likely by 2005.[17]

We know that everyone loses when young people are out of work. Young men and women lose the skills, confidence and quality of life that work provides. They are also more likely to be anxious and depressed. Those out of work when they are young will end up spending an average of two extra months a year without a job and earn £1800 to £3300 less per annum by their early thirties.[18] In addition, government loses their young people's

contribution to the tax system and parents end up having to support their children for longer. Pensioners and future pensioners
need the next generation to be productive workers to support
them in old age. Local businesses lose the extra revenue from
young spenders without family commitments.

1. Create better jobs

The answer to much of this is to create better jobs. Firstly
encouraging entrepreneurship – this means providing young
people with the infrastructure support – office space, adminis-
trative, legal or mentoring support – they need to start businesses.
It also means personal grants that give them the opportunity to
pursue an enterprise.

Secondly, supporting growth in high-value manufacturing
through the kind of local-driven growth agendas I explore in
Chapter 11. Thirdly, turning poor jobs into good ones – there is
no reason that care work, for example, should be poorly paid and
valued in our society. The kind of meaningful care that prevents
loneliness in old age or transforms young lives can never be per-
formed by a robot. As an ageing population we will need adult
social care workers and as women cement their place in the
labour market we will need childcare workers. Current projections suggest that the social care workforce could expand by as
much as 50 to 80 per cent by 2025, adding between 638,000 and
one million extra jobs.[19] It is largely un-unionised. It is zero-hour
contracts, poor pay and insecure employment. This could be
something we choose to properly remunerate and value. We
could end the poor employment practices in the sector, such as
zero-hour contracts. We could teach young people compassion
and we could introduce higher wages.

Fourthly, creating jobs in the green economy. In the United
States Green Jobs For All was set up to find a mutual agenda for
jobs, the environment and the economy. In 2009 'Clean Energy

Works' was born, a home energy-retrofitting programme designed to create growth and jobs while reducing carbon emissions. RecycleForce, also in America, is a social enterprise that recycles corporate and household waste. They use the profits from metal and other reusable material to help pay for training and employment opportunities for ex-offenders.

Finally, the IT professional workforce is predicted to grow by double the rate of average employment over the next decade.[20] Addressing the digital skills issue can turn new digital jobs into jobs for young people.

2. Tailored careers support

Too often young people describe the experience of unemployment as depressing and dehumanising. One young man in Bradford put it, 'There isn't a system to support you. Once you're on Job Seekers that's it: you're claiming it. You go in there, they ask you if you've applied for jobs. You say, yeah I've done five because the minimum you have to apply for is five – you can make any five up. You just write it down. They don't check your information, they're just happy with that.' He is looking for more from the systems supposedly designed to help. 'The Job Centre should do one-to-ones with you, bring you in more than to sign a piece of paper once every two weeks. They should sit down with you for an hour, help you apply, ring around places.' The Job Centre is trying to respond to this with more support for young job seekers and there is evidence this is working. However there is still a long way to go to give young people the kind of support they need. The current set-up has different systems working often in parallel without central coordination because of the lack of local authority powers.

It's not the fault of the Job Centre staff. They are overworked and oversubscribed. As the academic Andy Furlong, put it to me, 'There's a basic conflict between one person who's supposed to

be the guardian of the system and checking the rules and another
one to give you impartial advice.' Young people will always see
them as 'this is the person who can sanction me'.

We need to rethink our whole approach to youth unemployment. There needs to be a separate local authority-led
employment support service for sixteen- to twenty-five-year-
olds. No young person should have to walk into a Job Centre and
sign on.

These youth opportunity centres should consolidate careers
advice, partner with schools and colleges and support young
people to move on from school to work, training or university.
They should be available for post-university or college careers
advice, which is often when young people most need it. They
should be able to advise young people on their rights when it
comes to unpaid internships. Young people should walk into the
same buildings and use the same service whether their goal is to
be a doctor or a builder. Services would include advisers on hand
to give sustained, long-term support, to discuss options and refer
young people to courses to meet gaps in their knowledge and
skills where necessary.

This would be combined with a youth jobs guarantee, with
options available to young people facing unemployment – training opportunities, work experience and service projects. Young
people should be able to receive a training allowance to support
them through this period on the condition they take up one of
the opportunities available to them.

There would be an element of compulsion, but underwritten
by choice. If a young person is out of work for a certain amount
of time, they should be obliged to go on to a paid training, service or work experience scheme. Community service should not
be a punitive option but one of many positive opportunities available. The state should provide a stipend for young people who
want to spend a year serving their community, fostering a growth
in service schemes across different sectors.

This would end the crazy system that disincentivises young people from taking up training. At the moment, if young people want to take up education for more than sixteen hours a week they can no longer sign on, meaning young people are trapped in unemployment or low-skilled jobs.

Post-twenty-five, there should be investment in life-long learning, working with employers, colleges and trade unions. To pay for it local authorities should be provided with all the funding that currently goes into supporting youth unemployment in one coordinated grant. They should get this on the condition they demonstrate how they will partner with other boroughs. Extra resources should be put into areas of high deprivation to allow increased and tailored support. At the same time, further education funding should be devolved down to combined authorities, allowing more joined-up thinking between provision and the local labour market.

Employers can help fund this. The Institute for Public Policy Research suggests a new apprenticeship levy for large employers that can be devolved down to combined authorities (partnerships between local authorities) to fund vocational education and training for young apprentices.[21]

It will require a higher percentage of our budget to be directed towards youth unemployment. However, the current situation has high costs attached; a report in 2012 estimated that the net present value of the cost to the Treasury, even looking only a decade ahead, is approximately £28 billion.[22]

3. Reward young people for the work they do

Paid work is an important way to reward contribution. Unfortunately in the UK we have the fifth-largest share of low-paid work in the developed world.[23] 22 per cent of people earn below a living wage. Wages have been stagnating for low to middle earners over the last decade, but part of the effect of this has been offset by tax-credit. With wages continuing to fall and tax credits providing less support, the low paid are increasingly struggling to meet the basic cost of living. Low- to middle-income households are not expected to be any better off by 2017–18 than they were in 1997–8.[24] This stores up problems for the future. 69 per cent of these low earners have no pension and it reduces consumer spend in the short term as families are forced to spend more and more of their wages on essentials.

This particularly affects young workers. Research by the Resolution Foundation found that low pay stagnated for all workers between 1975 and 2012, but increased for young workers: 'the proportion of those earning less than one-half of median hourly pay accounted for by workers aged thirty and under increased from a low of one half (47 per cent) in 1996, to a peak of nine-in-ten (89 per cent) in 2012.'[25]

Increasing the minimum wage is one important tool in delivering a fairer society. In the past trade unions led the way in encouraging pay rises for working people. However, as their role weakens, especially in growing services industries, the state has to do more to increase pay. Furthermore, the cost of subsidising low wages in the private sector is picked up by taxpayers as the state spends more and more money on tax credits. The Resolution Foundation calculates that raising all wages to the living wage would save the public purse £2.2 billion, even when factoring in higher public service wages.[26] Therefore, a gradual increase in the minimum wage would reduce pressure on the public purse and make life easier for families. It would have other benefits too. One of the central reasons for the rise in anti-immigration feeling is a sense that it is driving down wages. The way to prevent this is strong and enforced legislation over pay that means no working person in this country is struggling on poverty pay. This should start with ending the unfair practice of a lower minimum wage for younger workers.[27]

A fair housing policy

This is a question of fairness between generations. An Intergenerational Foundation report shows that 'As housing wealth shifts irresistibly up the demographic scale, the "family home" is increasingly in the hands of an ageing population that is no longer actively raising Britain's families.'[28] The proportion of young people needing help from their parents went up from below 10 per cent in 1997 to 45 per cent in 2005.[29]

This means the transfer of assets to younger generations is a question not of hard work but of family money. The Resolution Foundation found that for young people under thirty-five ownership had fallen to 18 per cent; but this went up to 56 per cent for young people in the top half of the income distribution.[30]

The heart of the problem is we are not building enough houses. The state has reduced its commitment to house building and planning and the private sector has not filled the void.

House building as a national mission

Fundamentally we need to unlock a new wave of house building across the country. Only 13 per cent of the UK is built on, a lower proportion than countries with a similar population density such as Germany, Belgium or the Netherlands.[31] It means the state taking on an active and direct role in housing planning, investing not just in new homes but also new towns.

Currently housing is not recognised as part of our national infrastructure and loses out on vital investment despite the double benefit it brings. A Shelter report found that 'for every £1 spent on housing construction it is estimated that a further £2.09 of economic output is generated and 56p returns to the exchequer of which 36p is direct savings in tax and benefits'.[32]

Solving the housing crisis involves brave and long-term decisions. There needs to be a national plan backed up by investment.

We are paying for short-termism in the 1980s and 1990s with a backlog of housing demand with a housing benefit bill of more than twenty billion pounds.[33]

Local government also needs to be empowered to lead new housing projects. This means giving local authorities with coherent plans the freedom to borrow money to meet their housing needs. Local authorities are currently restricted by borrowing caps that bear no relation to standard prudential borrowing rules. It also means being stricter on developers sitting on land through taxation. It can be done. In Holland an active, state-led housing policy saw 455,000 new homes built between 1996 and 2005.

Helping young people on the housing ladder

We can't just build new housing; we need to ensure that first-time buyers have access to it. Increasing shared ownership schemes that reduce the deposit in favour of rental income is one strategy. The Conservatives have pledged to build a hundred thousand starter homes for people under forty at a discount of 20 per cent.[34]

Building new social housing

Social housing can't offer a safety net for most young people. Right to Buy massively reduced the stock of social housing: novelist and journalist James Meek estimates it represented £40 billion in its first twenty-five years, but that money was not re-invested in council housing stock.[35] At the same time, councils stopped building new housing.

An IPPR report found 'the number of social housing units has declined from 5 million in 1980 (or 30 per cent of the housing market) (Feinstein 2008) to 4.0 million (or 18 per cent) in 2011'.[36] Camden is not atypical as a London borough with a waiting list of twenty-six thousand, so when I meet young people there is little to offer any but those in the most desperate circumstances.

Regulating the private rented sector

In the short term, a fair policy for young people is one that sees reforms in the private rented sector and the introduction of secure tenancies and restricted rent rises. Local councils need new powers to tackle rogue landlords and drive up standards. One third of private-rented-sector properties fail to meet the government's Decent Home Standards.[37]

We have a highly unregulated and insecure private rented sector. It is no place to bring up children and I meet working private tenants every week who are facing eviction because they can't afford rent rises. The Resolution Foundation calculate that in 'a third of all local authorities, a low-income couple with one child on £22k would have to spend more than a third of their income to rent the least expensive two-bedroom property in the local area'.[38]

We also need to explore new classes of affordable rented accommodation for young people starting out in their careers, pursuing apprenticeships or setting up businesses, and a short-term affordable rent to give them a step up.

Making this a priority

There is no doubt that there will be upfront costs to the ideas put forward in this chapter. However, as we saw above, an investment approach focused on children and young people will save us money in the long term. It is our best economic growth strategy, our best community cohesion policy, our best crime policy, our best social care policy.

Political parties need to make this agenda a priority. Creating a fair agenda means being responsive to young people but it also means working with them. They need to be part of a dialogue about what constitutes fairness. They will be more likely to buy into a modern welfare state if they understand how reciprocity and fairness underpin it. This is about making it explicit that their concerns are being addressed, being transparent about policy-making and creating a scaffold between what individuals do and what the state rewards.

However, the state no longer has the capacity to create a fair society on its own. This requires government, civil society, the private sector and citizens to come together around a shared purpose.

Chapter 11

Finding a Common Purpose

We have to build a society where every person understands the contribution they are making to something bigger than themselves. They know that by stopping to talk to a young person in the street, or by volunteering at a local youth centre, they are building the kind of society they want to live in and hand over to future generations. Purpose is the difference between atomised individuals working in isolation and networks of connected individuals pulling in the same direction. It is the glue that connects individual citizens, businesses, government and civil society and gives meaning to the work of each individual part. A common narrative is no longer inherited, it has to be constructed and nurtured.

The most powerful ideas in a diverse and fragmented society will be those that unite. While the desire for consensus and conviction I heard from many young people may seem contradictory, it doesn't have to be. Big, aspirational ideas do not have to be divisive ones.

As Daniel Vockins, a young leader and social campaigner, put it to me, 'When you have moments that allow you to talk about [the common good], like the Olympics, then all of a sudden you see the flourishing of a re-engagement, and the idea that you can do things communally better, and that you can start to bring about an alternative politics and start to flower again.'

The spirit of 2015 has to be one of collaboration, openness and empowerment. This requires purpose-driven leadership at every level. This may seem simple but the reality is that many of our institutions actively work against this kind of leadership.

Purpose-driven leadership

The power balance has shifted and too many leaders are still trying to direct and not empower, and still believe it is possible to get away with saying one thing and doing another, rather than understanding that in a transparent world you have to live the values you promote. Too many are not putting the time into building coalitions and bringing people with them. They don't get what Jamal Edwards or Suli Breaks intrinsically understand: that you are only as powerful as your audience. This is what gives you relevance, not a title.

Modern leadership requires more than anything the ability to articulate a clear vision. A vision that unites diverse groups, a vision that inspires and a vision that calls on each individual's sense of purpose. It is an ability to tell a story that people want to be part of.

As Jennifer Bradley, co-author of *The Metropolitan Revolution*, put it to me, 'One of the things we talk about in the book is that metropolitan leaders need to build a network, they need to set a vision, and they need to find a game changer that can rally people.' If leaders are not able to provide authentic leadership and articulate a positive, uniting vision then the voices that will grow up in their place are those seeking to divide and play on people's fears.

They also need to have a genuine sense of purpose; they need to know why they are asking to lead. This may seem obvious, but too often it seems to young people that the gap between rhetoric and behaviour is a chasm. Leaders speak words like empathy, responsibility and purpose, but don't live them. Political leaders offer a shopping list to voters rather than a vision. Is it any wonder that young people think they are 'out for themselves' if they aren't able to clearly and consistently articulate who they are out for? Leaders need to go out and offer an honest appraisal of what they want for society, the limits of what they can achieve and what they need from everyone else. This means saying 'I don't know', admitting failures and mistakes.

Modern leadership in short is less about the leader. It isn't about one person saying 'I can do everything' but being honest about what they can't achieve. Jennifer Bradley tells me that they think in terms of the post-hero economy where networks are more important than any one individual. 'So what we wanted to tell people is what matters is the network. Because it's really unlikely that there is going to be one person who totally transforms everything. And that means that there's not one person to blame, and there is not one person to solve it. It's this whole group of people who have to spend a lot of resources, working together, acting together and kind of maintaining this network, this coalition.' Doing this has a dual benefit because it also gets over the blame culture. It rescues politics from the trap of high expectations and under-delivery. It shares accountability across a system and asks every part to take on responsibility, including citizens.

When it comes to modern political leadership, the informal power you have to set an agenda, convene and influence becomes as important if not more so than formal powers.

Purpose-driven leadership doesn't always have to come from politicians, it can come from and indeed has to come from campaigners, civil society and business leaders. All it requires is a sense of purpose that goes beyond the needs of an individual or organisation and expresses a common vision that others can buy into. Take Paul Perkins, CEO of a voluntary sector youth club, who carved out a promise zone for children, or Camilla Yahaya bringing together thousands of her peers around city safety. They put out questions for their community – do we want to stop poverty being a barrier to young people achieving their potential? Do we want safe streets? If so, what are we going to do about it?

As Matthew Taylor put it to me, 'We need leadership – but it's about demanding a different type of leadership. And demanding it again and again and again until, whatever the doctrinal policy differences are between the leaders, they recognise that they are being told to provide a different type of leadership that is authentic, that is inclusive, that is open. The disconnect now between the kind of leadership we need and the kind of leadership we're being offered is just . . . *enormous!* Enormous!' We need different forms of leadership to start to bridge this gap. Young people are going to accept nothing less. We can learn much from successful projects already in progress.

Purpose in practice

Finding a local purpose

Glasgow is one of the friendliest cities I've ever been to: everyone wanted to talk, often about politics. I got into long discussions with complete strangers about everything from Leonard Cohen to the Scottish referendum. I don't know if it is true, but one young man told me that in one year Glasgow was voted the friendliest place to visit but also the place you were most likely to get stabbed. 'We'll smile as we stab you,' he joked.

And nowhere has been more linked with knife crime than Easterhouse. Easterhouse is a large estate in Glasgow's east end, one of the poorest places in Europe and synonymous in the public consciousness with a history of territorial gang warfare. It has also gained notoriety for being the inspiration for Iain Duncan Smith's policies on welfare and poverty.[1]

Easterhouse is a lot more than the poverty it's known for. It is also the story of a remarkable battle led by the community, to end the territorial warfare that blighted the lives of the children living there. It started in 1989, when local people barricaded themselves into a shop and demanded support for their community. FARE (Family Action in Rogerfield and Easterhouse), the community organisation that grew out of that protest, now stands out as a beacon of optimism in a community still blighted by poverty.

When I visit FARE, the young people who show me round the purpose-built building are full of pride at a structure they feel belongs to them and their families. It is a building owned not just by one of Easterhouse's many 'territories' but by all of them. It is a testament to the community's work in defeating a gang culture that had been passed down from father to son.

Kevin* is fifteen years old, although he looks younger. He speaks with a kind of jaded wisdom, like he's seen far too much of the world. He tells me, 'I used to gang fight myself. So did everyone. Anyone that was my age was in a gang. They all thought they were cool. Like your dad would have been in the gang, your brother, your cousins. You follow their footsteps. You were born into it really.'

It was the upbringing common to kids in Easterhouse. It was what they saw out of their bedroom windows, what their older siblings got up to, the only life they knew. Seventeen-year-old Paul† tells me, 'It was your brothers and your family and your friends. When I was ten or eleven I used to watch it and I never used to go out because I was scared. I used to watch it from my window. And that's where it all happened. I could see them running and there were knives, there were everything.'

There was a whole structure and progression route within the gang culture. Kevin tells me, 'There were the wee ones and the big ones they called it. The wee ones would have been ten or

* Not his real name.
† Not his real name.

eleven fighting, ten or eleven. The big ones would have been fifteen upwards fighting.'

It all came down to postcodes, tiny little pockets of land. Walking through the schemes I have no idea where one post-code stops and another starts, but for the young people who grew up here these are powerful barriers built on family, friend-ship and tradition, but also on hatred, rivalry and revenge. These lines, invisible to me, might as well have been brick walls for them.

One of the workers at FARE told me, 'A couple of years ago fathers would maybe encourage their sons because it was repu-tation or status they have to maintain, that family have got a name and maintaining that name.' The young people tell me they know whose dad fought who and young boys felt a duty to settle old grievances. They can trace these lines even now; they know when they are crossing a boundary.

Challenging the gang culture was a triumph of partnership that included the council, the police, schools and crucially the com-munity. It was also a triumph for purpose-driven leadership: they all united around one driving mission to end the gang culture for the next generation. It started with the younger children. In the past each gang area had its own primary school. These were knocked down and many of the schools were amalgamated. It wasn't easy. One of the boys remembers being chased down the street with bottles flying as he tried to make his way home. FARE workers would have to stand at each end of the street to protect the children.

They worked with primary-school pupils who were at the edges of the violence, getting them to tell their stories through poems, posters and songs. They created banners with a call for change from some of the youngest victims. At the same time they were leading intensive programmes with the older children, for instance personalised 'Mere to me' (More to me) programmes. These fifteen-week, tailored interventions covered topics like sexual health, substance misuse or self-esteem counselling based on the particular challenges the young people were facing. They brought together teenagers from fifteen different gang areas in outward-bound activities, facilitated workshops so young people could put across their views, organised football games in different gang areas and created a shared youth club. Work was going on with the parents too. These were high-intensity interventions and slowly, through empathy and friendship, they knocked down the barriers.

It worked because it was community-driven and a lot of energy went into building up trusting relationships with staff at FARE.

Ultimately they were successful in meeting their purpose. The scars still run deep but the fighting has stopped.

One of the youth workers at FARE tells me that the change is revolutionary. 'It definitely has worked, no question, the difference in the area over the last five years is unbelievable. Trying to describe the difference is difficult because I think a lot of young people's views have completely changed from someone who was growing up fifteen years ago.' They have succeeded in breaking an embedded culture of violence.

You get the sense that FARE is a refuge and a home from home for these kids. One tells me, 'We sit in an old generator box, we call it the genie, that's where we sit if it is raining or whatever when the FARE is shut. But if the FARE is open we can come and sit in FARE and play table tennis or whatever.'

The community still faces huge challenges of youth unemployment, poverty and housing, but things are starting to change. In a way they see it as a victory that they can stop thinking merely about preventing violence but instead focus on building a different future for these young people.

FARE's work is shaped around the needs of the community: homework clubs, parenting classes, breakfast clubs and, increasingly, food banks. A worker told me, 'It is a community facility as well, not just about always supporting people but a place to have a chat with parents down the café, but if they do need additional services we support them.' For the young people that open door is important. 'It is for everyone. Walk in and walk out for teens, come when you want. If FARE wasn't here there would be a lot more trouble in the area.'

Kevin, who was hard drinking at ten and gang fighting at eleven, now volunteers. He tells me he can speak to the young workers in a way he never could with teachers at school. 'You get good relationships; you get to know them over the years and it's easier to speak to a member of staff than speak to a school teacher.'

The organisation maintains its link to the local community who barricaded themselves in all those years ago. One youth worker tells me, 'Local people sit on the board of the management on the committee and they still have a big say in what direction the organisation goes in. It's important to listen to what the community needs and try and develop a service that tries to meet that or support it.'

They have a deep infrastructure of community partnership and trust that they can use to continue to make a transformative impact. It is an example of how a powerful common purpose can defeat even the most intractable social issues.

In the Valleys another community faced the problems of long-term unemployment and poor opportunities. Alex Bevan, now in his mid-twenties, grew up in one of the poorest parts of Britain. His family's story was the story of the Valleys: both his grandfathers were proud miners and trade union activists. His mother was a hospital nurse and returned to work as a carer after bringing up her two sons on her own. In spite of the difficulties, he tells me he feels very proud of where he grew up – the community that was always there to support him, the history, the landscape and the music and literature that it inspired.

When MTV came to the Valleys to create one of their reality television shows, Alex and his brother felt incredibly angry at a media company that was coming, in their view, to exploit all the worst stereotypes. *The Valleys* is a programme that encourages a group of young people to get intoxicated, puts them in a house together and films the most extreme results. Alex told me, 'MTV saw an area that was prime for picking and that was us. From a UK perspective the Valleys is quite exotic, they don't know much about it, all you know is that the *Sun* and the *Mail* tell you once a year that Merthyr is full of scroungers; the rest was a blank canvas so you can do what you like with it. For the reasons I've just said, it's not a blank canvas for us. There's plenty that we love about this place.'

He was angry about everything it omitted to show. 'It's like a family, you can take the piss out of your own family but if somebody else does it about yours then you're going to stand up to them.'

He decided to do something about it. He started talking to shop owners, charities and bands to ask if they could help. He contacted someone else who had started an online petition on the same issue and asked if they could work together. They created a website and campaign called 'The Valleys Are Here' to show the other side of the Valleys using 'unabashedly vibrant, positive stories'. The campaign quickly picked up followers on social and mainstream media. Again there was a strong uniting purpose – to take on MTV and to show that the Valleys were more than the stereotypes they were projecting. Young people started to approach them, including Osian, a young film student who went on to make a film as part of the campaign.

They decided to use the film to give an alternative picture of the Valleys. 'The writers, the musicians, the artists, the ordinary people in that film didn't need MTV. And they live in the Valleys; they're people of the place.'

Thousands signed the change.org petition demanding that

5 per cent of the profits from *The Valleys* should go to the local charity Valley Kids. Over three hundred people packed into a sold-out venue for the first screening of the film, *The Valleys Are Here*, from twelve-year-olds to eighty-year-olds. They didn't stop MTV coming to Wales, but they did start a debate. Alex ended up head to head with Kerry Taylor, MTV's UK Director, on ITV news; his side of the story was also picked up by news outlets across Wales and the UK, including Radio 1 and the *Independent on Sunday*.

In the Valleys itself they mobilised a political spirit among a whole group of young people and they told a different story, one of potential and hope. It also created a network of young activists, youth workers and others leading positive activities in the local community, relationships that have outlived the initial campaign.

Alex is a Labour Party member and trade union activist, very much of the traditional political world. Yet as a young leader he understands that the starting point has to be an issue that goes beyond party politics to unite communities.

Purpose-driven leadership like Alex's and FARE's can be the spark that unlocks unknown resources in a community. It can unite towns, cities and regions.

In Oldham, Jim McMahon, a young Labour leader facing some huge challenges, decided to try a new approach. He had become a local councillor when he was just twenty-three and now at thirty-one is pioneering a new dynamic model of local government leadership. When he became leader of the Labour group opposition in a borough deemed one of the worst performing in Britain, he decided what was needed was not party politics but a long-term vision that everyone could buy into. He approached the opposition leaders about a joined-up approach.

Winning power in 2011 he took this further, embracing a cooperative model: 'Put very simply we work with the people of Oldham to create a shared future, using all the energy and resources we can muster towards the same aim.'[2]

They started with a 'cooperative conversation' with residents that fed through into a 'cooperative charter', which acts as their values framework and guide. This meant living the values they wanted to inspire, including the introduction of a living wage for employees and a new employee volunteering scheme.[3]

A key part of this was devolving power to people. This came in the form of six local partnerships across the borough, bringing together elected councillors and other public sector partners like the police and NHS to share budgets and make decisions for their local area. Crucially many of these new district partnerships include youth council representatives.[4] These district partnerships were designed to involve local people in shaping the decisions that affect them. Each included a new 'local town hall' in a building already used by residents, such as a library, providing an easily accessible base and a one-stop shop for services. Community development workers were employed to invest in building relationships with residents and new community dividend funds gave local people the opportunity to come together and run their own services. Formal decision-making is participatory, with residents able to ask questions online or in person. They also have new powers in the form of community call-ins where one hundred signatures from local residents can trigger a review of decisions made by the district partnerships.[5]

Oldham is recasting the role of councillor as a community champion. All councillors now have to undergo community leadership and budget training to be able to take on new powers. Community leadership means working as partners with residents and in 2012 the council launched a 'Love where you Live' campaign, which set out a positive vision of Oldham, celebrated citizens making a positive contribution and asked residents to pledge to do their bit to contribute to a better future for the borough.[6] They work with residents to find a mutual agenda, not just with the services they deliver but also for those they can influence. For example, they brought together nine thousand households in an energy-switching scheme that saved on average £170 pounds a year.[7]

This approach has also seen the council taking the lead on the challenges facing young people. 'Get Oldham working' is a partnership between the council, the voluntary sector and businesses to offer every young person leaving school a job, apprenticeship, work experience, self-employment, job shadowing, mentoring or volunteering opportunity.[8]

The new approach is working. Surveys conducted by the council show that satisfaction rates with the council have gone up from 22 per cent, one of the lowest in the country, to 65 per cent, the fastest-growing in the country,[9] and in 2014 Jim won the Council Leader of the Year award.

Jim's leadership models an empowering approach, transparent about purpose and process, embracing partnership and changing a culture from one of blame to one of shared responsibility.

Finding a local purpose: the case for devolution

Our current pattern of institutions works against the kind of purpose-driven leadership we see above. Too much power is held at the centre, preventing us designing solutions that meet the needs of a local area and putting a block on innovation and growth.

London is a great global city but it can't be our only great city. A Centre for Cities report found that since 2010, London has seen 79 per cent of Britain's net private sector jobs growth compared with 10 per cent for our next nine largest cities. One in three twenty-somethings who moved in the last few years moved to London.[10] This means cities across the UK lose the talent and creativity of their young, either through jobs they are overqualified for or because they end up migrating to London. A sustainable future for young people can't be the lucky few who make it to London and everyone else left behind. Growth has to be spread across the country to connect young people with opportunity.

From Bristol to Manchester, cities across the UK are recognising this and experimenting with purpose-driven leadership. However, they are held back by lack of power. The UK has the most centralised system of public finance of any major OECD country. Sub-national taxation accounts for only 1.7 per cent of Gross Domestic Product (GDP), compared with 5 per cent in France and 16 per cent in Sweden.[11] City halls collect 17 per cent of their own tax compared with an OECD average of 55 per cent.[12] Greater Manchester and Greater Leeds individually produce more than the whole of the Welsh economy, so the current situation is unfair and disjointed.[13]

A report from the Economist Intelligence Unit benchmarking the future competitiveness of cities found that, 'there is a strong correlation between the quality of a city's institutions and its overall competitiveness. This makes sense: a city's ability to tax, plan, legislate and enforce laws and its willingness to be held accountable by its citizens require strong institutions.'[14] By keeping power in the centre we leave our cities with one arm tied behind their backs as they seek to compete globally.

This view was supported by renowned economist Jim O'Neil, who concluded in a report for the RSA, 'The degree of centralised control in the UK is dramatic compared to other major economies, whether developed or developing, and it doesn't seem obvious as to why this makes good economic sense for either those that live in different parts of the country or the country as a whole.'[15]

A radical devolution agenda is the only way we are going to see the kind of growth and innovation that will give young people the opportunities they are looking for. In designing this we have the opportunity to devolve power in a way that works for the modern world and recognises the unique role of metropolitan centres in driving growth. Today metros, regions with an urban centre, drive 80 per cent of GDP globally[16] and 61 per cent of GDP in the UK.[17] They are also where the majority of young people in Britain live.

In their book *The Metropolitan Revolution*, Bruce Katz and Jennifer Bradley from Brookings Metropolitan Policy Program make the case for networked cities as the future engines of growth and social transformation in the US. This is partly out of necessity – there is no cavalry coming over the hill – but also because they are well suited for the modern world. 'In a world in which people live, operate, communicate and engage through networks, metros have emerged as the uber network: interlinked firms, institutions, and individuals working together across sectors, jurisdictions, artificial political border, and, yes, even political parties.'[18] They are also the right scale: 'large enough to make a difference but small enough to impart a sense of community and common purpose'.

UK cities are home to huge opportunities but they also present big challenges. 84 per cent of the most deprived neighbourhoods are in English cities.[19] Cities need more powers, not just for growth but also for dealing with problems of inequality, environmental degradation and care. At the moment local government often acts more like a conduit for central government decisions than a body that can shape a comprehensive local response. The majority of money passes through local councils as ring-fenced grants. At the same time local authorities have little control over other public-sector budgets in their area such as policing, NHS spend or out-of-work benefits. This means that the same individual can end up being supported by a whole range of services, not all of which pull in the same direction, without any one body taking a holistic view of that individual's needs.

This neutering of local government creates its own vicious circle. As local government has less power, local people and organisations become less interested and less willing to engage. In some parts of the country they fail to attract the kind of enterprising, reforming leaders they need, and quality falls. Central government becomes nervous about devolving power down to organisations that aren't able to take it on.

The fact that Britain has such an over-centralised state is a problem but it also presents an opportunity. We don't have to create a uniform top-down devolved structure but allow power to be passed down incrementally and organically. Power can be held at the appropriate level and city-regions can take on more powers as their capacity grows. In this way different solutions can be found in different areas, with some areas coming together as combined authorities and others developing a patchwork sub-regional combined authorities, as in London. Combined authorities are a positive example of local authorities coming together around shared boundaries. They work because they are bottom-up and they show where local leaders feel the need for more powers. The Greater Manchester Combined Authority came together in 2011 as a formal partnership of the ten Manchester boroughs to set a central vision on transport, regeneration and growth. They have been successful in pooling funds and investing in infrastructure.[20]

Part of this devolution has to be handing down fiscal powers to metros. There are different options depending on how ready a city-region is in terms of governance and experience. The RSA's 'Powers to Grow: City Finance and Governance' report suggests that there could be a spectrum for devolving powers from decentralisation – allowing cities to spend their grants from central government according to local need rather than centrally determined ring-fencing – through to fully devolved status, where they would have powers to retain business rates, revalue and set council tax bands, introduce and retain property taxes and introduce specific taxes (such as tourism). To gain new powers cities would be independently assessed to ensure they had in place the governance, accountability structures, leadership and potential for growth to succeed.[21] The answer from central government is not to impose a top-down model of devolution but allow cities and regions to come forward with their own models.

Devolving power can make it easier to unlock shared purpose
and engage young citizens, but this isn't going to happen if we are
devolving to bureaucratic mini-Whitehalls. Voting turnout for
local elections is currently far lower than national turnout. If
services are unresponsive and decision-making opaque it makes
no difference to young people or indeed older residents if it is
Town Halls or Parliament.

The fact that power is held locally is not alone going to engage
young people. It is also not going to ensure services are any more
efficient, responsive or innovative.

Local government needs to see itself as a tool to unlock the
power of citizens and other stakeholders such as businesses, public
services and the voluntary sector. This can lead to some radical
changes, such as pooling of budgets, scaling up responses across
authorities and new partnerships with the private sector. Local
government is well placed to facilitate the development of collective responsibility across these networks and holding the
different parts to account. It is also perfectly placed to set an over-
arching vision.

Local powers can help unlock the kind of mutuality discussed
in Chapter 9. One of Jennifer Bradley and Bruce Katz's case studies was in Chicago, where they overhauled their community
college system to deal with the endemic problem of high drop-
out rates. They linked community colleges very closely with
particular sectors of the economy and employers. The students at
one college are connected with IBM: they do their work experience there and gain an automatic interview if they complete a
certain amount of coursework. Jennifer puts it to me, 'It is the
notion of pipeline, this notion of being able to move smoothly
between experience in the classroom and experience in the
workplace.' It produces dual shared value for communities and
businesses.

Effective local government also means paying attention to
evidence. Too often policy decisions are made in isolation and

learning doesn't happen across different geographic areas and sectors. Disseminating and sharing evidence online should be much easier in today's world. One example is the Sutton Trust and Education Endowment Foundation toolkit for schools, which simply presents data on the kind of interventions that have most success in supporting young people on free school meals.

Transparency and openness about data is an important tool to empower citizens and encourage innovation. It also has the dual benefit of facilitating and deepening partnerships, removing barriers of mistrust. Camden's cabinet member for finance and technology policy, Theo Blackwell, believes that, 'Through "Big Data", data sharing and the use of technology to meet and reflect user needs, we can start to decentralise spending on housing, adult skills and regeneration and growth initiatives to their most appropriate level – be they city-regions, councils collaborating sub-regionally, to Town Halls directly or down to neighbourhoods themselves.'

To achieve this, councils have to work collaboratively across departments, resources need to be put into innovation and there have to be opportunities for residents to feed into decision-making. Part of Jim's success in Oldham lay in the way he paid attention to how he led, how councillors worked rather than just what residents were being asked to do.

We also need to pay attention to who leads locally. The changes I recommend in Chapter 8 around opening up political parties and selections will help. The kind of community leadership training that Oldham created ensures that locally elected officials have the skills to empower residents. The current local government set-up is much more suited to retired people than young people trying to start a career.

Local councils also need to have their own covenant with their local population so that citizens can hold elected leaders responsible for what happens in that area. Local elections have to be about local leaders, not national party politics. I am in favour of directly elected mayors, especially where more powers are devolved to cities as a means of ensuring strong democratic accountability. However, this should not be a one-size-fits-all approach; different governance and accountability arrangements are needed for different locations.

Young people are demanding more power, more responsive services and better leaders. It is my view that these changes will help deliver this, not just for young people but for everyone. Ultimately we need a long-term settlement with cities, regions and local authorities, which pays attention to local circumstances and gives a clear framework for gaining new powers.

Finding a national purpose

Finding a common purpose within democratic societies can be hard. As I showed in Chapter 2, the demands of short-term politics often win. This is the politics young people hate – the false dividing lines, the division for division's sake, where long-term thinking on the environment, infrastructure and public services is put off in the day-to-day battle for votes. We need cross-party forums to find agreement on long-term issues.

One potential solution is an independent productivity commission akin to Australia's, where parties refer long-term controversial decisions for cross-party analysis. The commission's independence is formalised by law and its deliberations underpinned by transparency, expert staff and rigorous scrutiny. Its remit has gradually expanded beyond its original purpose as an industry commission to include structural reform issues 'across all sectors of the economy, and in social and environmental as well as economic spheres'.[22] The commission provides cost-benefit analysis on all proposals and opportunities to have a public discussion with all stakeholders outside the to-and-fro of party politics.

An OECD report praises the model for the way 'it provides impartial, well-researched analysis of cost and benefits, along with advice and recommendations. The commission's process of public consultation and feedback gives the government an opportunity to gauge likely reactions and thus reduces the risk of reversals.'[23]

Former chairman Gary Banks thinks it provided 'government with a source of well-researched advice on structural reform that is impartial and concerned with the longer-term interests of the community as a whole. As noted, while governments face no shortage of information and advice, much of it can be self-serving or too narrowly focussed to allow for a balanced assessment.'[24] The commission has had success on developing policy on areas like private health insurance and the regulation of gambling industries.

The establishment of a similar commission in the UK could offer stability on elements of public service reform and long-term infrastructure projects such as the expansion of airports so that they aren't vulnerable to a reversal of decisions when a new government comes to power.

There will always be a debate between the different values and manifestos of political parties; however, it is necessary for parties to come together in the national interest on some issues. This will take more than structures; it will take leaders prepared to forgo short-term wins for long-term gains. Putting off the big challenges today will only punish future generations.

It also means changing the way policy is created. The era of prescriptive central targets and top-down politically driven reorganisations has to come to an end. Instead, policy development should be focused on the people providing and using services. Targets can exist but there should be room for autonomy and creativity.

At the same time the culture of politics has to change. Young people working in parliament tell me they find the atmosphere

stiflingly negative. If we look at some of the hallmarks of successful organisations – strong shared culture, focus on collaboration,
learning from failure – none of that exists in politics. As Matthew
Taylor, Chief Executive of the RSA, put it to me, 'It is the case,
I'm afraid, still, that politics, leadership in politics, decision-
making in politics, is thirty years behind the best practice in
private sector corporations. So, there is an issue here: if you're
talking the language of empowerment and relationship, and
respect, yet within the town hall people hate each other, don't
talk to each other, fight with each other, sitting in boring committee meetings, you've got a problem.'

We have to look at reforming how politics is conducted,
whether it is PMQs or political campaigning. I would like to see
a cross-party code of behaviour that is openly available and transparent to the public. When grown adults start heckling like
children or attacking each other's personal lives, they should be
held accountable.

Seeking a national purpose doesn't mean killing debate but
finding forums to have real debates rather than point-scoring exer-
cises. This includes the ideas we saw in Chapter 8 about civic days,
online policy discussions and more open policymaking, as well as
the citizen assemblies mentioned in Chapter 7. I would also look
at how we can open up and modernise the actual process of parliamentary decision-making which was become so deeply
associated with a politics that young people hate. Some ideas are
roving parliamentary sessions in some of our city-regions, screens
in parliamentary debates where the public could ask questions,
and the Prime Minster hosting bi-annual youth PMQs to the
youth parliament to show people a different face of politics.

Finding a global purpose

While a detailed discussion of global institutions is beyond the
scope of this book, we have to acknowledge that groups of young

people are increasingly taking a more global perspective, as we saw with some of the online communities and political activism. The challenges we face as a country increasingly require global solutions.

As well as handing power down we have to hand it up. So many decisions today take place at a regional and global level.

As we saw in Chapter 3, many young people are more pro-European and global in their outlook than older generations.[25] They want to see Britain as part of the world, to travel and live abroad. In Scotland the support for a 'yes' vote from many young people shouldn't be confused with an inward-looking perspective – polling from the Economic and Social and Research Council shows it was more likely to have the opposite effect. Only 27 per cent of the fourteen- to seventeen-year-olds they spoke to wanted to see the powers of the EU reduced or to leave the EU.[26]

Yet the whole tenor of public debate has moved towards an inward-looking, little-England agenda that doesn't represent the young. We cannot sacrifice young people's futures and the future of our country to the fears of a generation harking back to a world that no longer exists.

Far from leaving Europe, we need to be playing an active role in Europe, shaping and articulating its future. Civil society needs to be binding together local grassroots campaigns in networks that can challenge at a global level, whether this is as consumers holding transnational corporations to account, or as citizens holding nations to account on environmental concerns.

Empowered citizenship requires young people to understand how they can influence at every level. This is why local structures are so important, because they give young people a sense of their own power and belonging in a network. It is also why these local structures need to be open and connected rather than parochial, because they can help show young people how they can influence at a national or even global level.

A good place for us all to start is to think about our debt to the next generation. This offers a uniting purpose, a lodestar to reforming our institutions and a call to action.

A uniting purpose: inspiring a generation

As we look to the future we are faced with two possible paths. The first is to do nothing, to go on as we are, thinking in the short term, relying on older volunteers to keep our institutions going and paying lip service to the problem of youth disengagement. We could allow the lives of young people brought up in poverty and affluence to become increasingly removed from each other. We could continue to see the young through the lens of a problem that needs fixing. We could waste time and energy trying to reform them, sanction them and blame them.

My view is that this is a path that will end in failure. Our productivity will remain low and youth unemployment high, with many people beset by depression and ill health, unable to pass on a better future to their children. They will be susceptible to voices and movements with a divisive, revolutionary agenda. It is a future that is chaotic, one where we will watch our institutions slowly crumble or one day just disappear.

Inaction is a choice: a choice by government but also by all who pass off the wasted potential of our young as somebody else's problem. The alternative is to listen to young people. Listen to their critique of our institutions; listen to their anger, their despair and their alienation. Then listen again to their hopes, their dreams and their vision. Listen and start to take the action they want to see in our politics, our communities and our corporations. We can do what the organisers of the Olympics chose to do and take 'Inspire a Generation' as our guiding purpose as we look at the challenges we face.

What so many young people I meet can't get their heads around is why more people aren't more angry: angry about the lack of opportunities, angry about poverty, angry about the atmosphere of violence and neglect that so many young people are brought up in.

Vulnerable young people should not be an afterthought in our policymaking; they should be the driving purpose of our society. This means sweeping change in our political system. It is a challenge for everyone involved in a political party, a community group, a business, a school. We must ask: What can I do? How can I open the door to young people?

It means taking steps to hand over power, build relationships and create a mutual agenda. It means redistributing not just resources but also power, connections and opportunities. It means changing our mindset as individuals, taking the time to have a conversation, catching ourselves when we problematise the young.

The young bring with them a mindset that is optimistic, that is open to technological change and increasingly global. It is ultimately a progressive mindset, one that we can all embrace whatever our age. It requires us to have a big vision. Just as people in Harlem and Easterhouse said 'enough is enough', we have to do the same as a society. We have to believe that every young person can flourish, can live full, productive and creative lives. If everyone truly believed this then the stories in this book are a scar on all our consciences. We should not tolerate one young person out of work, let alone hundreds of thousands.

It won't be easy; it will involve risks and challenges. It will require a redirection of some of the spending in our economy. It will require some brave decisions. But by doing so we will unleash a torrent of energy and enthusiasm that could re-energise our economy, provide solutions to our social issues and reform our government.

I am highly optimistic about the next generation. They are the most educated, most tolerant, most entrepreneurial generation we have ever had. All they need is for us all collectively to have a bit of faith in them. Every time I have seen an organisation trust young people, they have risen to the challenge and exceeded all expectations.

We aren't starting from scratch. Across the country there are organisations showing us what can be done. There are young leaders ready and waiting to take on new responsibilities. If we begin to thread together this work we will have a movement with transformative power.

There is a moral case: it should be effort and talent that defines success in our society, not privilege. There is an economic case: it costs much more to allow the status quo than it does to challenge it. There is a political case: it is the only way we can safeguard our democratic institutions for the future.

In ten years' time we could be talking about a lost generation or about the generation that re-energised Britain. We've seen what can happen if we change our perspectives and work towards a shared vision. We just need to have the will, as individuals and as a society.

I started the first chapter with Franklyn Addo and I am going to finish with him because, as ever, the young people I have met say it better than I ever could.

'Change doesn't need to be explosive; one person broadening their horizons or changing their mind can be a revolution.'

Select Bibliography

Data Sources

British Election Study
British Social Attitudes Survey
Hansard Society Audit of Political Engagement
Ipsos MORI
Labour Force Survey
Ofcom Adults' Media Use and Attitudes Report
Ofcom Media Literacy Tracker
Populus
Prince's Trust Macquarie Youth Index
YouGov

Published Sources

Alakeson, Vidhya, 'Making a Rented House a Home: Housing Solutions for "Generation Rent"', Resolution Foundation (2011)

Andersson, Edward, Sam McLean, Metin Parlak and Gabrielle Melvin, 'From Fairy Tale to Reality: Dispelling the Myths around Citizen Engagement', Involve (2013)

Antoine, Danny, Elizabeth Berridge, Ellie Brodie, Danielle Grufferty, Sunder Katwala, Binita Mehta and Richard Miranda, 'Generation 2012: Optimism despite Obstacles', British Future (2012)

Bang, Henrik P., 'A New Ruler Meeting a New Citizen: Culture Governance and Everyday Making', in Henrik P. Bang (ed.), *Governance as Social and Political Communication* (Manchester: Manchester University Press, 2003)

————, 'Everyday Makers and Expert Citizens: Building Political not Social Capital', Australian National University working paper (2004)

Barber, Michael, Katelyn Donnelly and Saad Rizvi, 'Oceans of Innovation: The Atlantic, the Pacific, Global Leadership and the Future of Education', IPPR (2012)

Bartlett, Jamie, Sid Bennett, Rutger Birnie and Simon Wibberley, 'Virtually Members: The Facebook and Twitter Followers of UK Political Parties – A CASM Briefing Paper', Demos (2013)

Bell, David and David Blanchflower, 'Youth Unemployment: Déjà Vu?', IZA Discussion Paper 4705 (2010)

Benton, Thomas, Elizabeth Cleaver, Gill Featherstone, David Kerr, Joana Lopes and Karen Whitby, 'Citizenship Education Longitudinal Study (CELS): Sixth Annual Report. Young People's Civic Participation In and Beyond School: Attitudes, Intentions and Influences', National Foundation for Education Research research report 52 (2008)

Berry, Craig, 'The Rise of Gerontocracy? Addressing the Intergenerational Democratic Deficit', Intergenerational Foundation (2012)

'The Beta Generation: How Young People are Surfing the Crisis', vInspired (2013)

Birdwell, Jonathan and Mona Bani, 'Introducing Generation Citizen', Demos (2014)

———, Rutger Birnie and Rishab Mehan, 'The State of the Service Nation: Youth Social Action in the UK', Demos (2013)

'Broke, not broken: Tackling youth poverty and the aspiration gap', Prince's Trust (2011)

Camino, Linda and Cailin O'Connor, 'Youth and Adult Leaders for Programme Excellence, Promising Practices and Impact of Youth Engagement in Programme Decision-Making and Planning', Community Youth Connection (2005)

'Citizens at the Heart of Shaping Local Services', Consumer Focus/Optimisa (2010)

Cooper, Christine and Stephen Roe, 'An Estimate of Youth Crime in England and Wales: Police Recorded Crime Committed by Young People in 2009/10', Home Office (2012)

'The Cost of Exclusion: Counting the Cost of Youth Disadvantage in the UK', Prince's Trust (2010)

Denver, David T., *Elections and Voting Behaviour in Britain* (London: Philip Allan, 1989)

Dermody, Janine and Stuart Hanmer-Lloyd, 'Safeguarding the Future of Democracy: (Re)Building Young People's Trust in Parliamentary Politics', *Journal of Political Marketing*, 4:2/3 (2005)

Dermody, Janine, Stuart Hanmer-Lloyd and Richard Scullion, 'Young People and Voting Behaviour: Alienated Youth and (or) an Interested and Critical Citizenry?', *European Journal of Marketing*, 44:3/4 (2010)

Deviren, Figen and Penny Babb, 'Young People and Social Capital – Phase 2', Office for National Statistics (2005)

di Gennaro, Corinna and William Dutton, 'The Internet and the Public: Online and Offline Political Participation in the United Kingdom', *Parliamentary Affairs*, 59:2 (2006)

Dolphin, Tony, Kayte Lawton and Claire McNeil, 'Jobs for the Future: The Path back to Full Employment in the UK', IPPR (2011)

Dorling, Daniel, *Injustice: Why Social Inequality Persists* (Bristol: Policy, 2011)

Dweck, Carol S., *Mindset: The New Psychology of Success* (New York: Random House, 2006)

Edwards, Laura and Becky Hatch, 'Passing Time: A Report about Young People and Communities', IPPR (2003)

'European Youth: Participation in Democratic Life', Flash Eurobarometer 375 (2013)

'(Ex)aspiration Nation: A study on the aspirations and expectations of young people and their parents', BritainThinks/ResearchBods (2013)

'Fair Access to Professional Careers: A progress report by the Independent Reviewer on Social Mobility and Child Poverty', Cabinet Office (2012)

Farthing, Rys, 'The Politics of Youthful Antipolitics: Representing the "Issue" of Youth Participation in Politics', *Journal of Youth Studies*, 13:2 (2010)

Feldmann-Wojtachnia, Eva, Anu Gretschel, Vappu Helmisaari, Tomi Kiilakoski, Aila-Leena Matthies, Sigrid Meinhold-Henschel, Roland Roth and Pia Tasanko, 'Youth Participation in Finland and in Germany: Status Analysis and Data Based Recommendations', Finnish Ministry of Education/German Federal Ministry for Family Affairs, Senior Citizens, Women and Youth (2010)

Ford, Rob, Rachael Jolley, Sunder Katwala and Binita Mehta, 'The Melting Pot Generation: How Britain Became More Relaxed on Race', British Future (2012)

Fox, Ruth, 'What's Trust Got to Do With It? Public Trust in and Expectations of Politicians and Parliament', Hansard Society (2012)

Franklin, Mark and Bernard Wessels, 'Learning (Not) to Vote: The Generational Basis of Turnout Decline in Established Democracies', paper delivered at American Political Science Association annual meeting (2002)

Furlong, Andy and Fred Cartmel, 'Social Change and Political Engagement among Young People: Generation and the 2009/2010 British Election Survey', *Parliamentary Affairs*, 65:1 (2012)

Giddens, Anthony, *Modernity and Self-Identity: Self and Society in the Late Modern Age* (Cambridge: Polity, 1991)

Giner, Susana with Rhiannon Jones, 'Submission to the Leveson Inquiry: Fair press and accessible PCC for children and young people', Youth Media Agency (2012)

Gratton, Lydia, *The Shift: The Future of Work is Already Here* (London: Collins, 2011)

Grist, Matt, Jonathan Birdwell, Tom Gregory and Jenny Ousbey, 'Youth Labour's Lost', Demos (2011)

Halpern, David, *Social Capital* (Cambridge: Polity, 2005)

Halsey, Karen and Richard White, 'Young People, Crime and Public Perceptions: A Review of the Literature', National Foundation for Educational Research (2009)

Hannon, Celia and Charlie Tims, 'An Anatomy of Youth', Demos (2010)

Harris, Anita, Johanna Wyn and Salem Younes, 'Beyond Apathetic and Activist Youth: "Ordinary" Young People and Contemporary Forms of Participation', *Young*, 18:1 (2010)

Haste, Helen, 'My Voice, My Vote, My Community', Nestlé Social Science Research Programme (2005)

Held, David, *Models of Democracy* (Stanford: Stanford University Press, 2006)

——————, *Political Theory and the Modern State: Essays on State, Power and Democracy* (Cambridge: Polity, 1989)

Henn, Matt and Nick Foard, 'Young People, Political Participation and Trust in Britain', *Parliamentary Affairs*, 65:1 (2012)

——————, Mark Weinstein and Dominic Wring, 'A Generation Apart? Youth and Political Participation in Britain', *British Journal of Politics and International Relations*, 4:2 (2002)

——————, Mark Weinstein and Sarah Hodgkinson, 'Social Capital and Political Participation: Understanding the Dynamics of Young People's Political Disengagement in Contemporary Britain', *Social Policy and Society*, 6:4 (2007)

——————, Mark Weinstein and Sarah Forrest, 'Uninterested Youth? Young People's Attitudes Towards Party Politics in Britain', *Political Studies*, 53:3 (2005)

Howker, Ed and Shiv Malik, *Jilted Generation: How Britain has Bankrupted its Youth* (London: Icon, 2010)

Hutton, Will Hutton, *Them and Us: Changing Britain – Why We Need a Fair Society* (London: Abacus, 2011)

Inglehart, Ronald, 'Changing Values among Western Publics from 1970 to 2006', in Klaus Goetz, Peter Mair and Gordon Smith (eds), *European Politics: Pasts, Presents and Futures,* (Abingdon: Routledge, 2009)

'Innovating at the Point of Citizen Engagement: Making Every Moment Count', Govloop (2013)

'Intergenerational relationships: Summary of main findings', Calouste Gulbenkian Foundation/Ipsos Marketing (2009)

Jacobson, Jessica and Amy Kirby, 'Public Attitudes to Youth Crime: Report on Focus Group Research', Home Office/Institute for Criminal Policy Research (2012)

Jones, Owen, *Chavs: The Demonization of the Working Class* (London: Verso, 2011)

Keen, A. J., *Digital Vertigo: How Today's Online Social Revolution is Dividing, Diminishing and Disorientating Us* (New York: St Martin's, 2012)

Kippin, Henry, Heidi Hauf and Atif Shafique, 'Business, Society and Public Services: A Social Productivity Framework', 2020 Public Services Hub at the RSA (2012)

Kynaston, David, *Family Britain, 1951–1957* (London: Bloomsbury, 2010)

Lamb, Matthew, 'Young Conservatives, Young Socialists and the Great Youth Abstention: Youth Participation and Non-Participation in Political Parties', doctoral thesis, University of Birmingham (2002)

Lawton, Kayte and Matthew Pennycook, 'Beyond the Bottom Line: The Challenges and Opportunities of a Living Wage', Resolution Foundation/IPPR (2013)

Leach, Jeremy, 'The Poor Perception of Younger People in the UK – A Research Report from the Intergenerational Foundation', Intergenerational Foundation (2011)

Lent, Adam, 'Generation Enterprise: The Hope for a Brighter Economic Future', RSA Action and Research Centre (2012)

'Low Paid Britain 2013', Resolution Foundation (2013)

Lopes, Joana, David Kerr and Julie Nelson, 'Measuring the Impossible? Making a Start: Exploring the Impact of Youth Volunteering through Existing Longitudinal Research Data', vInspired/NFER (2011)

Madland, David and Ruy Teixeira, 'New Progressive America: The Millennial Generation', Center for American Progress (2009)

'Making the Connection: Building Youth Citizenship in the UK', Youth Citizenship Commission (2009)

Mannheim, Karl, 'The Problem of Generations', in Paul Kecskemeti (ed.), *Karl Mannheim: Essays* (London: Routledge, 1952)

Mokwena, Steve, 'Putting Youth Engagement into Practice: A Toolkit for Action', Commonwealth Youth Programme (2006)

Murray, Robin, 'The New Wave of Mutuality', Policy Network (2012)

'Old Enough to Make a Mark? Should the Voting Age be Lowered to 16?', Youth Citizenship Commission (2009)

Park, Alison, Caroline Bryson, Elizabeth Clery, John Curtice and Miranda Phillips (eds), *British Social Attitudes: The 30th Report* (London: NatCen Social Research, 2013)

———, Elizabeth Clery, John Curtice, Miranda Phillips and David Utting (eds), *British Social Attitudes: The 28th Report* (London: NatCen Social Research, 2012)

———, John Curtice, Katarina Thomson, Lindsey Jarvis and Catherine Bromley (eds), *British Social Attitudes – Continuity and Change over Two Decades: The 20th Report* (London: Sage, 2003)

'Pathways through Participation: What Creates and Sustains Active Citizenship?', Pathways through Participation (2011)

Pennington, Jenny, Dalia Ben-Galim and Graeme Cooke, 'No Place to Call Home: The Social Impacts of Housing Undersupply on Young People', IPPR (2012)

Phelps, Edward, 'Young Adults and Electoral Turnout in Britain: Towards a Generational Model of Political Participation', Sussex European Institute Working Paper 92 (2006)

Porter, Michael E., Greg Hills, Marc Pfitzer, Sonja Patscheke and Elizabeth Hawkins, 'Measuring Shared Value: How to Unlock Value by Linking Social and Business Results', FSG (2012)

Putnam, Robert, *Bowling Alone: The Collapse and Revival of American Community* (New York: Simon & Schuster, 2000)

———, Carl B. Frederick and Kaisa Snellman, 'Growing Class Gaps in Social Connectedness among American Youth', Harvard Kennedy School of Government Saguro Seminar: Civic Engagement in America (2012)

Puttick, Ruth, Peter Baeck and Philip Colligan, 'The Teams and Funds Making Innovation Happen in Governments around the World', Nesta/Bloomberg Philanthropies (2014)

Pye, Julia, Claire Lister, Jerry Latter and Lucy Clements, 'Young People Speak Out: Attitudes to, and Perceptions of, Full-Time Volunteering', Ipsos MORI/VResearch (2009)

Sandbrook, Dominic, *Never Had It So Good: A History of Britain from Suez to the Beatles* (London: Abacus, 2006)

———, *Seasons in the Sun: The Battle for Britain, 1974–1979* (London: Allen Lane, 2012)

——————, *White Heat: A History of the Swinging Sixties* (London: Abacus, 2008)

Schoon, Ingrid and Helen Cheng, 'Determinants of Political Trust: A Lifetime Learning Model', *Developmental Psychology*, 47:3 (2011)

Seldon, Anthony, *Trust: How We Lost it and How to Get it Back* (London: Biteback, 2009)

Sian, Katy, Ian Law and S. Sayyid, 'The Media and Muslims in the UK', Centre for Ethnicity and Racism Studies, University of Leeds (2012)

Skelcher, Chris and Jacob Torfing, 'Improving Democratic Governance through Institutional Design: Civic Participation and Democratic Ownership in Europe', *Regulation & Governance*, 4:1 (2010)

Skinner, Gideon, Chloe Forbes, Bobby Duffy and Daniel Cameron (eds), 'Understanding Society: Generations', Ipsos MORI (2013)

Sloam, James, 'New Voice, Less Equal: The Civic and Political Engagement of Young People in the United States and Europe', *Comparative Political Studies*, 20:10 (2012)

——————, 'Rebooting Democracy: Youth Participation in Politics in the UK', *Parliamentary Affairs*, 60:4 (2007)

Smets, Kaat, 'A Widening Generational Divide? Assessing the Age Group in Voter Turnout Between Younger and Older Citizens', doctoral thesis, European University Institute (2010)

——————, 'A Widening Generational Divide? The Age Gap in Voter Turnout Through Time and Space', *Journal of Elections, Public Opinion and Parties*, 22:4 (2012)

'Squeezed Britain 2013', Resolution Foundation (2013)

'The Start-Up Generation: Why the UK could be set for a Youth Business Boom', The Prince's Trust/ RBS (2013)

Stengel, Jim, *Grow: How Ideals Power Growth and Profit at the World's 50 Greatest Companies* (London: Virgin, 2011)

Stewart, Graham, *Bang! A History of Britain in the 1980s* (London: Atlantic, 2013)

Stoneman, Paul, *This Thing Called Trust: Civic Society in Britain* (Basingstoke: Palgrave Macmillan, 2008)

Strauss, William and Neil Howe, 'The Next 20 Years: How Customers and Workforce Attitudes Will Evolve', *Harvard Business Review*, 85:7–8 (2007)

——————, *Generations: The History of America's Future, 1584 to 2069* (New York: William Morrow, 1991)

Tapscott, Don, *Grown Up Digital: How the Net Generation is Changing Your World* (New York: McGraw-Hill, 2009)

Tough, Paul, *How Children Succeed: Grit, Curiosity and the Hidden Power of Character* (London: Arrow, 2014)

——————, *Whatever It Takes: Geoffrey Canada's Quest to Change Harlem and America* (New York: Houghton Mifflin, 2008)

Trikha, Sara, 'Children, Young People and their Communities: Summary of Top-Level Findings from 2003 Home Office Citizenship Survey', Department for Education and Skills/Home Office (2005)

Trippi, Joe, *The Revolution Will Not Be Televised: Democracy, the Internet and the Overthrow of Everything* (New York: ReganBooks, 2004)

Turkle, Sherry, *Alone Together: Why We Expect More from Technology and Less from Each Other* (New York: Basic, 2011)

'Valuing Young Voices, Strengthening Democracy: The Contribution Made by Youth Engagement', Local Government Group/National Youth Agency (2011)

'What Mutualism Means for Labour', Policy Network (2011)

White, Clarissa, Sara Bruce and Jane Ritchie, 'Young People's Politics: Political Interest and Engagement amongst 14–24 Year Olds', Joseph Rowntree Foundation/National Centre for Social Research (2000)

Whiting, Elizabeth and Rosalyn Harper, 'Young People and Social Capital – Phase 1', Office for National Statistics (2003)

Wilkinson, Richard G. and Kate Pickett, *The Spirit Level: Why Equality is Better for Everyone* (London: Penguin, 2010)

Willetts, David, *The Pinch: How the Baby Boomers Took Their Children's Future – And Why They Should Give it Back* (London: Atlantic, 2010)

'Young People and Their Communities: A Report by The Prince's Trust', Prince's Trust (2010)

'Young Voices "Stronger Together": A Report on the Local Youth Council Network by the British Youth Council', British Youth Council (2010)

'Youth Engagement to Strengthen Democracy: Roundtable Discussion 23rd March 2011 Report', Local Government Group (2011)

'Youth Unemployment: The Crisis We Cannot Afford', ACEVO Commission on Youth Unemployment (2012)

Notes

Introduction

1 According to one poll, more than half of adults agreed that Britain's children were beginning to behave like animals. 'The shame of Britain's intolerance of children', Barnardo's, 17 November 2008, <http://www.barnardos.org.uk/news/media_centre/press_releases.htm?ref=42088>.

2 'People in Western Countries Pessimistic about Future for Young People', Ipsos MORI Global Trends Survey (2014).

3 'The Distribution of Human Capital', Office for National Statistics, 20 August 2014, <http://www.ons.gov.uk/ons/rel/wellbeing/human-capital-estimates/2013/art-human-capital-estimates-2013.html#tab-The-Distribution-of-Human-Capital>.

4 Strauss and Howe, 'The Next 20 Years'.

5 As part of my research I looked at best practice in other countries, including a visit to the US where I visited the Brookings Institution, the New America Foundation, the Center for American Progress, Generation Progress, youth marketing and millennial marketing firm YPulse, Rock the Vote, the UN Foundation and 270 Strategies among others.

Chapter 1: The Myth of a Problem Generation

1 'Rapper rejects Cambridge Uni', *Sun*, 14 June 2011.

2 'Cambridge? No thanks, it hasn't got a music scene: What 17-year-old rapper told top university bosses', *Daily Mail*, 15 June 2011.

3 Sarah-Jayne Blakemore and Suparna Choudhury, 'Development of the Adolescent Brain: Implications for Executive Function and Social Cognition', *Journal of Child Psychology and Psychiatry*, 47:3 (2006).

4 Catherine Sebastian, Stephanie Burnett and Sarah-Jayne Blakemore, 'The Neuroscience of Social Cognition in Teenagers: Implications for Inclusion in Society', State-of-Science Review: SR-E15, UK Government Foresight Project, Mental Capital and Wellbeing (2009).

5 Marcel Proust, *In Search of Lost Time: In the Shadow of Young Girls in Flower* (1919; London: Penguin Classics, 2003).

6 Jamie L. Hanson, Amitabh Chandra, Barbara L. Wolfe and Seth D. Pollak, 'Association Between Income and the Hippocampus', *PLoS ONE*, 6:5 (2011).

7 Sandbrook, *Never Had It So Good*, pp. 435–40.

8 Ibid., p. 442.

9 Kynaston, *Family Britain*, p. 381.

10 Sandbrook, *Never Had It So Good*, p. 453.

11 Sandbrook, *White Heat*, pp. 205–7.

12 Ibid., p. 208.

13 Ibid., p. 577.

14 Ibid., p. 550.

15 Joe Hicks and Grahame Allen, 'A Century of Change: Trends in UK Statistics Since 1900', House of Commons Library Research Paper 99/111 (1999), p. 14.

16 Between 1960 and 1964, only 2.4 per cent of sixteen- to twenty-four-year-olds and 7.7 per cent of twenty-five- to twenty-nine-year-old women getting married had cohabited with a partner, but by 1975–9 it had risen to 17.2 per cent and 36.8 per cent. See Éva Beaujouan and Máire Ní Bhrolcháin, 'Cohabitation and Marriage in Britain since the 1970s', *Population Trends*, 145 (2011).

17 Sandbrook, *White Heat*, p. 557.

18 Sandbrook, *Seasons in the Sun*, p. 557.

19 Linda McDowell, *Working Lives: Gender, Migration and Employment in Britain, 1945–2007* (Chichester: Wiley-Blackwell, 2013), p. 154.

20 Sandbrook, *Seasons in the Sun*, p. 556.

21 Ibid., pp. 559–63.

22 Ibid., pp.565–7.

23 The BT share offer was oversubscribed five times over; 2.3 million people in Britain bought shares when the offer opened in November 1984. See Stewart, *Bang!*, pp. 280–1.

24 Ibid., pp. 301–3.

25 Ibid., p. 88.

26 Ibid., p. 89.

27 Cindi John, 'The legacy of the Brixton riots', *BBC News*, 5 April 2006, <http://news.bbc.co.uk/1/hi/uk/4854556.stm>.

28 77 per cent of those arrested were black. Stewart, *Bang!*, p. 88.

29 Sandbrook, *Seasons in the Sun*, p. 578.

30 Stewart, *Bang!*, p. 91.

31 Ibid.

32 Alwyn W. Turner, *Rejoice! Rejoice! Britain in the 1980s* (London: Aurum, 2013), p. 316.

33 Speech to Conservative Central Council, 27 March 1982. Transcript available at <http://www.margaretthatcher.org/document/104905>.

34 Leader's Speech, Blackpool 1976. Transcript available at <http://www.britishpoliticalspeech.org/speech-archive.htm?speech= 174>.

35 'Attitudes to Trade Unions 1975–2014', Ipsos MORI, 6 February 2014.

36 Stewart, *Bang!*, p. 183.

37 Ibid., p. 467.

38 In 1996/7 63 per cent of key stage 2 pupils were gaining level 4 in English and 62 per cent in maths; by 2009/10 this was up to 80 per cent. In 1997, 45 per cent of young people received five grades A* to C at GCSE; by 2010 it was 76 per cent. See Ruth Lupton and Polina Obolenskaya, 'Labour's Record on Education: Policy, Spending and Outcomes 1997–2010', Social Policy in a Cold Climate Working Paper 3 (July 2013), Centre for Analysis of Social Exclusion, London School of Economics and Political Science, p. 34.

39 Max Hastings, 'Years of liberal dogma have spawned a generation of amoral uneducated, welfare dependant, brutalised youngsters', *Daily Mail*, 5 August 2011.

40 'Statistical Bulletin on the Public Disorder of 6th to 9th August 2011 – September 2012 Update', Ministry of Justice (2012), p. 3.

41 Martin Evans and Raf Sanchez, 'London riots: daughter filmed "looting" trainers has shamed us, says mother', *Telegraph,* 10 August 2011.

42 Gareth Morrell, Sara Scott, Di McNeish and Stephen Webster, 'The August Riots in England: Understanding the Involvement of Young People', NatCen (2011), p. 7.

43 Tim Newburn, Paul Lewis and Josephine Metcalf, 'A new kind of riot? From Brixton 1981 to Tottenham 2011', *Guardian*, 9 December 2011.

44 Matt Griffith, 'Hoarding of Housing: The Intergenerational Crisis in the Housing Market', Intergenerational Foundation (2011), p. 5.

45 ONS figures quoted in Alex Morton (ed. Natalie Evans), 'Making Housing Affordable: A New Vision for Housing Policy', Policy Exchange (2010), p. 37.

46 Pennington with Ben-Galim and Cooke, 'No Place to Call Home', p. 2.

47 Ibid., p. 4.

48 Morton (ed. Evans), 'Making Housing Affordable', p. 37.

49 Alakeson, 'Making a Rented House a Home', p. 4.

50 Pennington with Ben-Galim and Cooke, 'No Place to Call Home', p. 3.

51 'Homelessness problems for under-25s up 57 per cent as recession takes its toll', 30 January 2014, <http://www.citizensadvice.org.uk/index/pressoffice/press_index/press_office-20143001.htm>.

52 Katie Schmuecker, 'The Good, The Bad and The Ugly: Housing Demand 2025', IPPR (2011), p. 2.

53 A YouGov survey conducted on behalf of Shelter found that 52 per cent of twenty- to thirty-four-year-olds living at home with their parents were worried about being held back from having an independent life. See 'The Clipped Wing Generation: Analysis of Adults Living at Home with Their Parents', Shelter Policy Library (2014), p. 22.

54 The two are related as young people in work struggle to find the resources to live independently; 75 per cent of twenty- to thirty-four-year-olds living at home with their parents are in work. Ibid., p. 9

55 James Mirza Davies, 'Youth Unemployment Statistics', Commons Library Standard Note SN05871 (2014).

56 'Youth Unemployment: The Crisis We Cannot Afford'.

57 Grist et al., 'Youth Labour's Lost'.

58 Nick Pearce, 'Youth unemployment and what to do about it', 30 June 2014, <http://www.ippr.org/nicks-blog/youth-unemployment-and-what-to-do-about-it>.

59 'Young People in the Labour Market, 2014', Office for National Statistics (2014).

60 The figures for the first quarter of 2013 were reflective of a long-term trend showing that large numbers of young people are stuck in part-time work because they are unable to find a full-time job. 31 per cent of eighteen- to twenty-four-year-olds and 19.8 per cent of twenty-five- to thirty-four-year-olds were in this position, compared with 15.5 per cent of those aged thirty-five to forty-four, 18.7 per cent of forty-four- to fifty-four-year-olds, 11.8 per cent of fifty-five to sixty-fours, 3 per cent of sixty-five- to seventy-four-year-olds, and 1.1 per cent of those aged seventy-five-plus. The same is true for temporary contracts, with 38.3 per cent of eighteen- to twenty-four-year-olds and 48.4 per cent of twenty-five- to thirty-four-year-olds in temporary employment because they couldn't find permanent work. Analysis of ONS Labour Force Survey data for first quarter of 2013.

61 Research from the Resolution Foundation estimates that 37 per cent of those employed on zero-hour contracts are between 16 and 24 compared with 12 per cent of the overall survey population. Matthew Pennycook, Giselle Cory and Vidhya Alakeson, 'A Matter of Time: The Rise of Zero-Hours Contracts', Resolution Foundation (2013).

62 Lawton and Pennycook, 'Beyond the Bottom Line', p. 23.

63 'More than three quarters of people think society has become more selfish', 21 May 2012, <http://www.mentalhealth.org.uk/our-news/news-archive/2012/12-05-20/>.

64 73 per cent of British businesses believe a skills crisis will hit the UK within the next three years: see 'The Skills Crunch: Upskilling the Workforce of the Future', Prince's Trust/HSBC (2014).
   British Future showed that 50 per cent were pessimistic about the

British economy in 2013 and 56 per cent thought that the recession has been so tough that 'Britain will be weaker because of it for years to come': see 'State of the Nation: Where is Bittersweet Britain Heading?', British Future (2013).

65 BSA polling in 2013 found that 45 per cent of respondents believed that British culture was undermined by immigration. See 'British Social Attitudes 2013: Attitudes to Immigration', NatCen (2013).

66 Quoted in Phoebe Griffith, Will Norman, Carmel O'Sullivan and Rushanara Ali, 'Charm Offensive: Cultivating Civility in 21st-Century Britain', The Young Foundation (2011), p. 19.

67 In a Demos-commissioned poll of one thousand fourteen- to seventeen-year-olds in England and Northern Ireland, 81 per cent of teenagers felt they were negatively presented in the media. 85 per cent thought it affected their employment opportunities, 62 per cent said it made them less willing to reach out to those not in their peer group and 58 per cent that it made them less actively engaged in their community. Birdwell and Bani, 'Introducing Generation Citizen', p. 21.

68 Fiona Bawdon, 'Hoodies or Altar Boys: What is Media Stereotyping Doing to our British Boys?', Women in Journalism/Echo Research (2009).

69 Quoted in 'Why is "chav" still controversial?', *BBC Magazine*, 3 June 2011, <http://www.bbc.co.uk/news/magazine-13626046>. Accessed 2 November 2014.

70 A 2014 Ofcom survey of two thousand adults and eight hundred children found that six- to seven-year-olds had higher digital confidence scores than forty-five- to forty-nine-year-olds. 'The Communications Market Report', Ofcom (2014), p. 35.

71 Yasmin Alibhai-Brown, 'So many young adults today are selfish monsters – and we parents are to blame', *Daily Mail*, 28 November 2013.

72 Anthony Mann, David Massey, Peter Glover, Elnaz T. Kashefpadkel and James Dawkins, 'Nothing in Common: The Career Aspirations of Young Britons Mapped Against Projected Labour Market Demand (2010–2020)', UKCES/Education and Employers (2013), p. 17.

73 'Mythbusting on Celebrity and Youth Aspirations', <http://celeb youth.org/mythbusting/category/myths/>. Accessed 2 November 2014. Findings from CelebYouth a two year research collaboration between Brunel University and Manchester Metropolitan University presented through data, stories and videos.

74 Luke Johnson, 'Too many young British job seekers do lack "grit". That's why we bosses end up hiring foreigners', *Daily Mail*, 21 August 2013.

75 'The Youth Inquiry: Employers' Perspectives on Tackling Youth

Unemployment', UK Commission for Employment and Skills (2011), p. 14.

76 Shiv Malik, 'Cait Reilly: "I'm no job snob, I hated being on bene-fits. They made me angry"', *Guardian*, 12 February 2013.

77 Alison Wolf, 'Review of Vocational Education: The Wolf Report', Department for Education/Department for Business, Innovation and Skills (2011), p. 78.

78 'Changing the Pace: CBI/Pearson Education and Skills Survey 2013', CBI/Pearson (2013).

79 M. Goos, A. Manning and A. Salomons, 'Explaining Job Polarisation in Europe: The Roles of Technology, Globalisation and Institutions', Centre for Economic Performance discussion paper 1026 (2010), cited in in Dolphin, Lawton and McNeil, 'Jobs for the Future', p. 22.

80 Lorna Martin, 'It's not all about you! How selfishness is ruining our society and turning our children into monsters', *Daily Mail*, 24 May 2010.

81 For example, in 2013–14 80 per cent of sixteen- to twenty-five-year-olds had taken part in some kind of volunteering in the last year, compared with an average for all adults of 74 per cent. For more detail, see 'Community Life Survey 2013 to 2014: data', Cabinet Office (2014).

82 'It's time to say ... NO MORE', *Sun,* 27 May 2008.

83 'Youth Justice Statistics 2012/13 England and Wales', Youth Justice Board/Ministry of Justice (2014), p. 9.

84 'Labels R 4 Jars, Not Young People: Research Summary July 2007', Frontier Youth Trust, Impact and 'Youth Work Matters' (Churches Together England).

85 Ibid., p. 2.

86 Guy Patrick, 'Family of yob victims', *Sun,* 4 August 2007.

87 'General Lifestyle Survey', Office for National Statistics (2011).

88 'Drinking Habits amongst Adults, 2012', Office for National Statistics (2013), p. 6.

89 'Smoking Statistics: Who Smokes and How Much', ASH (2014).

90 'Cameron "hoodie" speech in full', *BBC News*, 10 July 2006, <http://news.bbc.co.uk/1/hi/5166498.stm>.

91 These are Conservative proposals to restrict the right of those under twenty-five to claim certain benefits unless they take up offered train-ing or work; for mandatory sentences of six months for over-eighteens and four months for sixteen- to eighteen-year-olds caught in possession of a knife; and to cut housing benefits for under-twenty-fives.

92 'PM's Speech on the Fightback after the Riots', 15 August 2011.

Transcript available at <https://www.gov.uk/government/speeches/pms-speech-on-the-fightback-after-the-riots>. Accessed 2 November 2014.

Chapter 2: The Problem with Politics

1 A YouGov poll for British Future of 1005 seventeen- to twenty-one-year-olds eligible to vote for the first time in May 2015 found that they believed that 'young people' were the group senior politicians pay least attention to. 59 per cent felt they paid most attention to big business, 17 per cent to pensioners, 11 per cent to homeowners and only 4 per cent to young people. 'Voice of a Generation: What Do 2015's First-time Voters Think?', British Future (2014).

2 Aliyah Dar and Adam Mellows-Fraser, 'Elections: Turnout', Commons Library Standard Note SN01467 (2014), p. 4.

3 Ibid.

4 'How Britain Voted in 2010', Ipsos MORI (2010).

5 In 1992 67.3 per cent of eighteen- to twenty-four-year-olds voted compared with 38.2 per cent in 2005. In 1992 77.3 per cent of twenty-five- to thirty-four-year-olds voted compared with 47.7 per cent in 2005. Dar and Mellows-Fraser, 'Elections: Turnout', p. 4.

6 British Social Attitudes Survey. Answers to the question 'Do you think of yourself as a supporter of any one political party?'

7 Phelps, 'Young Adults and Electoral Turnout in Britain', p. 16.

8 55 per cent of people aged seventeen or eighteen, and 56 per cent of people aged between ninteen and twenty-four, are registered to vote. The Electoral Commission also found that 44 per cent of people not on the electoral register do not realise they are not registered. 'Evidence to Support Equality Impact Assessment at the Electoral Commission', Electoral Commission (2012), p. 7.

9 'Audit of Political Engagement 11: The 2014 Report, with a Focus on the Accountability and Conduct of MPs', Hansard Society (2014), p. 26.

10 '… among those aged under 35 who had *never* undertaken any form of non-electoral activity, reported turnout was 46 per cent; among those who had undertaken three or more, turnout was reported at 58 per cent. Consequently, non-electoral participation should be seen as an *add-on* to voting, and not as a substitute': cited in John Curtice and Ben Seyd, 'Is there a Crisis of Political Participation?', in Park et al. (eds), *British Social Attitudes 20*, p. 103.

11 Andy Furlong and Fred Cartmel's paper analysing the results of the 2009/10 British Election Survey came to the conclusion that 'if young people perceive the older generation as having little concern for issues

that affect them profoundly, such as unemployment, they would be broadly right in their assessment'. Furlong and Cartmel, 'Social Change and Political Engagement among Young People', p. 16.

12 The Hansard Society audit data shows that young people are the least likely to contact their elected representatives (30 per cent compared with 65 per cent of fifty-five- to sixty-four-year-olds, and 55 per cent of over sixty-fives). 'Audit of Political Engagement 11', p. 17.

13 According to ibid (p. 57), only 21 per cent of eighteen- to twenty-four-year-olds and 23 per cent of twenty-five- to thirty-four-year-olds felt they had influence over local decision-making, compared with 31 per cent of fifty-five- to seventy-four-year-olds.

14 Sarah Birch, Glenn Gottfried and Guy Lodge, 'Divided Democracy: Political Inequality and Why it Matters', Institute for Public Policy Research (2013), p. 2.

15 See Sloam, 'New Voice, Less Equal', p. 3.

16 Henn and Foard, 'Young People, Political Participation and Trust in Britain', p. 55.

17 A nationwide study of young people who had just entered the electoral register in 2002 showed that social class 'exerted a statistically significant influence – young people from middle-class, managerial/professional households were significantly more interested in politics than those from manual, unskilled or working-class households'. It also influenced trust: 'Young people from middle-class households reporting much less scepticism than their manual, unskilled or working-class counterparts.' Henn, Weinstein and Hodgkinson, 'Social Capital and Political Participation', p. 471.

18 Only 26 per cent of eligible voters who had lived in their current residence for less than one year are registered to vote. Only 56 per cent of eligible voters renting from a private landlord are registered to vote, compared with 78 per cent of social housing tenants, 87 per cent of people living in their own home with a mortgage and 89 per cent of people who own their home outright. Berry, 'The Rise of Gerontocracy?', p. 35.

19 Farthing, 'The Politics of Youthful Antipolitics', p. 185.

20 A 2009 YouGov poll of fourteen- to twenty-five-year-olds found that 44 per cent were not in favour of lowering the voting age compared with 31 per cent who were. YouGov/Citizenship Foundation Survey Results (2009), <http://iis.yougov.co.uk/extranets/ygarchives/content/pdf/Citizenship_FINAL.pdf>. Accessed 13 September 2014. Also in 2009, research conducted by Jigsaw for the Youth Citizenship Commission found a 3 per cent majority of eleven- to twenty-five-year-olds in favour of lowering the voting age. 'Old Enough to Make a Mark?'.

21 In 1992 turnout was 77.7 per cent and in 2005 65 per cent. Dar and Mellows-Fraser, 'Elections: Turnout', p. 4.

22 Held, *Political Theory and the Modern State*, p. 125.

23 Research from Ipsos MORI found that less than 25 per cent of people generally trusted politicians to tell the truth from 1983 to 2011. This did reduce between 2008 (21 per cent) to 2011 (14 per cent). See <https://www.ipsos-mori.com/Assets/Docs/Polls/Veracity2011.pdf>.

24 Respondents to the 2009/10 British Election Survey were asked to rate on a scale of 0 to 10 their trust in different institutions. Gen Y gave politicians a low mean score of 3.1 which was very similar to older generations (Gen X 3.1, Boomer 2.9 and Silent 3.0). See Furlong and Cartmel, 'Social Change and Political Engagement among Young People', p. 25.

25 Schoon and Cheng, 'Determinants of Political Trust'.

26 Only 29 per cent of eighteen- to twenty-four-year-olds and 23 per cent of twenty-five- to thirty-four-year-olds agreed that when people like them got involved in politics they really could change the way the UK was run. 'Audit of Political Engagement 11', p. 53.

27 Decline in party affiliation over generations has been particularly stark in the UK. Analysis by Ipsos MORI of seventeen European countries shows that the UK has the widest dispersion between generations in levels of party affiliation. In the UK there was a thirty-six-point difference between the pre-war generation and Gen Y in the UK compared with a thirteen-point difference for Sweden. See <http://www.ipsos-mori-generations.com/Party-Politics-Europe>.

28 Gerri Peev, 'Is this the most humiliating political interview ever? Paxman can be a Rottweiler when quizzing politicians. But when he got his teeth into hapless Treasury minister Chloe Smith, OUCH!!', *Daily Mail*, 27 June 2012.

29 Emine Saner, 'Why don't we trust politicians?', *Guardian*, 19 October 2012.

30 Robert Winnett, 'David Cameron calls for "good clean" election fight', *Telegraph*, 28 December 2009.

31 Smets, 'A Widening Generational Divide? Assessing the Age Group in Voter Turnout Between Younger and Older Citizens' and 'A Widening Generational Divide? The Age Gap in Voter Turnout Through Time and Space'.

32 Maya Agur and Natalie Low, '2007–08 Citizenship Survey: Empowered Communities Topic Report', NatCen/Department for Communities and Local Government (2009), p. 121.

33 This age group were also less inclined than average to agree that Parliament holds government to account (20 per cent compared with

34 per cent overall). 'Audit of Political Engagement 10: The 2013 Report', Hansard Society (2013), and 'Audit of Political Engagement 11'.

34 See Henn, Weinstein and Hodgkinson, 'Social Capital and Political Participation', p. 473.

35 Beck and Beck-Gernsheim, *Individualization*, p. 158.

36 Farthing, 'The Politics of Youthful Antipolitics', p. 190.

37 Charles Pattie, Patrick Seyd and Paul Whiteley, *Citizenship, Democracy and Participation in Contemporary Britain: Values, Participation and Democracy* (Cambridge: Cambridge University Press, 2004) and Pippa Norris, 'Young People and Political Activism: From the Politics of Loyalty to the Politics of Choice', 2003, available at <www.pippanorris.com> and ibid., p. 189.

38 Segmenting refers to studying the different attitudes that young people have towards political institutions with regards to a classification according to their engagement in political activity. 'Democratic Engagement and Participation: Segmenting the 11–25s', Youth Citizenship Commission/Jigsaw (2009), p. 6.

39 Sloam, 'Rebooting Democracy'.

40 Deviren and Babb, 'Young People and Social Capital – Phase 2', p. 3.

41 Sloam, 'Rebooting Democracy'.

42 According to Deviren and Babb, 'Young People and Social Capital – Phase 2' (p. 6), 6 per cent of sixteen- to twenty-four-year-olds have taken part in a protest – 2 per cent more than all adults.

43 Jack Sommers, 'Scottish Independence Poll: Were Youngest Voters Less Likely To Vote For Independence?', *Huffington Post*, 29 September 2014. http://www.huffingtonpost.co.uk/2014/09/30/scottish-independence-young-vote_n_5882160.html

44 Dr Jan Eichhorn, Prof Lindsay Patererson, Prof John MacInnes and Dr Michael Rosie, 'Briefing: Results from the 2014 Survey on 14–17 year old Persons Living in Scotland on the Scottish Independence Referendum', Applied Quantitative Methods Network (2014), pp. 5–6.

45 This compares to 22 per cent of fifty-five- to sixty-four-year-olds who, despite being less frequent internet users, are more likely to have contacted a councillor or MP online. 'Ofcom Media Literacy Tracker 2012 – Adults – 24th September to 2nd November 2012', Ofcom (2013), p. 339.

46 Polling for the 2014 Hansard Audit of Political Engagement found that 10 per cent of eighteen- to twenty-four-year-olds had created or signed an e-petition in the last twelve months. 'Audit of Political Engagement 11', table 9. Ofcom 2012 media literacy tracking data showed that 19 per cent of sixteen- to twenty-four-year-olds had ever signed an online petition and their 2013 data had it at 15 per cent:

'Ofcom Media Literacy Tracker 2012', op. cit., p. 339, and 'Ofcom Media Literacy Tracker 2013 – Adults – 16th October to 22nd November 2013', Ofcom (2014), p. 257.

47 In the 2012 Ofcom data, 36 per cent of sixteen- to twenty-four- year-old internet users had at some point gone online to look at a political or campaign website. 'Ofcom Media Literacy Tracker 2012', p. 303.

48 Evgeny Morozov, 'Foreign Policy: Brave New World of Slacktivism', NPR, 19 May 2009, <http://www.npr.org/templates/story /story.php?storyId=104302141>. Accessed 13 September 2014.

49 Only 2 per cent of sixteen- to twenty-four-year-olds have ever helped organize a petition: Deviren and Babb, 'Young People and Social Capital – Phase 2', p. 6. According to Ofcom's 2013 media tracker just 1 per cent of sixteen- to twenty-four-year-olds sign an online petition every week, and only 4 per cent do so at least every three months. 'Ofcom Media Literacy Tracker 2013', p. 257.

50 Thomas Hannan, 'UKYP smashes records as over 875,000 11–18 year olds vote in make your mark ballot', UK Youth Parliament website, 13 October 2014, <http://www.ukyouthparliament.org.uk/2014 /news/ukyp-smashes-records-865000-1118-year-olds-vote/>.

51 Benton et al., 'Citizenship Education Longitudinal Study', p. v.

52 Sloam, 'Rebooting Democracy', p. 555.

53 Curtice and Seyd, 'Is There a Crisis of Political Participation?', p. 103.

54 Ibid., pp. 93–107.

55 Ruth Milkman, Stephanie Luce and Penny Lewis, 'Changing the Subject: A Bottom-Up Account of Occupy Wall Street in New York City', Murphy Institute (2013).

56 According to research by the Sutton Trust, 35 per cent of MPs elected in 2010 attended independent schools, up 3 per cent from 2005. See <http://www.suttontrust.com/wp-content/uploads/2010/05/ 1MPs_educational_backgrounds_2010_A.pdf>. The average age of an MP elected in 2010 is fifty. 62 per cent of MPs elected in 2010 were white men over forty: Matthew Keep, 'Characteristics of the New House of Commons', House of Commons Library Research (2010).

57 In 2010 22 per cent of MPs were women (143), a number which has been gradually increasing over the last twenty years. 'Women in the House of Commons', House of Commons Information Office fact-sheet M4 (2010), p. 7.

58 Kelly Kettlewell and Liz Phillips, 'Census of Local Authority Councillors 2013', National Foundation for Educational Research/Local Government Association (2014), p. 35. Councillors are also disproportionately white (96 per cent), male (67.3) and older,

with 46.6 per cent retired. Of the councillors in work the vast majority were in managerial or professional roles (39.2 per cent in managerial or executive positions and 32.5 per cent in professional or technical roles).

59 Lee Moran, 'And the councillor for the wild party is . . . 23-year-old Tory politician slammed for her boozy photos on Facebook', *Daily Mail*, 30 August 2011.

60 YouGov/Citizenship Foundation Survey Results (2009), <http://iis.yougov.co.uk/extranets/ygarchives/content/pdf/Citizen ship_FINAL.pdf>. Accessed 13 September 2014.

61 Dermody, Hanmer-Lloyd and Scullion, 'Young people and Voting Behaviour', p. 428.

62 Matthew Taylor, 'Take me to your (normative) leader', <http://www.matthewtaylorsblog.com/uncategorized/take-me-to-your-normative-leader/>. Accessed 13 September 2014.

63 Henn and Foard, 'Young People, Political Participation and Trust in Britain', p. 63

64 Ibid., p. 9.

65 In 2013 90 per cent of councillors said they wanted to become a councillor to serve the community. Kettlewell and Phillips, 'Census of Local Authority Councillors 2013', p. 33.

66 Only 35 per cent of eighteen- to twenty-four-year-olds believe that most politicians go into politics because they want to make a difference. 'Audit of Political Engagement 11', p. 84.

Chapter 3: Project Me

1 Giddens, *Modernity and Self-Identity*, p. 5.

2 Inglehart, 'Changing Values among Western Publics from 1970 to 2006', p. 131.

3 Giddens, *Modernity and Self-Identity*, p. 228.

4 According to Ipsos MORI analysis of BSA data, 54 per cent of Generation Y place themselves in the political centre – higher than all older generations. See <http://www.ipsos-mori-generations.com/Generation-not-quite-right>.

5 'David Cameron's Conservative Party Conference speech: in full', *Telegraph*, 10 October 2012.

6 '(Ex)Aspiration Nation', p. 7.

7 'Broke, Not Broken', p. 8.

8 Ibid., p. 11–12.

9 Tracy Shildrick, Robert MacDonald, Andy Furlong, Johann Roden and Robert Crow, 'Are "Cultures of Worklessness" Passed Down the Generations?', Joseph Rowntree Foundation (2012).

10 'RBS Enterprise Tracker, In Association with the Centre for Entrepreneurs: 3rd Quarter 2014', Populus/RBS (2014), p. 27.

11 'The Start-Up Generation'.

12 Daniel Pink, *Drive: The Surprising Truth About What Motivates Us* (Edinburgh: Canongate, 2010).

13 British Social Attitudes Survey. Answers to the question 'About sexual relation between two adults of the same sex. Do you think it is always wrong, almost always wrong, wrong only sometimes, or not wrong at all?'

14 Ford et al., 'The Melting Pot Generation', p. 2.

15 British Social Attitudes Survey. Analysis of question 'Do you agree or disagree that ... Immigrants generally are good for Britain's economy?'

16 YouGov/*Sunday Times* Survey Results (25–6 September 2014), <http://cdn.yougov.com/cumulus_uploads/document/j77kqbuqsf/YG-Archive-Pol-Sunday-Times-results-260914.pdf>. Accessed 28 September 2014.

17 'The American–Western European Values Gap', Pew Research Center (2011), p. 1.

18 '(Ex)aspiration Nation', p. 7.

19 Ibid.

20 'RBS Enterprise Tracker', p. 27.

21 Ibid., p. 32.

22 David Bell and David Blanchflower, 'Youth Unemployment'.

23 'The Prince's Trust Macquarie Youth Index 2014', The Prince's Trust/Macquarie (2014), p. 14.

24 Antoine et al., 'Generation 2012', p. 20.

25 YouGov/*Daily Telegraph* Survey Results (26–8 January 2010), <http://cdn.yougov.com/today_uk_import/YG-Archives-DT-Class-280110.pdf>. Accessed 28 September 2014.

26 British Social Attitudes Survey. Analysis of question 'How much do you agree or disagree that ... government should redistribute income from the better-off to those who are less well off?'

27 'The Prince's Trust Macquarie Youth Index 2011', The Prince's Trust/Macquarie (2011), p. 9.

28 Antoine et al., 'Generation 2012', p. 12.

29 British Social Attitudes Survey. Analysis of question 'About the government choosing between these three options. Which do you think it should choose? Reduce taxes and spend less on health, education and social benefits *or* keep taxes and spending on these services at the same level as now *or* increase taxes and spend more on health, education and social benefits?'

Chapter 4: Searching for Community

1 Putnam, *Bowling Alone*, p. 27.
2 Statistics from Halpern, *Social Capital*, pp. 212–16.
3 See: Peter A. Hall, 'Social Capital in Britain', *British Journal of Political Science*, 29:3 (1999); Paola Grenier and Karen Wright, 'Social Capital in Britain: An Update and Critique of Hall's Analysis', International Working Paper Series, 14, Centre for Civil Society, London School of Economics and Political Science (2003); Halpern, *Social Capital*.
4 Lucy Lee, 'Religion: losing faith?' in Park et al. (eds), *British Social Attitudes 28*, p. 181.
5 'Race, Religion and Equalities: A Report on the 2009–10 Citizenship Survey', Department for Communities and Local Government (2011), p. 22.
6 Whiting and Harper, 'Young People and Social Capital – Phase 1', p. 11.
7 Amanda Anderton and Rachel Abbott, 'Youth Engagement – Deliberative Research 2CV for Youth Citizenship Commission', Youth Citizenship Commission (2009).
8 Putnam, *Bowling Alone*, p. 19.
9 BSA data shows that in 1983 31 per cent of people did not belong to a religion; by 2010 it was 50 per cent. This was particularly marked for the Church of England, down from 40 per cent to 20 per cent. Park et al. (eds), *British Social Attitudes 28*, p. 173.
10 According to the 2009 Department for Communities and Local Government Citizenship survey 80 per cent of Muslims, 70 per cent of Hindus, 66 per cent of Sikhs, 66 per cent of Buddhists and 32 per cent of Christians actively practised their religion. See also Cara Seddon, 'Lifestyles and Social Participation – Social Trends 41', Office for National Statistics (2011), p. 28.
11 Putnam, *Bowling Alone*, p. 22.
12 Leach, 'The Poor Perception of Younger People in the UK'.
13 2009 analysis from Children and Young People Now showed that 76 per cent of coverage of children and young people is negative. Giner with Jones, 'Submission to the Leveson Inquiry'.
14 'Intergenerational Relationships', p. 16.
15 'Young People and Their Communities', p. 1.
16 Willetts, *The Pinch*, pp. 129–30.
17 Lisa F. Berkman, Thomas Glass and Ian Brisette 'Social Integration, Social Networks, Social Support and Health' in Lisa F. Berkman and Ichiro Kawachi (eds), *Social Epidemiology* (Oxford: Oxford University Press, 2000).
18 'Loneliness Research', <http://www.campaigntoendloneliness.org/loneliness-research/>. Accessed 27 September 2014.

19 Anthony Heath, Mike Savage and Nicki Senior, 'Social Class, the role of social class in shaping social attitudes' in Park et al. (eds), *British Social Attitudes 30.*

20 Ibid.

21 Research from the Independent Schools Council shows that the independent sector educates 7 per cent of pupils in England and 6.5 per cent of pupils in the UK: <http://www.isc.co.uk/research>.

22 Alan Smithers and Pamela Robinson, 'Worlds Apart – Social Variation Among Schools', Sutton Trust/Centre for Education Employment Research, University of Buckingham (2010), p. i.

23 'Broke, Not Broken', p. 5.

24 Matthew Bennett and Meenakshi Parameshwaran, 'What factors Predict Volunteering among Youth in the UK?', Third Sector Research Centre briefing paper 102 (2013).

25 'Young People and Their Communities', p. 1.

26 In the Prince's Trust 2014 Youth Index 47 per cent of young people said that isolation drove young people to join gangs and 59 per cent cited the lack of a positive role model. 'The Prince's Trust Macquarie Youth Index 2014', The Prince's Trust/Macquarie (2014).

27 Halpern, *Social Capital*, p. 260.

28 'British Social Attitudes 2013: Attitudes to immigration', NatCen (2013).

29 Bobby Duffy and Tom Frere-Smith, 'Perceptions and Reality: Public Attitudes to Immigration', Ipsos MORI (2014), p. 21.

30 Sean Demack, Deborah Platts-Fowler, David Robinson, Anna Stevens and Ian Wilson, 'Young People and Community Cohesion: Analysis from the Longitudinal Study of Young People in England (LSYPE)', Centre for Regional Economic and Social Research and the Centre for Educational and Inclusion Research, Department for Education (2010).

31 'Young People and Prejudice Survey', BBC/ComsRes (2013).

32 Kerry Moore, Paul Mason and Justin Lewis, 'Images of Islam in the UK: The Representation of British Muslims in the National Print News Media 2000–2008', Cardiff School of Journalism, Media and Cultural Studies (2008), p. 3.

33 Putnam, *Bowling Alone*, p. 23.

34 Nissa Finney and Ludi Simpson, *'Sleepwalking to Segregation'?: Challenging Myths About Race and Migration* (Bristol: Policy Press, 2009), p. 104.

35 Halpern, *Social Capital*, p. 261.

36 Ibid., p. 240.

37 Ibid., p. 223.

38 Trikha, 'Children, Young People and Their Communities', p. 5.

39 'Measuring National Well-being – Our Relationships, 2012', Office for National Statistics (2012).

40 In 2013–14 42 per cent of sixteen- to twenty-five-year-olds informally volunteered at least once a month – more than the 35 per cent average. 67 per cent had done so at least once in a year, compared with an average for all ages of 64 per cent. 'Community Life Survey 2013 to 2014: Data', Cabinet Office (2014).

41 The data is the breakdown of informal volunteering for all ages, but these are activities young people are most likely to do. Becky Hamlyn, Alice Fitzpatrick, Emma Coleman and Keith Bolling, 'Giving of time and money: Findings from the 2012–13 Community Life Survey', Cabinet Office (2014), p. 4.

42 Finney and Simpson, *'Sleepwalking to Segregation'?*, p. 96.

43 Steve Ballinger and Sunder Katwala, 'EU migration from Romania and Bulgaria: What does the Public Think?', British Future (2013), p. 13.

44 Mark Hutin, 'Young People Help Out: Volunteering and Giving among Young People', Institute for Volunteering Research (2008), p. 4.

45 'My American Accent', <http://www.youtube.com/watch?v=LpJ3yzUPbL0&list=TLi-2H6y_mOu8GDSv_ioqD6orYuXM4w08X>.

46 'I'm Scared', <http://www.youtube.com/watch?v=_56nx3eHK4c>.

47 <http://charliemcdonnell.com/im-scared/>.

48 'I'm Scared, too', <http://www.youtube.com/watch?v=BeCB4UOT6cQ>.

49 'July 18: Accio Deathly Hallows (no spoilers)', <http://www.youtube.com/watch?v=CvvFiZyEyTA>.

50 'Nerdfighters: Insider View from a YouTube Persona', <http://www.youtube.com/watch?v=CvvFiZyEyTA>.

51 'What Would Sachs Say? The Cyclone Tragedy and Poverty', 6 December 2007, <http://uncultured.com/2007/12/06/what-would-sachs-say-the-cyclone-tragedy-and-poverty/>.

52 'Hashtagnation: Marketing to the Selfie Generation', Prosumer Report, Havas Worldwide (2014).

53 Tomio Geron, 'Airbnb and the Unstoppable Rise of the Share Economy', *Forbes*, 11 February 2013.

54 Quoted in 'The State of the Sharing Economy May 2013', The People who Share (2012), p. 3.

55 'UK Consumer Earnings from Sharing 2012: A Global Sharing Day Consumer Survey', <http://www.compareandshare.com/compare/assets/File/GlobalSharingDay_ConsumerSurvey2012_report.pdf>. Accessed 28 September 2014.

56 'Housing Aspirations', Ipsos MORI Generations, <http://www.ipsos-mori-generations.com/housing>. Accessed 28 September 2014.

57 Rachel Griffiths, 'The Great Sharing Economy: A Report into Sharing across the UK', Cooperative UK (2011), pp.7–9.

58 Hutin, 'Young People Help Out', p. 4; Sarah Kitchen, '2007–08 Citizenship Survey: Volunteering and Charitable Giving Topic Report', Department for Communities and Local Government/Office for National Statistics (2009).

59 A YouGov poll found that only 12 per cent of eighteen- to twenty-four-year-olds feel they are influenced by religious leaders, compared with 38 per cent who are influenced by politicians and the 77 per cent influenced by their friends. Will Dahlgreen, 'British Youth Reject Religion', YouGov, 24 June 2013, <http://yougov.co.uk/news/2013/06/24/british-youth-reject-religion/>. Accessed 28 September 2014.

60 Ibid. 25 per cent believe in God, 19 per cent said 'I don't, but do believe there is a spiritual greater power', 18 per cent don't know and 38 per cent do not believe in any god or greater spiritual power.

Chapter 5: Declining Social Mobility

1 'The Social Mobility Summit: Report of the Summit held at the Royal Society, London 21–22 May 2012', Sutton Trust (2012), p. 6.

2 59.9 per cent of pupils achieved A★ to C grades in English and mathematics at sixteen in England. 'Attainment of the Basics at Age 16', Department for Education.

3 'Social Mobility and Education Gaps in the Four Major Anglophone Countries: Research findings for the Social Mobility Summit, London, May 2012', Carnegie Corporation of New York/Sutton Trust (2012).

4 Leon Feinstein, 'Very Early', *CentrePiece*, 8:2 (2003), pp. 24–30.

5 Anthony Heath and Clive Payne, 'Twentieth Century Trends in Social Mobility in Britain', Centre for Research and Social Trends (1999).

6 John Goldthorpe and Clive Payne, 'Trends in Intergenerational Class Mobility in England and Wales, 1972–1983', *Sociology*, 20:1 (1986), pp. 1–24.

7 John Goldthorpe and Colin Mills, 'Trends in Intergenerational Class Mobility in Modern Britain: Evidence from National Surveys, 1972–2005', *National Institute Economic Review*, 205:1 (2008), pp. 83–100.

8 Ibid.

9 Ibid.

10 Jo Blanden, Paul Gregg and Stephen Machin , 'Intergenerational Mobility in Europe and North America', Centre for Economic Performance/Sutton Trust (2005); 'The Social Mobility Summit'.

11 Abigail McKnight and Eleni Karagiannaki, 'The Wealth Effect: How Parental Wealth and Own Asset-Holdings Predict Future Advantage', in John Hills, Francesca Bastagli, Frank Cowell, Howard Glennerster, Eleni Karagiannaki and Abigail McKnight (eds), *Wealth in the UK: Distribution, Accumulation and Policy* (Oxford: Oxford University Press, 2013).

12 'New Opportunities: Fair Chances for the Future', Cabinet Office (2009), p. 17.

13 'Social Mobility and Education Gaps in the Four Major Anglophone Countries'.

14 Analysis by the Sutton Trust found parents in the richest fifth of houses are four times more likely to pay for extra classes outside of school than the poorest fifth: <http://www.suttontrust.com/ newsarchive/richest-parents-four-times-more-likely-than-poorest-to-pay-for-extra-classes-for-their-children/>.

15 Paul Gregg, Susan Harkness and Stephen Machin, 'Poor Kids: Trends in Child Poverty, 1968–96', *Fiscal Studies*, 20:2 (1999), p. 167.

16 Stephen Nickell, 'Poverty and Worklessness in Britain', *Economic Journal*, 114:494 (2004), p. C14.

17 Jo Blanden and Stephen Machin, 'Up and Down the Generational Income Ladder in Britain: Past Changes and Future Prospects', *National Institute Economic Review*, 205:1 (2008), pp. 101–16.

18 'Unleashing Aspiration: The Final Report of the Panel on Fair Access to the Professions', Cabinet Office (2009), p. 19.

19 Robert Wilson and Katerina Homenidou, 'Working Futures 2010–2020: Main Report', UK Commission for Employment and Skills (2012).

20 'Divided We Stand: Why Inequality Keeps Rising', OECD, (2011), p. 349; also see 'An Anatomy of Economic Inequality in the UK: Report of the National Equality Panel', Government Equalities Office/Centre for Analysis of Social Exclusion (2010), p. 39.

21 'Divided We Stand', p. 357.

22 Ibid., p. 17.

23 Steven Kennedy, 'Social Mobility: Missing an Opportunity?', House of Commons Library Research (2010).

24 John Hills, Francesca Bastagli, Frank Cowell, Howard Glennerster, Eleni Karagiannaki and Abigail McKnight, 'Wealth Distribution, Accumulation and Policy', Centre for Analysis of Social Exclusion brief 33 (2013), p. 1.

25 Wilkinson and Pickett, *The Spirit Level*; Joseph E. Stiglitz, *The Price of Inequality*, (New York: W. W. Norton, 2012).

26 'Conception to Age 2 – The Age of Opportunity: Addendum to the Government's Vision for the Foundation Years: *"Supporting Families in the Foundation Years"*', WAVE Trust/Department for Education (2013), p. 39.

27 Tom MacInnes, Hannah Aldrisdge, Sabrina Bushe, Peter Kenway and Adam Tinson, 'Monitoring Poverty and Social Exclusion 2013', Joseph Rowntree Foundation (2013), p. 26.

28 'Conception to Age 2 – the age of opportunity', p. 3.

29 Jane Waldfogel and Elizabeth Washbrook, 'Early Years Policy', in 'An Anatomy of Economic Inequality in the UK'.

30 'Conception to Age 2 – The Age of Opportunity', p. 17.

31 L. Alan Sroufe, Byron Egeland, Elizabeth A. Carlson and W. Andrew Collins, *The Development of the Person: The Minnesota Study of Risk and Adaptation from Birth to Adulthood* (New York: Guildford Press, 2005).

32 Angela Duckworth and Martin Seligman, 'Self-Discipline Outdoes IQ in Predicting Academic Performance of Adolescents', *Psychological Science*, 16:12 (2005), pp. 939–44.

33 A literature review on available evidence found that parental involvement was more important even than school quality: 'The most important finding from the point of view of this review is that parental involvement in the form of "at-home good parenting" has a significant positive effect on children's achievement and adjustment even after all other factors shaping attainment have been taken out of the equation. In the primary age range the impact caused by different levels of parental involvement is much bigger than differences associated with variations in the quality of schools. The scale of the impact is evident across all social classes and all ethnic groups.' Charles Desforges with Alberto Abouchaar, 'The Impact of Parental Involvement, Parental Support and Family Education on Pupil Achievements and Adjustment: A Literature Review', Department for Education and Skills (2003).

34 98 per cent of all mothers taking part in the survey, and 96 per cent of mothers with minimal or no formal qualifications, want their children to go to university. Figures quoted in Alison Wolf, 'Review of Vocational Education: The Wolf Report', Department for Education/Department for Business, Innovation and Skills (2011), p. 24.

35 A Joseph Rowntree Foundation study looking at four disadvantaged areas of Glasgow found that parents had high aspirations for their children based on a realistic understanding of their strengths; what they lacked was knowledge and resources. Peter Seaman, Katrina Turner, Malcolm Hill, Anne Stafford and Moira Walker, 'Parenting and Children's Resilience in Disadvantaged Communities', Joseph Rowntree Foundation (2006).

36 Elizabeth A. Dowler, Moya Kneafsey, Hannah Lambie, Alex Inman and Rosemary Collier, 'Thinking about "Food Security": Engaging with UK Consumers', *Critical Public Health*, 21:4 (2011), pp. 403–16. Research in 2004 found that just under half of parents had gone without food to meet the needs of their children. 'Going Hungry: The Struggle to Eat Healthily on a Low Income', NCH: The Children's Charity (2004), p. 20.

37 'An Anatomy of Economic Inequality in the UK', p. 332.

38 'Conception to age 2 – The Age of Opportunity', p. 20.

39 Ilan Katz, Judy Corlyon, Vincent La Placa and Sarah Hunter, 'The Relationship between Parenting and Poverty', Joseph Rowntree Foundation (2007), p. 17.

40 Howard Meltzer, Rebecca Gatward, Robert Goodman and Tamsin Ford, 'The Mental Health of Children and Adolescents in Great Britain', ONS (2000), p. 99.

41 Tough, *How Children Succeed*, p. 17.

42 Waldfogel and Washbrook (2012), cited in 'Social Mobility and Education Gaps in the Four Major Anglophone Countries', p. 12.

43 Research from the Social Mobility & Child Poverty Commission found that in the best performing schools 67 per cent of the poorest pupils gained five good GCSEs compared with just 21 per cent in the lowest results. 'Cracking the Code: How Schools Can Improve Social Mobility', Social Mobility & Child Poverty Commission (2014), p. 12.

44 Ibid.

45 Barber, Donnelly and Rizvi, 'Oceans of Innovation', p. 46.

46 Anthony Mann, David Massey, Peter Glover, Elnaz T. Kashefpadkel and James Dawkins, 'Nothing in Common: The Career Aspirations of Young Britons Mapped against Projected Labour Market Demand (2010–2020)', UKCES/Education and Employers (2013).

47 'On the Margins? A Qualitative study of White Camden Households at Risk of Exclusion from Education and Employment', Centre for Urban and Community Research, Goldsmiths College (2005).

48 Pamela Meadows, 'Young Men on the Margins of Work: An Overview Report', Joseph Rowntree Foundation (2001).

49 Dweck, *Mindset*.

50   Lisa A. Harrison, Chiesha M. Stevens, Adrienne N. Monty and Christine A. Coakley, 'The Consequences of Stereotype Threat on the Academic Performance of White and Non-white Lower Income College Students', *Social Psychology of Education*, 9 (2006).

51 Dorling, *Injustice*, p. 48.

52 Eric Turkheimer, Andreana Haley, Mary Waldron, Brian D'Onofrio and Irving I. Gottesman, 'Socioeconomic Status Modifies Heritability

of IQ in Young Children', *Psychological Science*, 14:6 (2003), pp. 623–8.

53 In contrast, 90 per cent of those praised for their effort wanted to take on a new more challenging test. Dweck, *Mindset*, pp. 71–2.

54 Tough, *How Children Succeed*, pp. 184–5.

55 Research from the Sutton Trust shows that 31 per cent of graduates report working for no pay. 'Internship or Indenture?', Sutton Trust research brief (2014).

56 'Changing the pace: CBI/Pearson Education and Skills Survey 2013', CBI/Pearson (2013), p. 56.

57 'Fair Access to Professional Careers', p. 5.

58 Research commissioned by the Sutton Trust estimated that a six month unpaid internship will cost a single person living in London a minimum of £5556 (or £926 a month): 'Internship or Indenture?', op. cit.

59 Wilson and Homenidou, 'Working Futures 2010–2020', p. xi.

60 YouGov/NUS Survey Results (28–30 November 2012), <http://d25d2506sfb94s.cloudfront.net/cumulus_uploads/document/05tns8c27q/YG-Archive-NUS-results-121130-internships.pdf>. Accessed 1 October 2014.

61 A 2011 YouGov poll found that only 10 per cent of young people and 12 per cent of managers knew that unpaid internships may be illegal. Becky Heath and Dom Potter, 'Going for Broke: The State of Internships in the UK', Internocracy (2011), p. 8.

Chapter 6: The Revolution Will Be Digital

1 Data in this paragraph is from 'Adults' Media Use and Attitudes Report', Ofcom (2014).

2 Joichi Ito, 'In an Open-Source Society, Innovating by the Seat of Our Pants', *New York Times*, 5 December 2011.

3 William H. Dutton and Grant Blank with Darja Groselj, 'Cultures of the Internet: The Internet in Britain', Oxford Internet Survey 2013 Report, Oxford Internet Institute (2013), p. 48

4 Andrew McAfee, 'What Will Future Jobs Look Like?', TED Talk; transcript available at <https://www.ted.com/talks/andrew_mcafee_what_will_future_jobs_look_like/transcript>. Accessed 5 October 2014.

5 Ibid.

6 'Jobs and Growth: The Importance of Engineering Skills to the UK Economy', Royal Academy of Engineering Econometrics of Engineering Skills project report (2012), p. 23.

7 'NeverSeconds blogger Martha Payne school dinner photo ban lifted', *BBC News*, 15 June 2012, <http://www.bbc.co.uk/news/uk-scotland-glasgow-west-18454800>.

8 Jessica Leber, 'Too Young to Fail', MIT Technology Review, 3 February 2012, <http://www.technologyreview.com/news/426789/too-young-to-fail/>.

9 'Millennials: The Challenger Generation', Prosumer Report vol.11, Havas Worldwide (2011), p. 20.

10 While low numbers create their own websites and blogs, more sixteen- to twenty-four-year-olds maintain a website or blog (34 per cent) and spend time contributing to other websites (40 per cent). 'Ofcom Media Literacy Tracker 2013 – Adults – 16th October to 22nd November 2013', Ofcom (2014), p. 346.

11 'A level and other level 3 results in England: academic year 2012 to 2013 (provisional)', Department for Education (2013).

12 'New Figures Reveal Crash in Computer Science Degrees', Next Gen Skills, 20 March 2012, <http://www.nextgenskills.com/new-figures-reveal-crash-in-computer-science-degrees/>.

13 'Technology Insights 2012', e-skills UK (2012), p. 42.

14 Douglas Carswell, The End of Politics and The Birth of iDemocracy (London: Biteback, 2012), p. 160.

15 Ibid., p. 159.

16 'Adults' Media Use and Attitudes Report', Ofcom (2013), p. 101.

17 'Conspiracy theories rife in classrooms', Demos, 30 September 2011, <http://www.demos.co.uk/press_releases/conspiracytheoriesrifein-classrooms>; Jamie Bartlett and Carl Miller, 'The Power of Unreason: Conspiracy Theories, Extremism and Counter-terrorism', Demos (2010) and 'Truth, Lies and the Internet: A Report into Young People's Digital Fluency', Demos (2011), p. 5.

18 'Adults' Media Use and Attitudes Report', Ofcom (2014), p. 62.

19 'Humanity and Sanity: The Full Text of John Robbins's Repudiation of Thrive and its Conspiracy Theories.', Thrive Debunked, 26 June 2012, <https://thrivedebunked.wordpress.com/2012/06/26/humanity-and-sanity-the-full-text-of-john-robbinss-repudiation-of-thrive-and-its-conspiracy-theories/>.

20 Michael Kelly, 'The Road to Paranoia', New Yorker, 19 June 1995.

21 Viren Swami and Rebecca Coles, 'The Truth is Out There: Belief in Conspiracy Theories', Psychologist, 23:7 (2010), pp. 560–3.

22 Daniel Jolley and Karen M. Douglas, 'The Social Consequences of Conspiracism: Exposure to Conspiracy Theories Decreases the Intention to Engage in Politics and to Reduce One's Carbon Footprint', British Journal of Psychology, 105:1 (2014), pp. 35–56.

23 Bartlett and Miller, 'Truth, Lies and the Internet', p. 7.

24 'Conspiracy theories rife in classrooms – a new report from Demos', Nominet Trust, <http://www.nominettrust.org.uk/news-events/news/conspiracy-theories-rife-classrooms>.

25 'New News, Future News: The Challenges for Television News after Digital Switch-over', Ofcom (2007), p. 61.

26 'Ofcom Media Literacy Tracker 2012 – Adults – 24th September to 2nd November 2012', Ofcom (2013), p. 429.

27 Amanda Lenhart, 'Teens, Smartphones & Texting', Pew Research Center's Internet and American Life Project (2012), p. 22.

28 YouGov/Prince's Trust Survey Results (29 October–13 November 2012), <http://cdn.yougov.com/cumulus_uploads/document/irijwkt1rd/YG-Prince%27s-Trust-Archive-results-131112-social-networks-bullying.pdf>.

Chapter 7: Building Relationships

1 'London Citizens Mayoral Accountability Assembly 2012', 23 April 2012, <http://www.citizensuk.org/2012/04/london-citizens-mayoral-accountability-assembly-2012/>.

2 See <http://hcz.org/results/>.

3 'Kids Company Annual Report & Accounts: Year Ending 31 Dec 2013', <http://kidsco.org.uk/download/Annual_Report_2013.compressed.pdf>.

4 Marc Stears, 'Everyday democracy: Taking centre-left politics beyond state and market', IPPR (2011).

5 Quoted in ibid.

Chapter 8: Sharing Power

1 Held, *Models of Democracy*, p. 263

2 Ibid., p. 276.

3 Matthew Taylor, 'The Power to Create', RSA, 8 July 2014. Transcript and audio available at <http://www.thersa.org/events/audio-and-past-events/2014/the-power-to-create>. Accessed 5 October 2014.

4 Puttick, Baeck and Colligan, 'The Teams and Funds Making Innovation Happen in Governments around the World'.

5 Ibid.

6 Feldmann-Wojtachnia et al., 'Youth Participation in Finland and in Germany', p. 20.

7 'Good Practice in Youth Information', European Youth Information and Counselling Agency (2014).

8 Andersson et al., 'From Fairy Tale to Reality', pp. 17–19.

9 Brian Boyer, 'What happens next?', Brickstarter, 15 January 2013, <http://brickstarter.org/what-happens-next/>.

10 'We need to generate more demand for Civic Technology' Nesta, 21

July 2014, <http://www.nesta.org.uk/blog/we-need-generate-more-demand-civic-technology>.

11 'Young mums in Swansea get organised', Movement for Change, <http://www.movementforchange.org.uk/young_mums_swansea_get_organised_payday_lending>.

12 Andrew Sparrow and Paul Owen, 'Labour conference and Ed Miliband's interview on the Andrew Marr show: Politics live blog', *Guardian* online, 22 September 2013, <http://www.theguardian.com/politics/2013/sep/22/labour-conference-and-ed-milibands-interview-on-the-andrew-marr-show-politics-live-blog>.

13 Trippi, *The Revolution Will Not Be Televised*, p. 119.

14 David Brindle, 'The strength of the public vote', *Guardian*, 8 March 2011.

15 A 2008 longitudinal study focused on youth participation in and beyond school found that the most important student level factor linked to positive attitudes to civic engagement was their belief in their own personal efficacy. More important than gender, class and age was their belief that they could make a difference. Benton et al., 'Citizenship Education Longitudinal Study', p. viii.

16 Quoted in Henn and Foard, 'Young People, Political Participation and Trust in Britain', p. 54.

17 'Audit of Political Engagement 10: The 2013 Report', Hansard Society (2013), p. 4.

18 Feldmann–Wojtachnia et al., 'Youth Participation in Finland and in Germany', p. 45.

19 Ibid., pp. 43–4.

20 According to an independent evaluation by Ipsos MORI 84 per cent of NCS participants report feeling more positive about people from different backgrounds and 89 per cent report a better understanding of those from different backgrounds. 72 per cent say they are more likely to help out locally. Caroline Booth, Daniel Cameron, Lauren Cumming, Nicholas Gilby, Chris Hale, Finn Hoolahan and Jayesh and Navin Shah, 'National Citizenship Service 2013 Evaluation', Ipsos MORI (2014).

21 Work by the Education Endowment Foundation and the Sutton Trust assessing the evidence of educational interventions shows that the two strategies that have the greatest impact on young people's learning are those that give more responsibility to the learner. Feedback to students that let them manage their own learning and 'meta-cognition and self-regulation' strategies that help students to set goals and monitor and evaluate their learning. They require students to be self-aware, able to assess their strengths and weakness and adapt their strategies accordingly. See <http://education

endowmentfoundation.org.uk/toolkit/feedback/>.

22 Amelia Paterson, Jen Lexmond, Joe Hallgarten and David Kerr, 'Schools with Soul: A New Approach to Spiritual, Moral, Social and Cultural Education', RSA Action and Research Centre (2014), p. 12.

Chapter 9: Helping Me, Helping You

1 Birdwell and Bani, 'Introducing Generation Citizen', p. 70.
2 'Talent Edge 2020: Building the recovery together – What talent expects and how leaders are responding', Deloitte (2011), p. 10.
3 'The Millennial Survey', Deloitte (2011), p. 8.
4 Birdwell and Bani, 'Introducing Generation Citizen', p. 70.
5 'Millennials: The Challenger Generation', Prosumer Report vol.11, Havas Worldwide (2011), p. 21.
6 'State of the Global Workplace: Employee engagement insights for Business Leaders Worldwide', Gallup (2013), p. 21.
7 Dame Carole Black's review of the health of Britain's working age population found that sickness absence and worklessness of the working-age population connected with ill health costs over £100 billion each year. 'Working for a Healthier Tomorrow' (2008).
8 An analysis by the Institute for Employment Studies and the University of Liverpool of 58,700 fit notes (notes issued by doctors to employers about employees fitness for work) distributed to 25,000 patients by forty-nine GP practices between October 2011 and January 2013 found that 35 per cent of these were for mild to moderate mental health disorders including stress, anxiety and depression. Chris Shiels, Jim Hillage, Emma Pollard and Mark Gabbay, 'An Evaluation of the Statement of Fitness for Work (Fit Note): Quantitative Survey of Fit Notes', Department for Work and Pensions (2013).
9 Stengel, *Grow*, pp. 7–8.
10 Porter looks at three different ways they can do this; first 'reconceiving products and markets', which looks at how a product or service can add value in itself and address need. Secondly 'redefining productivity in the value chain', which is how internal operations can be better managed to save costs, invest in the environment and increase productivity – for example better paid or trained employees. Thirdly 'enabling cluster development', which is the benefit that comes from investing in local communities and infrastructure.
11 'RBS Enterprise Tracker, in association with the Centre for Entrepreneurs: 3rd Quarter 2014', Populus/RBS (2014), p. 28.
12 'Social Impact Report May to December 2012', Livity (2013).
13 See <http://creativeaccess.org.uk/about-us/history>.

14 Porter et al., 'Measuring Shared Value', p. 14.

15 Ibid., p. 13.

16 'Tackling Corporate Tax Avoidance in a Global Economy: Is a New Approach Needed?', House of Lords Select Committee on Economic Affairs report (2013).

17 Atif Shafique, Henry Kippin and Ben Lucas, 'Oldham's Co-operative Council: A Social Productivity Framework', 2020 Public Services Hub at the RSA (2012), p. 62

18 'Gateway to Growth', CBI/Pearson (2014).

19 'Millennials: The Challenger Generation', Prosumer Report vol.11, Havas Worldwide (2011).

20 McKenna Pope, 'Hasbro: Feature Boys in the Packaging of the Easy-Bake Oven', Change.org petition, <https://www.change.org/p/hasbro-feature-boys-in-the-packaging-of-the-easy-bake-oven>.

21 'Trade Union Membership 2013', Department for Business, Innovation & Skills statistical bulletin (2014), p. 37.

22 'Delivering for Young Workers: A Unions21 debate', Unions21 (2011).

23 Ibid.

24 'Productivity in the Public Sector: What Makes a Good Job?', PwC (2014), p. 11.

25 Cooperative ownership can be an effective tool to incentivise young employees across the public and private sector. In August 2012 the Oxford Centre for Mutual and Employee-owned Business ran an online survey of employees of Association of Financial Mutuals member organisations and found that '85 per cent of employees under twenty-five agreed or strongly agreed that this organisation is run in the interests of its members/customers.' The same proportion agreed with the statement 'I am proud of the ethical reputation and record of this business.' William Davies and Jonathan Michie, 'Measuring Mutuality: Indicators for Financial Mutuality', Centre for Mutual & Employee-owned Business, University of Oxford (February 2013).

26 Lib Peck, 'Cllr Lib Peck: The Young Lambeth Co-operative – Shifting Power to Communities', Co-operative Councils Innovation Network, 30 June 2014, <http://www.coopinnovation.co.uk/blog/cllr-lib-peck-the-young-lambeth-co-operative-shifting-power-to-communities/>. Accessed 4 October 2014.

Chapter 10: What's Fair?

1 Hutton, *Them and Us*, pp. 61–2.

2 Duncan O'Leary, 'Something for Something: Restoring a Contributory Principle to the Welfare State', Demos (2013).

3 Ruth Lupton and Polina Obolenskaya, 'Labour's Record on Education: Policy, Spending and Outcomes 1997–2010', Social Policy in a Cold Climate Working Paper 3 (2013), Centre for Analysis of Social Exclusion, London School of Economics and Political Science.

4 'The Damage: Warning: Dismantling Council Services Will Seriously Damage Our Lives and Our Communities', UNISON (2014).

5 Jacob S. Hacker, 'The Institutional Foundations of Middle-class Democracy', Policy Network (2011) and 'The Free Market Fantasy', Policy Network (2014).

6 The costs of ignoring these problems are high. Children with behavioural problems that remain untreated cost on average £70,000 by the time they reach twenty-eight, which is ten times the cost associated with children who don't experience these issues. See 'The Youth Justice System in England and Wales: Reducing Offending by Young People', Report by the Comptroller and Auditor General HC 663, Ministry of Justice (201), p. 4.

7 The Early Intervention Foundation summarises some of the evidence and examples of integrated support for families in Clare Messenger and Donna Molloy, 'Getting It Right For Families: A review of integrated systems and promising practice in the early years' (2014).

8 'Conception to Age 2 – The Age of Opportunity: Addendum to the Government's Vision for the Foundation Years: *"Supporting Families in the Foundation Years"*', WAVE Trust/Department for Education (2013), p. 5.

9 The Early Intervention Foundation use analysis by the Social Research Unit at Darlington to show both the evidence for interventions and the savings they accrue. For example Family Nurse Partnerships involving an intensive visitation programme during pregnancy and the first two years of a child's life by nurses for at-risk first-time mothers is estimated to have a social benefit–cost ratio of 1.94, meaning for every pound spent on it £1.94 of social benefit are generated. The same applies for early intervention with older children: functional family therapy, a family-based therapy intervention for young people at risk of delinquency has a cost–benefit ratio of £12.32 for every pound spent. See <http://investing inchildren.eu/node/65> and 'Making an Early Intervention Business Case: Evidence and resources', Early Intervention Foundation (2014).

10 Character capabilities are more important than ever in determining young people's life chances as they are increasingly rewarded in the labour market. Research by the IPPR showed that personal and social skills were thirty-three times more important in defining the life chances of children born in 1970 than they were for those born in

1958. J. Margo and M. Dixon, *Freedom's Orphans: Raising Youth in a Changing World* (London: IPPR, 2006.)

11　Reid Hoffman and Ben Casnocha, *The Start-up of You: Adapt to the Future, Invest in Yourself, and Transform Your Career* (New York: Crown Business, 2012), quoted in Barber, Donnelly and Rizvi, 'Oceans of Innovation', p. 26.

12　'Strong Performers and Successful Reformers in Education: Lessons from PISA for the United States', OECD (2010), p. 123.

13　This includes early years. A 2014 research summary for the Sutton Trust found that qualified staff with access to professional development is integral to the success of early education interventions. 'Sound Foundations: A Review of the Research Evidence on Quality of Early Childhood Education and Care for Children Under Three – implications for policy and practice', Sutton Trust (2014).

14　In Pearson's 2012 'Learning Curve' report they acknowledged that while the two leading education systems (Finland and South Korea) were in many ways very different, one thing they have in common is the high status of teachers and the strong focus on teacher training and recruitment. 'How the World's Most Improved Education Systems Keep Getting Better', McKinsey's 2010 analysis of the reform of twenty education systems around the world, found that the education systems that moved from 'good to great' invested heavily in teachers as professionals. They improved even further when focused on teachers supporting other teachers and encouraging innovation.

15　See Mona Mourshed, Chinezi Chijioke and Michael Barber, 'How the World's Most Improved Education Systems Keep Getting Better'. The authors found that the education systems that make the transition from 'great' to 'excellent' focused on collaborative peer-led learning for teachers and principals. Furthermore, Professor John Hattie's wide-ranging review of evidence on pupil learning 'Learning Power' found that 'The remarkable feature of the evidence is that the biggest effects on student learning occur when teachers become learners of their own teaching.' Teachers empowered and learning together is what makes a successful education system.

16　London went from being the lowest-performing region in the country in 2002 to the highest-performing for disadvantaged pupils by 2014, who are now 38 per cent more likely to get five good GCSEs including English and maths than elsewhere.

17　Nick Pearce, 'Youth unemployment and what to do about it', 30 June 2014, <http://www.ippr.org/nicks-blog/youth-unemployment-and-what-to-do-about-it>.

18 'Youth Unemployment: The Crisis We Cannot Afford', p. 13.

19 Dolphin, Lawton and McNeil, 'Jobs for the Future', p. 32.

20 'Technology Insights 2012', e-skills uk (2012), p. 7.

21 Kayte Lawton, Graeme Cooke and Nick Pearce, 'The Condition of Britain: Strategies for Social Renewal', IPPR (2014).

22 'Youth Unemployment: The Crisis We Cannot Afford', p. 4.

23 Matthew Whittaker and Alex Hurrell, 'Low Pay Britain 2013', Resolution Foundation (2013).

24 Ibid.

25 Ibid., p. 19.

26 The Resolution Foundation estimated that if all employers paid the London Living Wage it would save the government £3.6 billion with higher tax revenues and lower spend on benefits; even when taking account of higher public-sector wages they estimated a £2.2 billion saving. 'Squeezed Britain 2013', p. 19.

27 In 2014 the national minimum wage for those aged over twenty-one is £6.50, while eighteen- to twenty-year-olds get £5.13, under-eighteens £3.79 and apprentices £2.73. While a temporary lower wage for those in quality training makes sense, the blanket approach means young people often get paid less for doing the same work.

28 Matt Griffith, 'Hoarding of Housing: The Intergenerational Crisis in the Housing Market', Intergenerational Foundation (2011), p. 17.

29 Pennington with Ben-Galim and Cooke, 'No Place to Call Home', p. 12.

30 Vidhya Alakeson and Giselle Cory, 'Home Truths: How Affordable is Housing for Britain's Ordinary Working Families?', Resolution Foundation (2013), p. 11.

31 Simon Tilford, 'Why British Prosperity is Hobbled by a Rigged Land Market', New Geography, 31 March 2013, <http://www.new-geography.com/content/003609-why-british-prosperity-hobbled-a-rigged-land-market>.

32 Pete Jefferys, Toby Lloyd, Andy Argyle, Joe Sarling, Jan Crosby and John Bibby, 'Building the Homes We Need: A Programme for the 2015 Government', Shelter/KPMG (2014), p. 72.

33 Ibid., p. 27.

34 'First-time buyers under 40 to get 20% off under Tory plan', BBC News, 27 September 2014, <http://www.bbc.co.uk/news/uk-politics-29387866>.

35 James Meek, 'Where Will We Live?', London Review of Books, 36:1 (2014).

36 Pennington with Ben-Galim and Cooke, 'No Place to Call Home', p. 13.

37 Department for Communities and Local Government English Housing Survey 2012–13, quoted in 'Shelter's response to the review of property conditions in the private rented sector', Shelter (2014), p. 4.

38 Alakeson and Cory, 'Home Truths', p. 3.

Chapter 11: Finding a Common Purpose

1   Mary Ann Sieghart, 'Profile: Work and Pensions Secretary Iain Duncan Smith', *BBC News,* <http://www.bbc.co.uk/news/uk-politics-11565723>. Accessed 19 October 2014.

2   See <http://jimmcmahon.co.uk/oldham.html>.

3   See   <http://www.oldham.gov.uk/info/200572/co-operative_oldham/1189/our_co-operative_approach>.

4   Atif Shafique, Henry Kippin and Ben Lucas, 'Oldham's Co-operative Council: A Social Productivity Framework', 2020 Public Services Hub at the RSA (2012), p. 28.

5   Ibid.

6   Barbara Brownridge, 'Creating a Co-operative Council for Oldham' in Caroline Julian (ed.), *Making It Mutual: The Ownership Revolution that Britain Needs* (London: ResPublica, 2013), p. 196.

7   Ibid., p. 197.

8   'Stunning £1million launch donation to get Oldham working', <http://www.oldham.gov.uk/press/article/391/stunning_1_million_launch_donation_to_get_oldham_working>. Accessed 19 October 2014.

9   'Satisfaction with Oldham Council', <http://www.oldham.gov.uk/homepage/628/how_are_we_doing>. Accessed 19 October 2014.

10 'Cities Outlook 2014', Centre for Cities (2014), p. 7.

11 Tony Travers, 'Local Government's Role in Promoting Economic Growth: Removing Unnecessary Barriers to Success, An Independent Report Commissioned by the LGA', Local Government Association (2012), quoted in 'Powers to Grow: City Finance and Governance', 2020 Public Services Trust at the RSA/City Growth Commission (2014), p. 6.

12 Hansjörg Blöchliger and Oliver Petzold, 'Taxes of Grants: What Revenue Source for Sub-central Governments?', OECD Economics Department Working Paper No. 706 (2009), cited in 'Cities Outlook 2014', p. 10.

13 'Cities Outlook 2014', p. 10.

14 'Hot spots 2025: Benchmarking the Future Competitiveness of Cities', Economist Intelligence Unit (2013), p. 3.

15 'Powers to Grow', p. 2.

16 Ibid., p. 10.
17 'Cities Outlook 2014', p. 6.
18 Bruce Katz and Jennifer Bradley, *The Metropolitan Revolution: How Cities and Metros are Fixing Our Broken Politics and Fragile Economy* (Washington, DC: Brookings Institution Press, 2013), p. 6.
19 'Cities Outlook 2014', p. 2.
20 Plans were announced in November 2014 for a move towards a directly elected Mayor for Greater Manchester with powers over transport, housing and planning alongside new powers for the combined authority, a welcome step in the right direction. See <https://www.gov.uk/government/news/manchester-to-get-directly-elected-mayor>.
21 'Powers to Grow', p. 8.
22 Gary Banks, 'Structural Reform Australian-style: Lessons for Others?', Productivity Commission (2005), pp. 17–18.
23 Michael Wise, 'Opening Markets to Competition', in *Making Reform Happen: Lessons from OECD Countries* (Paris: OECD Publishing, 2010), pp. 39–68.
24 Banks, 'Structural Reform Australian-style', p. 19.
25 48 per cent of eighteen- to twenty-four-year-olds would remain in the EU, compared with 36 per cent of all adults. Antoine et al., 'Generation 2012', p. 20.
26 Dr Jan Eichhorn, Prof Lindsay Patererson, Prof John MacInnes and Dr Michael Rosie, 'Briefing: Results from the 2014 Survey on 14–17 year old Persons Living in Scotland on the Scottish Independence Referendum', Applied Quantitative Methods Network (2014), p. 8.

Acknowledgements

I'd like to thank the brilliant team at Little, Brown for everything they did to make this book happen, and for always being willing to go the extra mile. In particular Tim Whiting, who believed in the book from the start; Claudia Connal for all her support and the many hours she spent discussing the text with me; Zoe Gullen for her tireless attention to detail; and Zoe Hood for her enthusiasm in promoting the book.

My agent Ed Victor, who first suggested I write a book and whose faith in me and constant support are the reason I managed to actually do it.

I had so much help from so many quarters that I could never list everyone but there are some people I have to mention. Jake Leeper, whose deep passion for social change and research skills gave me so much rich material, and Helen Williams, who is a political genius and to whose hard work and brilliant mind this book owes an enormous debt.

Daniel Farrell and Sarah Lawrie from, in my view, the UK's top focus-group agency, Leftfield, who believed in the book so much they gave their time to help me recruit focus groups around the UK and without whose support the book would never have happened.

I'd like to thank the many youth workers, teachers and charity workers who supported the project and helped introduce me to young people, with special thanks to Mick Chandsoor, Simon Jones, Farhaan Mumtaz, Chloe and Marsha Powell, Jimmy Wilson, Abdi Ahmed, Ibrahim Isse, Haroon Shirwani, and the brilliant team at Birmingham Youth Television.

I would like to thank DJ Collins, Leon Feinstein, Peter Hyman, Dennis Kavanagh, Jamie Bartlett, Bobby Duffy, Adam O'Boyle, Charles Handy and Theo Blackwell, who all took the time to read chapters and give smart and thoughtful feedback, and Tessa Jowell, who gave me support over many breakfast meetings.

I owe a huge debt to many other thinkers and practitioners who generously shared their ideas with me, and I would like to particularly mention David Held, Neil Jameson, Will Hutton, Matthew Taylor, Andy Furlong, Greg Nugent, Anthony Seldon, Andrew Cooper, Sophie Livingstone, Stella Creasy, Sally Gimson, Michael Lynas, Michael Sani, Paul Perkins, Nicola Howson, Aditya Advani, Cllr Lib Peck, David Milner, Kate Ward and, in the US, Ruy Teixeira, Michael Lind, William Galston, E. J. Dionne, Christopher Caldwell, Jennifer Bradley, William Antholis, Anna Greenberg, Marlon Marshall, Lynda Tran, Edward Saatchi and Heather Smith. Special thanks to David Kamenetzky, Anna-Lena Kamenetzky-Wetzel and John Thornton who championed the book in the US and were so generous with their time and ideas.

Many of the ideas in this book are inspired by those I work with in Camden. The officers at Camden Council's Children School and Family Department led by Martin Pratt, who every day model the commitment to children and young people I speak about in my book. Our council leader Sarah Hayward and cabinet member for children Angela Mason, whose commitment and drive ensure that vulnerable children are a political priority. Martin Cresswell, who pioneers many of these ideas and taught me so much about education. My brilliant fellow Kentish Town councillors, Meric Apak and Jenny Headlam-Wells, who have been endlessly patient. The other Camden Labour councillors who have done so much to support the book, with special mention to Peter Brayshaw who passed away before he could read it but who dedicated his life to making the world a better place for future generations. Sam White, the head of William Ellis, where

I am a governor, who taught me about the transformative impact of a purpose driven school leader. My own school, Camden School for Girls, which gave me a brilliant comprehensive education and teaches girls from all backgrounds that they have a right to be heard.

I have to thank my wonderful friends who have always followed me on every crazy campaign and this was no exception. My Camden girls, Natalie Whitty, whose huge intellect and incisive judgement helped improve many chapters; Naomi Lyon, who has been an inspiration to me since I met her at eleven and who let me share our story; Alisa Franklin for her many insights on empathy; and Zareen Walker for her unrivalled organisational skills. Abhishek Advani, whose positivity kept me going through many late nights. Amar Radia for patiently answering all my questions, Kyro Brooks for his constant encouragement, Drazen Jorgic for his sound advice, Sab Sandhu for working with me to pull all my ideas together and contributing her own. Helena Cookman, Greg McEwan and Sophie Husseini for their help transcribing interviews. Ahana Advani for her help with research. Sofia Ahmad, Leila Mulloy, Greg Deeley, Sukhjeet Khalsi, Amy Cameron, Joel Samuels, Lucy Ellery, James De Kauwe, Maria Florut, Ferghal McTaggert, Clair Weaver, Ana Irofte and everyone else who all helped in more ways than I can mention and put up with my perennial absence without giving up on me.

My second family, the Campbell/Millars: Alastair for the robust and winning motivation techniques, writing advice and endless support, Fiona for the encouragement and the passion she shared with me for children and education and Rory, Calum and Grace for always having my back. Margaret McDonagh, who is the bravest person I know and who has supported me in this as she has everything else. Matthew Freud for everything he taught me about purpose, who with Sarah Eglise and everyone at the Brewery created a space dedicated to purpose and generously let me write in it. I only hope I did it justice.

I am forever grateful to my family, and if I needed any reminder of the importance of the relationship between generations it would be the richness, wisdom and joy my wonderful grandparents Mavis and Gordon Rebuck bring to my life. My mum, whose belief in me is the rock that everything else rests on and who always supports everything we do with complete dedication and unconditional love, and my sister Grace, who helped me in every way imaginable, is always my most enthusiastic supporter and lights up every room she enters. I don't know how to thank them, only to say I am lucky to have the two women I most admire as my closest family. And finally my dad, whose example lives with me always and who I wish was here to read this.

But most importantly I want to thank the young people I spoke to who gave me their time, their trust and their stories. There are too many to name here but they fill the pages of this book and they have been a constant inspiration. This is their book and I hope it gives them the platform they deserve.

Index

Georgia Gould is a Labour Party councillor for Kentish Town ward in the London Borough of Camden. Elected when she was twenty-four, she is now the borough's cabinet member for young people.